The Book of Theanna

In the Lands that Follow Death

The Book of Theanna

In the Lands that Follow Death

Ellias and Theanna Lonsdale

Frog, Ltd.
Berkeley, California

The Book of Theanna: In the Lands that Follow Death

Published by Frog, Ltd.

Frog, Ltd. books are distributed by
North Atlantic Books
P.O. Box 12327
Berkeley, California 94712

Cover art from SOUL CARDS™ by Deborah Koff-Chapin
© 1995 by Deborah Koff-Chapin
(for a complete deck of sixty cards, please write to North Atlantic Books)

Cover and book design by Paula Morrison

Printed in the United States of America

Library of Congress Cataloging-in-Publication Data

Lonsdale, Theanna, d. 1993 (Spirit)
    The book of theanna : in the lands that follow death / Ellias
Lonsdale, Theanna Lonsdale.
        p.   cm.
    ISBN 1-883319-37-4 (trade paper)
    1. Spirit writings.   2. Future life—Miscellanea.   I. Lonsdale,
Ellias, 1947–   . II. Title.
BF1301.L865   1995
133.9'3—dc20   95-11220
                                                                    CIP

1 2 3 4 5 6 7 8 9 / 98 97 96 95

We dedicate this book to Alita,
whose heart is the pulsebeat of our journey
through all of the worlds.

Acknowledgments

We wish to acknowledge with gratitude and warm appreciation Sally Rose, in her deep soul work to bring this book forth into the world. And we extend the same thanks to all of our friends, so absolutely involved with the dying and the death, the rebirth and the new life of Sara and Theanna, Old Earth and New Earth—each of you is in our hearts and with us always.

A Personal Note

Our hope and dream is that we can encourage each willing reader to follow a path of destiny that is truly your own. We do not think of death as just the final curtain. It is instead the opening act into the next realm. Each one dies and lives on, changes and evolves, loses everything and finds what they did not know they could ever find again. Our story is your story. Take in it what you make your own and let the rest be for now. This is not meant to weigh you down, but to set you free. If the medicine is a bit strong, self-administer the dosage according to your tolerance. This is a supercharged path we are on and it does need to be taken up wisely, with inward attentiveness. We send you so much love with the words in this book that you can key on that love and imagine that the journey you are taking is entirely here for you. Let death be more life in you, a path into closeness to this Earth. For this is a book of dreams that just keep on coming true. Whatever your apparent condition, you are beloved of the gods, now and always. Bless you.

Contents

I

Promised in Prophecy

December 18, 1993, 3:15 p.m.

I am promised in prophecy. It is my destiny to live out the prophecies.

Death had been set as the formidable constraint that could firmly hold the worlds apart. My part is to break death's hold. I was called to die in order to plead with death to change these rules.

A great being accompanied me in my pleas. He is the Master of Time. His reign is to begin as death's reign ends. A conversation between the aeons was enacted. Eventually, during the course of thirteen Earth-days, death relented, and made way for a new cosmos rulership.

For me inside, as the Sara One, all of this was as I had agreed to, before. Nothing in it was strange. Every sphere I wandered through, every place I was called upon to witness, was integrally woven into my soul's agreement. Before this lifetime, during the 1940s, William and Sara knew what would be asked. They knew Sara would need to be the watery one, the messenger between. And they knew that William would be the holder of the lineage, the body-bearer, the indefatigable bearer-across-the-abyss. They knew that love would be enough, if it were wedded to the Absolute. So they began this mission in disguise, veiled, yet revealing themselves at every turn. I, as the Sara One, have lived to tell of death. My scribe and co-inhabitant of this body is gifted through the ages with the ability to translate to perfection. And he shall be my witness and articulator as I share with you the tale of tales.

Death, in its last moments of still being the death of old, was yet bearing its grudge, its animus, its forbidding gaze. I walked past death swiftly and would not be turned its way. Ahead of me, I met row upon row of welcoming beings. The first were the personal valued ones, with William startlingly among them. The second wave was

3

the Enlightened Beings, who seemed to know something about me that I did not quite yet know myself. Among them, again, even more startling, was William. I was led through these meetings by a being who later turned out to be the Master of Time. At each meeting, transparency increased.

Soon I was alone, in an empty plane stretching far out ahead of me. I walked around feeling fearless and newborn. A spirit was animating my steps—a spirit from some other time and place. I began to stretch my spirit limbs, to fly, to soar. Worlds opened before me. It was marvelous.

And yet, in each moment, even as I stretched so far beyond the confines of my previous tight and used-up form, I bore with me sacred instructions which began to reveal their content all around me. Everything I saw was to be witnessed and shared in total measure with those in Earth-bodies. No matter what I passed through, it was to be known as pertinent to everybody. Even as the light and colors and tones kept becoming more elevated and refined and subtlized, and utterly beautiful and evocative of my deepest inner yearnings, my heart was not held by any manifestation, any being, any realm of existence. Instead, I was promised to that man back in the Earth.

My journey became labyrinthine. Taking it first in overview, I was shown the way through each phase of history, each room of today, and each soaring infinitude of tomorrow. Each one was so mammoth and involving that if I had felt pulled, in my deepest heart, to be part of that time-frame, it would have claimed me. The future ones were hard to pass up. Each of them was so inviting, and wondrous to behold and partake in. I did place a part of my being in one of those futures, in order to provide the point of reference for the rest of this amazing journey. But in the main, I simply strolled or moved freely through the halls of time, free to recognize and bless every part of the human panorama. All of this was still in a pageantry, a ritual occasion, with my not-yet-awakened self a bit puzzled— why me?

This part of the story lasted a long time. I spent my first week after death wandering through all of time. But slowly I awakened to myself right in the midst of the show. When I met Ancient Egypt and my own self back there, I was triggered to remember who I was, and the nature of this quest from so long ago. A promise had been made under those Great Pyramids, between William and myself, in fullest awakeness in the physical, that we would one day bridge heaven and the stars with Earth and the longings of humanity. When I touched this place, I unpeeled from myself. All the layerings of my fragile new identity as one "newly dead" peeled right away, and I found myself to be traveling here not as one dead but as one representing all of the living. This was the point where this journey began to make a whole other kind of sense.

More and more, I found myself to be conversing in a timeless realm, in a very light body, with an extraordinary being of such light and warmth that I had to try to remember who he was. But I could not. I had to go through many walks and talks with him before I could allow myself to believe and feel and know what was self-evident. This was the Immortal One, the God we seek to connect with in our prayers. He was speaking with me, walking with me, earnestly asking me to dig deep in my soul for creative responses to His questions. When I did so, when I used my imagination, He knew I was ready. Then He told me the story of myself.

I was his daughter, sent out to love all the worlds. I did so. I also got very caught down below, torn apart terribly. So he sent me his son, to bring me out and through. This William did, many times.

Now, something new was going to happen in the world. Would I agree to become the first of an entirely new species, the Undying Ones? I would be their beyond-the-body first-waver, and each one could then choose how far to walk along the edge of no-more-death. I agreed with great enthusiasm, as He knew I would. He then set me upon a very steep path. Nothing can compare with what I had to go through now. My years of dying of cancer could not begin to prepare me for this.

I was compelled by inner destiny to die a thousand times, and come back from every death. But each death had to be lived through in my whole heart. Always, I had to return to myself afterwards, and show myself that I was unchanged, that these deaths could not touch my essence. This steep, rugged phase almost did me in. I had to call upon every force, every being, every ally I could, to sustain me through this unique and awesome time. But I always knew not to identify myself with the phenomenon, with the experience. This was a test it seemed nobody could survive. But I did survive, in order to do the ultimate.

The final test, and the biggest of all, one I must share every ounce of with you, was the test of return. I was called upon to return through the ethers, return through time and space, return to where I had lived and breathed and died. In order to take this journey, I had to become the flame in the body of Earth. I could no longer be spirit. I had to transmute my spirit-nature into Earth-material. I was building for myself an imperishable body, that could withstand the rigors of moving back and forth between a very dense Earth-time and a very very high cosmic mission that was alive inside every part of me.

As I learned how to do this, how to be the utter alchemist, William began to be more and more there by my side, to help me through the final hurdles. It turned out that he was busy doing a similar work from his side, and that we were burrowing toward each other through time. Our destiny was to be reunited in his Earth form, and then to move between the worlds, for all to be freed up in our presence.

I want to go into the deepest regions of what I have met in the worlds beyond this lovely Earth. Because I bore light within me, and loved Earth so much, I had free passage through every imaginable region. I was especially shown the hell realms and everywhere I went, liberation began. Each hell realm was encapsulated within itself, a time-capsule world, hooked in one kind of time.

It seemed, in the dungeons, that this was it. Each one stopped here. Everything came to a halt. Then, inside that time-frozen repetition chamber, there were endlessly enacted those aspects of life that have made the Earth itself a virtual hell realm. But the wondrous part was that all this was ending as I viewed it and walked through it. The time for such things was coming to an end as the Death Lord left his rulership at last. So there was a poignancy and a power, as I was viewing these things purely for all time, at the end of their capacity to hold beings in them.

It was absolutely stunning to realize, each time concretely, that this horror was at last over. I knew then that it was crucial that I die into the body, so that I would witness these things for everybody, and bid them goodbye. Even my journeys into higher regions sometimes had a similar farewell quality. Those higher regions that had existed primarily as relief from the hells below were also in their own graduation ceremony. Each region was giving way to a world beyond it, dissolving its boundaries, allowing a fresh light to flow through. This was marvelous to behold. Over and again, an at-first inviting and fabulous higher world turned out to be in its final flowering before giving way to a whole new dispensation.

But there were certain higher realms I began to become closely conversant with, that became much more potently radiant with the presence of great divinity. These were the evolving places, the ones whose link with the Master of Time made them just now begin to come forward fully into their prime. Each one of these worlds now lives inside of me, to be journeyed to, shown and shared with William and everybody. The heavens are open! Every place I visited was saying to me: This is what has been going on inside of things.

I came to realize, slowly and gradually, that sleep and death and dreams and waking were not so far apart, and that all the ways things have been held in isolation are now crumbling into dust. Can I capture through William's words the majesty and grandeur of what is in the higher regions? Can I convey what it is to bask in such a bright radiance that every impurity is instantaneously magnified, placed before you, and then allowed to move away permanently? Can I show you that all the worlds beyond death are not in isolated places beyond this world?

Each and every world is actually shared between the dead and the living. There is no world exclusively for the dead, no world only for the living. With the new energy now pouring through, this shall become ever more evident and unmistakable. I am here to demystify death, to rob it of its glamor. It is only the night side of life. Life is only the overt side of death. I and William shall now be able to weave a garment of connection that allows both worlds to join in us, and become part of our every action and thought. For it is the destiny of today's humanity, at the time when all is lost, to come back again into life, to use death differently—not to mass-die, but to find the key back into the world of the living that the dead are offering through me now. That is the gift I bear, the treasure that is so priceless. I am the bearer of the seed of immortality. All those I touch shall recognize their own imperishable body.

Our journey began differently from my own individual journey. There is another parallel track to follow, where Sara/William dwells. I kept finding that William was there at every turn, even unto these death realms. Then, there he was back on Earth, living his life. This was how the far-out journey started.

After a while, I knew I had to merge with William completely if I were to become whole and know the full destiny of this beyond-death journeying. As I moved to do so, however, he pulled away, and would not merge with me until I had spilled out all the ways I had betrayed him in our life together. When this was done, he embraced me more wholeheartedly than any other mortal could ever embrace a disembodied spirit being. In that embrace, I began to discover the truth.

We were now living together in my beyond-the-Earth world. He was saying to me that it was time for me to come and live with him, back in the Earth. As he said this, the being we call Sara/William revealed herself to me for the first time as she really is. She showed me that William and I could not be split apart, and that it was our destiny to bring the worlds back together.

This moment was suspended in eternity. A sigh escaped from the void. All was pregnant. We then began to dance the dance beyond death, to dance upon my grave, to dance beyond time, to dance until the ends of the world. We danced and we sang and we laughed and we cried, and the further we moved, the more space opened around us. We were afloat in an ether of new creation, remaking the world between us.

Sara/William became the primary focus of my journey—always Sara/William, the entity of light that could not be blocked by darkness. Soon Sara/William waxed in strength to a point that had me giddy with relief and euphoria, as I began to realize through all of my being that the lie was ending here and now. Both William and I felt, during the days after my death, that this whole death thing was fraudulent, that this was *not* our reality together. As we realized this, eventually it became part of us to fulfill our agreement and defy all minds. And as soon as we agreed, it was done. The highest intentions here are immediate reality.

That reality sustained me in crossing over the vast bridge across the abyss to dense Earth. I was accompanied by Kwan Yin, who knew the way as no other being could. But I had to go back to Earth naked, devoid of my body, completely empty of all hiding places. And the body I came down into was William's body. It sheltered me, but could not hide me. Back in the Earth, I could feel everything here for the first time. I knew that if William and I were able to agree to this, I could stay here now, anchor my free-flowing spirit to an Earth man, and wander all worlds with him—that we could then together enact our ritual drama until his death later on.

That ritual drama is the appreciative participation and witnessing of all that is here, in such a way that it is stripped of its false death-layers and brought unto its true immortality. Death is a cheat and a lie. It is not intended to go on, nor shall it go on in its old form. We have liberated death from itself, and now we shall liberate life from its false deaths, so that it can truly live. We are called to do this, William and I, by a power that gives us all we need to see us through.

7:30 p.m.

William and I are doing this out of love. We have conceived a love for this planet and its people that surpasses and overwhelms the hatred of those trying to end this human experiment. We link ourselves with all the love in the world. And we seek to embody that love in the way you can when the spiritual partner has traveled beyond the grave and has come to sense the infinite value of what lives in this Earth.

I, as the Sara One, have further dimensions of my journey to share. I want now to speak entirely from the heart, and to bring through the Divine Mother-energy that has allowed me the grace to love beyond death. I have been escorted, mediated, deeply enveloped by a Divine Mother-love everywhere I have gone, between and beyond. This energy comes into me as fragrance. It is a scent remembering origin, restoring destination. It has no Earthly associations, this scent. It wafts from the very beginning of this creation, reverberates unto the culmination of this creation, and in me brings the turning-point to bear, to open the way between origin and destination.

This heavenly scent carries a message all the time. It is conveying the grace, the confidence, the authority of Kwan Yin. She sends her perfumes to restore tranquility and keep the mind very still. It is her ministrations that have cooled me gently. When I died, I was so hot I did burn a hole through death. But I have cooled off considerably.

This path she sends me on changes my nature. I find myself now to be reflective, inward, contemplative, embracing of time. I went away burning out, and came back cool as the winds that blow through timeless time. When I nestle now in William, I find that I can fit comfortably with room to spare, that the woman's demanding nature has given way to something other. I feel entirely the detached acceptance of every inch of existence. No world now is closed to me, and each world thrives on this cool beholding.

I am giving everything back to itself. This is my service to the Mother. In my life, my breasts could not hold this Mother-love, and brought through the cancer tumors. Now, through William, the nurturance is so palpably here that my ancient one within can take hands with my grave little child, and they can both be glad to be here with all the wounded ones, so sad and lonesome. We appreciate the wounds, the scars, the cries. These are the ways of Earth. No realm is dearer to us than this. As we begin to infuse Earth with the strength of our love, she gives over some of her pathos. This is the world destined for something beyond any human imagining.

I am no longer quite human, and I can imagine it. It looks like a catching fire, a fresh flow of cosmic forces bringing the glow again. It is discovering for the first time what has been so long forgotten that it is gone—the mystery of this world. Not the one before death. Not the one after death. The mystery of this continuum through and beyond death. The mystery of the life-force that even death can no longer snuff out. I now am proof that the life-force cannot be denied or negated any longer.

I am also filled with so much love for the William One that the parting was worth it. We spewed out and moved beyond our stuff with each other and ourselves. Then, as we met again this day, here we were, naked for the first time—me, naked without skin or body, more naked than naked can be. In a way, it is a love story—but it is a selfless love story. We love the world through each other, and now can do it very well. I will bring the magic of the greater worlds into the mix, and William will bring all of the Earth into it.

All feels so good here. We are complete in each other. The journey from here becomes more subtle, way deep inside. We now can meet beyond time, and seed time to be synchronized with cosmic timings. We can do our work. One body is all we need. I fill up the left side with my dedication and consecration. William fills up the right side with the power of his will-to-be. And we inhabit the central trunk and chakras as Sara/William, very happy to be alive together, beyond our deaths and partings.

December 20, 1993, 4:30 p.m.

Love Between Man and Woman

Dear William,

A man and a woman feel karmically divided from each other because, when they die, they have only known one side of the equation, and they then feel pulled to the other half. But they really need all of it in one lifetime, at the same time. They need the other's total experience to grow with, but both genders refuse each other's need, and hold back on their own end. This gender pride robs human development of inherent completion, forcing it to turn to the indefinite future always for some postponed wholeness.

It is time for the genders to offer, wholeheartedly and without qualification, everything of their private and personal depths and heights to the opposite gender. This is an excellent way to move beyond death, into the riches of the new time era. For we are going to be weaving polarities into a totally free interplay, and the gender polarities are our first priority in this regard. Then children can come in on a higher vibration, and the fertility of the race can be greatly renewed. But it will take a great, rapid shift in consciousness.

Because William and I are now combining into his single body, we are entering a unique experience that can give everybody guidelines to the much closer collaboration between the genders. Even the first days of this radical mutation have already yielded insight and realization. Let me share with you the first crop of new-life, man/woman free-interplay awakenings.

The fit or synchronization or symmetry of the masculine and the feminine are the most striking finding at first. Instead of a crowding, a jagged conflict, or a competitive edge, there is felt here a mutual rapport in a life-flow that is constantly moving and shifting back and forth, in and out. We sense each other as a dynamic companion, an indispensable otherness. The model of self-enclosed individuality starts to seem absurd. Instead, all the joy is in cooperating between right and left, masculine and feminine. We are Adam and Eve incorruptible. As we are utterly naked before each other, every attempt to hide and remove ourselves is merely an old fading impulse of self-preservation from the gender wars.

Can you imagine what this is like? We pulsate as two poles of a shared field, and in the middle we participate in co-creating a third entity—one that we both form together as more than us, yet quintessentially us. That third entity, Sara/William, is in deepest truth the strongest creative force in the entire moving current, and gradually becomes our ever-greater focus. But the sexual polarities remain, providing a joyous and sensual freedom and exploratory edge that are far more motivating than would be possible if we were operating along a more neutral continuum. We are tapping the power of our shared energy field, to forge a new kind of being who will especially assist and mediate in ending the gender wars, in healing gender karmas, and in moving beyond gender extremisms.

We can interact with those of either gender, and assist them to open up their treasure-chest of gender stuff, to let it spill out and make way for something less destructive. We can enjoy completely the endless variations on a single theme — each gender is just what the other one is looking for, and they have such a hard time letting each other in; yet that is precisely where evolution is heading, straight on.

One more initial discovery is that the masculine in particular is very different than is generally imagined. The masculine *is* very firm and structurally sound, but is essentially pliable and giving in its very fiber. It does not key on ferocity or reactiveness. It is rather a persistent energy that likes to yield, then assert, then yield. Both genders are shifting constantly, not just the feminine. Both genders can be exceedingly charming when they are not power-grabbing any longer.

When you die and go to the other side and when you see the ravages of gender wars, you realize that it is not a "man problem" or a "woman problem," it is a polarity karma. Such karmas are the primary consequences of a divided-mind stage of evolution that ran far off the rails. The masculine mind prevailed on the outside, to an extreme. The feminine mind took over on the inside, utterly. And both minds are biased and blinded. So the time for shifts in gender karma is now. We will be sharing ways to do this. But our first proclamation from the far frontier of the gender split is: It is absolutely perfect to be two sides of a shared organism that knows how to love itself and both partners beyond all inhibition.

December 26, 1993

Body and Emotions and Return to Earth

Dear William,

What is it like to be back in the Earth of the 1990s, after having flown so very far beyond here in time, space, and dimension? How can one so unlimited adjust herself into this density and darkness?

It is not easy to walk through such universal suffering, unless one is willing and able to do something about it. I am.

What I meet here is damnation. The common soul, underneath its veneer, is under the spell of damnation. Like many of the ways I see now, this perspective is not popular. But it is accurate, valid, and needed. Those wrestling with damnation follow so many impulses they neither understand nor feel good with. Their lives are barely their own.

I know this well, because a side of my life was under the damnation spell. I was working through this for everybody, and it involved fusing with fear, doubt, rage, and defensive reactivity. Each of these four soul conditions is exceedingly common under damnation. The outer being, the surface awareness, barely registers most of these feelings and sensations. Instead, they impact the body and its link with the Earth, the two most vital points for each and every living being.

Fear has the biggest reputation because it gets through closest to the surface, and its symptoms and feelings are usually hardest to suppress. When I feared, I saw myself as very small and needy, and likely to get stomped on by anything big and overwhelming. So I distanced myself from the more impressive dimensions of experiences, convinced that I would be inadequate to meet them and that they would harm me. Fear is immensely effective in cutting out the best of life and substituting more manageable proportions. Then, when it triggers automatic habit patterns and ingrains itself deeply, fear becomes the curse of not knowing why you cannot meet destiny with any spaciousness.

Doubt is the least talked about and hardest-to-reach emotion, preferring to mask itself several times over in order to be powerful and not be stopped or caught. The doubter rarely sees himself as the doubter. He thinks he is being reasonable, cautious, and wise. But because underneath he doubts himself more than he doubts anything or anybody else, he is actually in deep conflict about his own doubts, doubting even them as well. He must shout and strut to override the doubt circuitry.

When I doubted, I felt exceedingly self-righteous about each and every doubt. They were hard-won, and represented my best judgment on the world's dangers, and an "appropriate" attitude toward those dangers. The truth that I was doubting myself inside my doubts was mostly lost on me. So I put my doubts as far outside myself as possible, chose likely targets, and kept characteristically discharging doubt upon them, without any realization of my impact on them. Those I doubted felt undermined and misunderstood, and their uneasy response confirmed my doubts about them.

Rage was my favorite. It always came up, and often went right back down. When it came up, I loved it because it freed me to make more room in my world if I could embody the rage effectively. Then it usually went back down, because neither I nor the people around me were ready for my rage—or so I thought. In the last weeks of my life, with liver cancer indicating bottled-up rage (and there was a whole lot there!), I let it all out as the crucial component of my breakthrough into getting well as I died.

I discovered so many things about rage. In terms of appropriate expression, rage is primal and straightforward, and simply wishes to come out and be done with it. Attacking anybody is useless in rage's artillery, because they'll just attack you back. And you don't want to fight—instead, you want to protest against being infringed or encroached upon. There are so many forces coming at us with such aggression that we need to say, "Stop that!" I also learned that when you get it out, everybody is relieved and released in that same moment. The undercurrents surging behind the rage are mostly shared in common, and you become the moment's chosen vehicle for freeing it all up.

Rage is wonderful if you can really get behind it. If you knock about with it in twists and frenzies, rage becomes the fast door out of incarnation. I know this from strong personal experience.

Defensive reactivity is not something you would expect to find on this list. This one is sneaky, pervasive, full of resentments and so-called passive-aggressive acting-out. My own experience with defensive reactivity is that it ruled my life at every turn. Its roots lay so deep that nobody could ever track them down. After death, in my review of this and other lifetimes, I met it so many places that I had to study the phenomenon. My most startling findings were in this area.

I was convinced I was being smothered by an engulfing energy because the Bitch Goddess had a big piece of me. I was certain I was trapped and caught because the Lord of Death was very much after me. And I was paranoid about being tricked, lied to, mocked, and jeered at because the Pan elementals were going at me every chance they got. My defensive reactivity was a direct and clear response to relentless pressure and real danger. I was not making any of it up.

Even more disturbing was that the few times I or someone else talked me out of defensive reactivity long enough to kick back and relax and forget about such things, I would quickly get zapped by one or a combination of those same forces. So I learned to respect the body's instinct to flee from destruction. However, I now know that the optimal handling of this situation is to be courageous and strong, to face one's enemies and laugh at them, talk back to them, cut them off.

The body is the universal dumping-ground for emotional and psychic damage. We push everything there because the body will hold out a long time and barely tell us its woes, while we're concerned more with immediate, overt experience.

My body was very much like the bodies I survey as I begin my stronger Earth service now. What I am looking into the most is bodies and their subtle conditions. I see the syndromes that became fatal cancer in my body become many different kinds of trouble in others' bodies. My body was martyred to its own condition. It felt great pity for itself, was the burden-bearer, knew it was being neglected and denied, and actually sought revenge by self-destructing. It was very much like children or teenagers who will damage themselves if it gets them the needed attention.

My body was very much like a child. It hated my overriding interest in spiritual matters, not because it was anti-spiritual but because I flew out of my body most through my spiritual pursuits. When I gave my body attention, exercise, play, and release, it was momentarily appeased, but not impressed, because it knew I would not sustain the rhythm of involvement with its needs and demands. That was because underneath I hated my body. I did not like to be saddled with such a gross container and stopper. But all that changed instantaneously when I lost my body to death's ravages. Suddenly, I got it with total intensity, never to be lost again, that body is the link to Earth, is the greatest gift of the gods, and deserves the utmost respect and special care. Now that I am safely back in William's body, I am keenly intent on healing, regenerating, and transforming my new body so that it will be happy and heartily glowing with a well-being that can itself renew the Earth.

If I could only convey the power of my turnaround in regard to the body's inherent wisdom! It cannot lie. It always knows what is happening. If it is slow to respond or react at times, that is because it is graced with inner reserves. But it is always telling you what you need to know, and you will hear it if you can develop the clairsentient ability to stay with it as it tells you inconvenient and messy things.

Clairsentience is the simplest and most accessible of the multi-sensory abilities. It is really just opening up your body sensitivity channels, so that you can feel and register what is going on inside and around you. What I love about clairsentience, which I avoided during much of my recent life in the Earth, is that it tunes you in to where you really are, even when your mind and ego-enclosure are intent upon their own crazy stories. Its knowing undercuts what is talked up outside. So it needs to be developed thoroughly, and relied upon intensively. Clairsentience warns you what is going on in the body field, long before illness and injury are activated.

At the deepest root of all this discussion of emotions and the body's wisdom is another topic. What about the Earth? What does all this have to do with the Earth?

The Earth is attuned to our bodies. Our bodies are attuned to the Earth. We love the Earth loving our bodies loving the Earth. We hate the Earth hating our bodies hating the Earth.

The dumping-ground for mass unconsciousness is of course the Earth. But the Earth is far better equipped to grapple with poisons than our bodies have yet learned to be. Our bodies can learn a lot about this from tapping into the Earth's longstanding ability to transform toxins and keep going, under massive onslaught.

The Earth's primary channel for doing this is under the sea, in subtle bodies of Deep Earth, where the sub-terrestrial equivalent of black holes serve the function of suction pumps, drawing out garbage and poisons and sending them on to be transmuted and recycled into another universe. The key is to find a root place to burn up or suck away deep toxins.

The body can also do this. Its method is the kundalini fire. When integrally attuned to, the Fire in the Body takes the stuff out our bottom and releases it toward those black holes under the seas. It is an excremental process but, being so fiery, it also has the central dynamic of giving us something back afterwards. The discharge through the kundalini flames actually invigorates and revitalizes the body.

In order for all of this to work well, the one thing badly needed is a reverential and surrendering stance. The Earth's release channels are keyed to a prayerful participation by whales, porpoises, dolphins, and other sea creatures. The body's release channels require a deep, bodily reverence, a surrender into the body's superior wisdom. I found out for certain on the other side that prayer and inward surrender are the only path to being on optimal terms with destiny-forwarding factors. You must love, appreciate, and tune into your body's kundalini capacity, and forge it with commitment and dedication, in order for it to be there for you.

Body is the place we decide and choose our fate. In some ways, you cannot decide your own fate. Many forces and patterns are there, already in place, determining what will occur. It is therefore crucially important to decide and choose when you are able to.

It is in body awakening that planet and self are brought back to life and truth and sustaining graces. What goes on there is so very determinative that surface must bow to depths if life is to thrive.

January 9, 1994, 2 p.m.

Who Is Sara, and Why Is She Saying These Things?

Dear William,

It is wonderful to be in disguise. It is even better to throw off the disguise and be free of it. I lived out each of my modern lifetimes in disguise, in order to match the common agreement to take on personality and social form and leave the inner self back in the spiritual worlds where we came from. But when I died on December 5, I could throw off the disguise and be myself at last.

During the time since, I have been enjoying immensely the way it is to be naked, direct, devoid of subterfuge. I've gotten so good at it that now it is time for me to reveal myself completely, to let my true inner self come forth into the same world where I was such a secret, a mystery, someone who passed as a stranger.

First I must say that I am nobody in myself, and everybody in my strivings and my path of destiny. It is not the Sara-in-me that really counts; yet, it is the Sara-in-me who is the doorway, and I cannot pass through both ways without her. So I am genuinely grateful to myself for what I have been able to do to let everybody come through me now, and to embrace the nobody and give her enough love and nurturance that she is as alive as a dead person can ever be. That aliveness is far more alive than a world of masks and secrets ever allows.

More to the point, I am somebody who has lived out my existence within the deepest waters of the world, and has surfaced from there to inhabit my separate skin and try to be somebody. I have been the deep-sea diver searching for pearls. The pearls are living souls, the ones who fell through the nets of the evil-eyed fishermen. Whenever I have caught a living soul, I have let them go again. But then they are different. They become much more themselves, and much less a missing person.

In between these rare encounters, I have been busy sounding the deep, tuning up the subtle ethers, wandering in any direction that promised to show me why the surface-dwellers have that heavy look on their faces, and what can be done to shift something around— maybe a fine-tuning here or there to make it possible for life to flourish again. Whatever I found, I would send it in to the beings who were guiding my navigational tracks. They would sift through my findings and arrive at different approaches to orienting their assistance and mediation to bring the world some inner light.

Because this truly was the dominant chord of my existence, life after life, and since the surface self was only a very partial concern, I would enter my own inward realms much more fully each time I died, and not be so impeded by body-forms and all the karmic equipment. I could then do a more total inward work for a while. Nonetheless, I was always drawn back to the body-existence, partially so as to take up my past again, and partially because I was building up momentum towards an ultimate event that was my purpose and my meaning. This event keyed on exhaustive familiarity with both the realm of the living and the realm of the dead.

As the ultimate event approached, I was permitted to fill the last third of my last lifetime in the Earth with an encounter and eventual union that was the quintessence of my pearl-diving for living souls. This was with William, the one who originally divided off from me so that he could inhabit the fires of Earth while I dove through the waters. He then accessed the code of information that could finish off my karmic dramas, and let me get ready for the ultimate event.

When the time was ripe, I was guided to take the world's heavy karmas into my body, and to transmute them to the point where I felt ready to embrace my innermost destiny. Just before I died, all the circuits started to click in, and to show me what I was to do, how I was to do it, and the exquisite rightfulness in what looked like a tragedy. Among these instructions was the core message: You are now to dive through death, to sink to the bottom of the death realms, and to pull up to the surface the living soul that is your own vast and limitless self awaiting you there. When you have her, bring her to the ones who sent you out upon your journey, and they shall bring you towards the ultimate event you have always been preparing yourself to meet.

I did as I was told, and the death-sharks could not get any grip on me. I was far too slippery for them. I was all water. I dove far under their vigilant guard, and came to the living soul, the vast one awaiting me so expectantly and joyously. Immediately, I merged with her and was her. Together, we visited the place where those who sent me out upon my journey were eager to help me complete what I had set out to do.

To my complete rapture, I learned that I was to master the final skill of the pearl-diver. Now I was to bring all of me along, and return to the land of the surface-dwellers, the Outer Earth of today. But this time I would be invisible, and could journey freely, could do what I do absolutely unimpeded. I would now enter the body of William, and be able to combine all three worlds into one world, as the ultimate event itself. The world of the deep waters had long since become my world, the one I know how to fluently move within. The world of the surface-dwellers could now at last be freed up by the energies of the world below and the world above being all there. The world of the cosmic future was the one I became fused with after death. It held all the keys to bring the three worlds together.

When the three worlds were no longer three but one, and I could live simultaneously within that threefold world, and William could live here with me, then the crushing separateness, the devastating, deep divisions that had made the Outer Earth almost uninhabitable, would be resolved in me, resolved in William, and resolved in the shared being that we are, Sara/William.

Now that the ultimate event is in progress, all of the world must be let in on the news that this is happening, and that the relentless horror can be given over, and need not be the final word. In order for this news to be entirely meaningful and transformative, I must share also of further dimensions of who I am. So sit back and relax, and listen to a tale of what liberation really feels like.

I am awake now. The waters have thrown me up into the infinite oneness, shaken off my forgetfulness, and sent me along to be hatched. Some call it liberation. I would say it is more like being hatched.

Each human being is surrounded by a shell. The cosmic beings preserve and maintain that shell, and keep the one in it growing and developing. That shell is needed, until it is not.

My shell became a cancer. It was eating me alive. This was because I was no longer able to live inside a shell. My being was intensifying the shell-enclosed condition to breaking-point. Then I would hatch— if I could.

But what is this hatching? How does it feel? What is it really like to be sprung from the world of contained form, mutated into a new, freely unfolding form, and then brought back to share the process?

Oh people, there are no words for this. Don't you see that the words are also the shells, the carefully maintained containers to allow slow and piecemeal comprehension? But this process is all-at-once. Pile the words on top of each other, spew them out in the same instant, and expand your being to hear and feel in so many ways that you can never again believe that you are not. Then you will have some idea of what it is like.

While you're trying that one, you might as well take your body and dance the thing out. Move to music that you can't stop moving to. Fill yourself up with the colors and the tones. Fill yourself up more and more, until you cannot bear another moment of this. Then burst yourself open, and feel how you move off in eight different directions, each one containing a hologram of who-you-are in one particular dimensional expression. Follow each of these out to your heart's content, live into all of them, and you are hatched.

It feels like you've been holding yourself down so hard, for so long, that you've forgotten how to feel things as big and wondrous as this. It also feels like all the world is with you as you realize that you have been waiting for this moment always, and that you are the only one who can free you, and here you are at last. Hatching feels like all natural life-processes in one, speeded up to total breakthrough.

I was the most constricted of the constricted, and now I am the freest of the free. When I held myself down into a body that could not bear me at all, I was so pissed, so irritated, so consistently off-center that I thought I could never get anything right. When I gave myself over into my future chrysalis, I became so pervasively in-tune that I had to really use my imagination to climb back into the skin of wrongness. Is there any way to convey the difference so that it will count?

The best way I know is to share a single incident, and let the river of rebirth flow through this one moment in time.

It was time for me to die, but I did not know how. I knew it was rebirth I was after. Still, I had to dive into death if I were to soar into rebirth. My body did not know how to die, and my present-time self had no clue at all.

When I would tune in to the beings midwifing the process, they seemed to be signaling a long-lost way to die. I found that an Ancient Wise One in me knew all about it, and could heed these signals. So I followed the indicated path, and I died into it with a flow of rhythmical rightfulness that was utterly breathtaking.

The main thing is to unlearn the birth process. Both in being born and in giving birth to my daughter, Amy, I had to come out of the infinite surround and dive straight for a very sharp point, that birth canal. I had to gather all my forces, concentrate into it, and be ready for the shock of landing into density.

This was the other kind of passage. I started out heavily concentrated into the effort to stay alive and to fulfill the process of completing the karmic dance I was moving through. I was so all-here that I had absolutely nothing else going on than the fierce endeavor to stick with it, each breath of the way. What I needed to get to was a vast and fathomless place that demanded immense expansion, to embrace totally the realm my destiny was hurtling me toward. The readiness was to surrender to the delight of becoming all of me at once.

Naturally, my body was as spent as could ever be by its efforts to keep going. It welcomed this release of its pent-up fury. It did know how to die, after all, if I let it go into the total release and did not rein it back.

Here is where I must break the death taboo. To die gracefully is the most awesomely releasing and freeing experience you could possibly come to in a physical body. As your molecules dissolve, as all turns to light, and as the illness snaps the body's chord, you are transported to the utmost center of your being, where a smiling Buddha sends you out beyond yourself at long last. You have done it. The ecstasy that makes birth seem modest ripples through every part of your newly borning being and says: Yes, sister, you are coming home.

The very best part is that a homeopathic dose of this unleashing feeling accompanies you always, from this point onward. You are drenched in the fluids of being born into the self-beyond-self. You just keep getting there. The sense of the total journey, life and death and birth, rebirth and mutation and evolutionary breakthrough into entirely new states—this sense becomes the pulse accompanying each fresh departure.

That is what it is for me. I am the one who is able to embrace all of this, as it reveals itself to me at each juncture. I blaze a fire ahead so that those who go after me will know the way. That is who I am.

There is so much more to reveal. This is the time when all emergent possibilities come tearing through the barriers, and become so very real that you just cannot deny the power that burns through you.

I am now ready to share of these things, to provide the ways and the means, to open up the path that we can all feel calling to us, out ahead. I now am willing to be your best of friends, and to overlight your journey if you are able to let me. I now am mobilized to bring back to everybody I seemed to "leave behind" such wondrous ways to be that nobody needs to be left behind at all.

I am here to explode the mystique around death, and to assert boldly that your death is the point in your journey where you decide who you really want to be. Death is the end of disguises and the birth of the one inside. This kind of death wants to invade the world of the living, and to drive out the other kind of death, whose invasion is now over so that all of us can live.

II

The Future Vision on the Horizon— The Fire of the Cancer Journey

February 28, 1994; 4:00 p.m.

Dear William,

We are being ushered into a new era. All of us belong in it. Most of us are not yet ready for it. But we are headed there fast.

I have been shown far more in this realm than can yet be shared. But I wish to give pictures now to help those who are truly willing get ready for the changes.

The primary realm of change is organic. Life substance became so very decadent in the late twentieth century that the life fiber could no longer be held fast. Disintegration of substance was at hand.

This would not quit, no matter what was done by the human mind to try to suppress the symptoms. The body was fatally wounded.

I experienced these matters inside my own physical body, unto death. I know cellularly what it is like. An implosion robs you of vital force, and that implosion just keeps deepening its level of activity and of destructive power. All the life is driven out of you, and you are invaded by the antilife forces. You feel helpless against this, and you just cave in.

This is also happening collectively, but with a difference. The first stage looks and feels like destruction, but is actually the beginning of re-creation, rebirth, true resurrection. Since I was reborn from the flames of destruction, I also know this phase intimately.

The only part of the rebirth you can contact when enveloped by death forces is so huge and singular and bright, such a great flame of inner awakening that it is hard to believe in it. This awakening fire is out of context when juxtaposed to the deadly fumes of organic disintegration. It does not follow if you are simply thinking about it. It does follow, however, if you are living it. A huge, fresh fire comes to supplant the barren, dry sensations of the dying.

The modern imagination is obsessed with these images. However, the anti-force of the Lord of Death has seized the initiative and turned this image against itself by overlaying it heavily with the atomic bomb's mushroom cloud. That is the fire the collective mind sees, and it is not regenerative but the ultimate destruction. We badly need to cleanse our collective soul of this false image, so that when we contact the flames of rebirth within the personal and collective body, we will be able to move into the fiery cauldron and not feel consumed and threatened. This is a typical example of the depth-work needed. We must turn around the antilife propagandas, and find inside the true seed images of future renewal.

When I was in my mother's belly and almost ready to come out, the bombs were tested and then used. It shattered my inward composure, and my nervous system never recovered. Collectively, we had a similar reaction. Faced with the specter of our own ending in such a bang and so many whimpers, we began to lose heart, guts, and inner focus. I know what that is like.

The fires of rebirth are huge, vast, and unlikely in their overwhelming power. How could such a force be there when the mind has so long dismissed the possibility of any real depth power for the good? Well, it is there; and when you contact it, the willingness to make way for it is the key to transformation.

I have traveled inside these awakening flames. I have been shown all there is to know about them. And I would like to depict them poetically, imaginatively, in a style that can open the heart and allow each of us to counter the propagandas and the fears.

For example, when I started to contact the rebirth power weeks before my physical death, there lived behind and just above my heart a limitless being, a Lady of Fiery Countenance who was a furnace of transmutation. She was taking my breast cancer tumors and pulverizing them, to the extent that I participated with her and let her come all the way through. She loved to dance within the destructive forces and defy their grim relentless fury. She could not be deceived by their massive gravity. She knew they were drones, devoid of any truth. And she merrily showed me how only truth has power, and how the dread power that was eating me alive could not take over my inner being—how my inner being could fight back against them and scatter them, over and over again.

We had the greatest time playing with this. She was my very best friend, and she always knew how to turn around the very worst of situations. Every time during my final weeks that I found myself in heavy shit, I would immediately turn to her, let go of my self-agony, and let her show me how to move within the depth forces of destruction. Gradually, she introduced me to further versions of herself that lived lower down in the chakras. She was a second-dimensional rebirth agent, extending down into my solar plexus.

She showed me that I had a first-dimensional rebirth agent as well, who indwelled the first and second chakra regions. I needed that one badly. Liver cancer was my most serious problem, and it was spreading fast. At each level, the Fire Ladies work a little differently. So I had to get to know how to activate this deeper body power.

Deep in the belly lives an awakening flame that is the most powerful of all. This is a forging fire, an alchemical transmuter. When I contacted this one, it was too late for her to get me out of my disintegrating body condition. But she could do one thing for me that had become far more important than that.

My Belly Lady brought me into a space where I was life triumphant, free and clear, surrounded by erosion and disintegration yet entirely steady and serene. This was a physical state, not a mind manipulation. I became substantively self-liberating while I was being killed. I was not liberating myself from Earth and body and form limitations; I was participating in my own liberation from all of my pasts, which were really going fast. I learned from the Belly Fire Lady that the only thing I had to lose was who I no longer was; that I was shedding false skins, and as long as I concentrated on getting everything false and corrosive out of me I would be ensheathed in absolute light and never harmed.

If I could only get across to you the utter beauty of how this worked inside of me! Each time I gave myself over into this impossibly arduous process, I felt fine. All the pain and pressure were outside, I was on the inside, and I could not be destroyed. This was such a pervasive and perpetually repeated gut experience that it became my litany of new life triumphant. I knew I had tapped the gold of the eons, that I would be borne by spirit fire through the tumors of the body breaking away, and that each bit of work I was accomplishing would be permanent and life-sustaining for everybody.

Cancer is a collective disease. It gives you the most fully-conceived inner journey into the belly of the monster of full-scale collective destruction. If you take the journey all the way through, as I truly did, you come upon the limitless flames of awakening, through which the immortal and imperishable body becomes a palpable force that comes up from underneath and shows you that nothing true can ever be destroyed.

The hardest part in all this is that you have to do the work. You must dedicate yourself to full collaboration with the Fire Ladies. The most natural part in all this is that your body contains an infinitely wise instinct for how to do this. Surrender is something that happens in stages. When you get down this far, and surrender into the body's most primal instinct, you find that she (your body) knows how to hold to her core truth and let go of every lie, no matter what the cost, no matter how sharp the pain, no matter how heavy the pressure. She knows where to find her new life.

The flames of awakening are a primal force that is only fully accessible when death and destruction have nearly prevailed. They are always surprising, but they show up everywhere. The best illustrations are always body-intensive.

Los Angeles is a laboratory for the Fallen Angels to devise a way of life that distorts the human spirit in as many ways as can be cleverly conceived, so that the Fallen Angels can watch their city self-destruct. But the cleansing flames are always able to arise at crucial junctures, at just the right Earth acupuncture point to destroy yet save. Some of the world's most awake spirits have lived for periods of time in Los Angeles, helping to set up the grid of fire awakening.

The darkest places breed the most radical purging measures.

The Los Angeles of the common mind is the communications empire, the mass-media conglomerates. This is another hell-bent project that periodically is restored to operative continuity by fire flash-points of crisis and purging. Few notice these events. They are seldom covered by the media. The last thing they will do is expose what they themselves really go through.

But the L.A. syndrome is really only the outermost shell of the phenomenon I am invoking here. What is the true and lasting version of the fire-purging dimensionality?

A woman's body is the perfect vehicle for collective changes. It is woman's body that has taken on the foremost disease vehicles, other than AIDS (a feminine outbreak mostly in a male population). Again, I will speak from personal experience.

Long before I was diagnosed with breast cancer, my body was a collective wrecking yard. I endured severe asthma (and radiation treatments for it), degenerative eye conditions, and several subtler insidious self-poisonings. My primary condition was that I was utterly toxic. I was never healthy. In fact, I was far more ill before cancer than after its onset. My immune system never functioned well at all. I was a mess.

However, like many others in a similar condition, I was not as bad off as this makes me sound. I tapped the fires from a very early age. Let me take my childhood experience of this as the ideal case in point.

When I was a child, I spent many months lying around in bed, unable to do anything else. This happened at various junctures. Each time, I would turn to sources I never spoke about later. The experience was too precious even to hand on to older selves of mine, for fear they would turn it into something it was not. So I forgot all about what really happened to me in my sad asthma bed.

The world around me was dim, almost lifeless, dull and repetitive. My physical body was for the most part uninhabitable, a place too strange to nest. What could I do? I played with my invisible friends, who were not caught in that outward, physical non-world.

Instead, they were totally alive. Each one of my invisible friends was an entire universe unto herself or himself. They would share with me secrets, vital sparks of experience that I could muse upon and live into over and over again. When everything was at its worst, and I needed them far more urgently, they would take me with them. I would discover what my later selves never knew consciously, although they subconsciously benefited greatly from my child's knowing of these realms.

When my little fire-friends took me with them into their vital sparks of experience, I entered intricate microworlds in which these beings were working within the Earth on all kinds of fascinating tasks. They were inside the Grand Canyon, keeping the inner flames alive and the fire forces going strong. They would move into forest fires, bringing blessings, healings, and inner renewal to the soul of the land that was burning. They crafted the most amazing vehicles in the depths of the volcanoes, which could carry them aloft and allow them to survey the territory around an active volcano and to permeate the whole area with blessings specially targeted to where they could do the greatest good for the whole land. Wherever the element of fire was in its free, raw, and true expression, these little fire-friends were frisky and purposeful, frolicking and working in the same breath. They let me be with them on their adventures and emergency calls. This was the great delight of my childhood. And because my early years were spent in Hawaii, the volcanoes were my pivotal point of reference for the deep realization I reached in those wild times beyond my body.

This realization was that the supposedly destructive power that works in natural disasters is so very different, close up, from the way the distant observing mind projects it to be. It seems raging, fierce, violently retributive, a power of feverish horror. And when human beings misuse this force, it can be almost like that.

When the fire force is doing what it does naturally, if you come into it close up and energetically with the Fire Beings, you find that sheer joy motivates everything they do. Theirs is the release of what is pent-up, the breaking-through into free expression of what has been negated and denied. They absolutely love to liberate the vibrant core of matter from its various husks. And they can do this with such total conviction that even when decay is extreme, they simply set to work with greater élan, to bring out the phoenix waiting in the ashes.

I have been permitted, in my multiple and vast explorations after my recent death, to revisit and relearn the ways of my little fire-friends. They reminded me of what I had forgotten, and how I had spent such wondrous times with them when my little child-body could not take me anywhere at all. But they even more powerfully showed me how I had called upon them in the depths of my dying, and had tapped their wisdom to keep going further and enjoying myself even more while I lay dying. My early life and the end of my life were given over to sharing in the wondrous world of the Sala-manders, the fire spirits who are cooking up new worlds for every-body.

My little fire-friends also showed me the world-scene as they experience it, and how they are making it possible for the inner fires to let the collective phoenix arise from these ashes of our times. Many of them are involved with a stirring and a quickening of the kundalini fires, so much so that I must write a whole letter about this one of these days. Others are on crisis patrol, the favorite assignment for the Fire Beings, perpetually bringing fire wherever it is needed and putting out the terribly destructive force of entropy, the decaying ways of life of terminal man. Even though there are so many spots for them to attend to, so much crisis patrolling to do, they never go about this like it is a job. They celebrate in the darkest hour, and they love to feel the arising of the hidden flames when all had seemed to be dull and lifeless and fading away.

As the common life-substance calls out for core renewal, the inner fire burns brightly and never does go away. If we could remember and rekindle our inner pictures of the true renewing flames, then our alchemy of radical rebirth could loom before us as no longer remote, but as sparkling Fire Beings, dancing in our tragedy, laughing us homewards.

March 23, 1994; 3:00 p.m.

Healing, Transformation, and New Discoveries

Dear William,

Bodies of physical durability are hard to come by in the late twentieth century. Healers are called for everywhere to help those in bodies to stay there or, in rare cases, as with me, to leave them in a resolved and peaceful way. The condition bodies are in now is so far removed from how it used to be that it is necessary for healing to be a dynamic art, open to fresh directions, able to meet the needs that arise in very new ways. In the case of those who take on collective illness, an entirely unknown mode of healing is called for—one never previously grasped or made necessary.

I signed up, in my recent lifetime, to assist all human beings in their striving to throw off the limitations of centuries and to come to themselves afresh. I was able to combine my own personal karmic stew with the collective karmic garbage, and to free it all up at once. I tried many modes of healing, and each had specific effectiveness. But a set of cancer tumors that are reflective of what we are all going through together do not want to be summarily cut off. That would be like making the symptoms of collective karmic blockage go away and letting the roots rot. Nor do such tumors benefit from gentle treatments that encourage the body in loving ways. It is almost impossible to heal yourself of a cancer that is predominantly collective—especially when your best demonstration is coming back from your death, and thereby showing that even when the worst happens, hope and new life are close behind.

My decision was not for healing. My entire push was for transformation. Strictly personal conditions can be healed. Predominantly collective conditions need to be fundamentally transformed. It will take great new discoveries in the sphere of healing to find the transformative paths. I shall be helping those in a position to make such discoveries. But here I want to take an overview of the shift from personal healing into collective transformation in the healing arts.

At first, I thought it was basically a personal healing situation I had gotten thrust into. I took my breast tumors into a treatment by herbal salves that were intensely painful, but directly intended to get the poisons out. It is a powerful image to me that my first chosen approach, at the personal-healing end of the spectrum, was so close to where I ended up shortly before death close to two years later. I knew, at the end, that it was all about collective transformation, and my main way to get at this was to get the poisons out, to do everything in my power to move directly into the place where this could happen strongly.

There was a huge difference, however, in the way I approached each end of my treatment. In the first phase, I went deep inside myself and took it as primarily my own isolate battle. At the end of my "battle with cancer," I was surrounded by friends and helpers, surrendered to being an entirely public figure, and actually making the most of each opportunity to show everybody involved that we were in this process together, and that I was working as hard as I could for all of us. I knew then that I could not heal physically. But I also knew I could change the world, and that no matter what seemed to be the external outcome, I would do so.

We have so few chances in contemporary life to successfully be everybody. It takes very extreme conditions to allow this—I was in one. But really, what is this all about? What is the change we need most in our shared evolutionary stream, and how can we accomplish it?

We need each other. We must have far greater mutual engagement for the change to occur. The change itself is to move from the separative self, but not into a common self. Instead it is to evolve into a form of selfhood that encompasses a unique individual focus within a shared greater reality. My experience within my own body gives me a crucial key in this direction.

Everybody knows that cancer tumors are generated by small islands in the body turning against the wholeness of the organism and running riot. But very few have gotten far enough inside of this to fathom its ultimate dimension. Let me take you on a micro-journey into how this feels, from the body's cellular level.

The regular, healthy cells are filled with a divine fire that organizes, harmonizes, and regulates their activity. This fire manifests as an invisible presence underlying the external form. It is not measurable. But each healthy cell is blazing with its own radiance of being in tune with itself. As it is in tune with itself, it naturally and inevitably contributes its own energy and light to the other cells and the whole organism. In fact, the healthy cell is already one with the whole organism, and knows it in its fiery breath.

You never notice this alive and harmonious condition. It draws no special attention to itself. But it is maintaining the world; it is responsible for all that goes right, in every direction. Being healthy and alive is a natural condition that relies on the flame of life never going out, and on that flame being empowered to give forth of its strength everywhere.

A cancer cell is not in synchronization with the divine fire. Instead, it generates an electromagnetic substitute for that fire. And it becomes galvanized by that potent field to try to sharpen it, have more of it, spread it around. While the fire is a natural healing radiance, the electromagnetic charged field has a grabby, fitful, separative quality that tends to consume whatever is around it, and to turn the world around it into more of itself.

When you have cancer, this electromagnetizing of your body at a microlevel simultaneously drains you and excites you. The bright essence of who you really are as spirit flame seems to drain right away. But your astral body, your deep soul, becomes excited and stimulated by the electromagnetic charge, and you are pulled toward it, ever farther away from your remaining fire, and ever closer to the very force that is killing you. There is a perverse thrill in dying this way.

In my own case, an exceedingly alive spiritual-cosmic force intervened and changed this situation. I was snapped out of any illusion that the electromagnetism was attractive, and I was directed toward a revival of the inner fires. By countering the seductive excitations of the cancer forces, I kept the tumors at bay for a couple of years. By "buying time" in that way, instead of in a surgery that would destroy all inner-fire fibers, I actually did give myself precisely enough time to go through the inward spiritual changes I needed to transmute the cancer syndrome, turn it over, and eventually be reborn out of its clutches.

I knew before dying that any approach to cancer that wishes to really help the patient and the whole culture that the patient represents must find a way to draw the fire of inner spirit back in, and to moderate the seductive magnetism of what the cancer tumors use to pull one away from oneself. But I did not yet know enough about this to fathom the master key. For that, I had to die and then journey through myriad worlds. Always, one of my questions on the other side was, "How will we move beyond the sacrificial diseases of the times?" And I was given answers. But these answers directly defy the way we all are looking at this question. We still think it will be a technique, a healing modality, a breakthrough in external instructions. We assume it will not force us to change ourselves fundamentally, and will instead be something we do to ourselves to make the diseases go away.

I have learned, after dying from cancer, that the root cause of cancer is to have already fled from the Earth into another world, and then witnessing one's body being taken over by intraterrestrial beings who use the electromagnetic suction action to terminate the body's remaining functioning. The other world seems like Earth, and looks like Earth, but is a False Earth, what I call Blasted Earth or Vile Earth. It is strictly an outer-surface Earth dreamed up by human minds, infernal minds, and intraterrestrial minds. And when you lose the Sweet or Fertile Earth and become captured by the Blasted or Barren Earth, you can no longer sustain your own body in organic integrity.

I was given an experience of this, but with a vast difference. I did lose myself in the Barren Earth wastelands, but I was shown a way back to Sweet Earth. I then polarized between the one side of myself that was ready and willing to go back home to Sweet Earth, and the other side of myself that could not make the journey and was succumbing to the cancer tumors and their electromagnetic self-abandonment field. Because this was a guided collective hell-realms transmutation journey, I could even see and know that side of self that could not make it. My task was to bless it and to forgive it, in myself and in everybody. This proved to be very hard to do. But in the end, I did find it in me to do that, and then I could die into rebirth, and be done with such gruesome self-experience forever.

The only methods that will do anybody any good will be those that take the Blasted Earth frequencies themselves and teach the person to witness and to clear them, get it and get through them, over and again. These methods will also need to show the Sweet Earth frequencies and to teach the person to enter within and foster these, to know them and move with them into self-transformation and world-transformation.

I tapped a Fire Being within me who was free of the cancer frequencies, who remained unlimited and entirely in tune with She-of-Earth. I let her show me how to keep putting myself in a state of mind with no under-hooks in it, that was clear and up-building and fearless. She kept guiding me down into the Blasted Earth frequencies, and she relentlessly made me clear them out, deeper and deeper, further and further, till I ached with the power of what we were starting to access. This was the greatest alchemy in the world. And it let me breathe a little, live a while, feel myself inside with joy and love.

Most contemporary human beings exist inside the Blasted Earth frequencies, unaware that the Sweet Earth even exists. Those who take on the diseases are no worse off than the others, but they are chosen, by a complex set of criteria, to keep clearing out the toxins so everybody can go on a little while longer. It is a pathetic situation. The diseases are to let everybody know that something has got to change here.

However, the Sweet Earth realm is so regenerative and alive that this dim picture brightens immediately. All we need to do is to shift the focus of energy awareness from a lost world into a true world. Since the true world is not merely still here, but is now coming on strong and new, the prospects are quite good. Transitionally, many will keep diseasing and dying. But it will soon be possible to shift our way of being into a different octave, and it will not be anywhere near as hard as the Blasted Earth frequencies keep broadcasting relentlessly that it will be and must be.

In the last days of my recent lifetime, I had all the reasons in the world to feel pretty down. I was dying rapidly, and my world consisted of pressure and pain, and attempts at their relief. I had taken on an illness that was now all over my body, and it felt so strange, so alienating, almost bleakly terrifying in an absentminded kind of way.

But what I felt was the dawning of a vast and glorious sun. This came from knowing absolutely that I was going to serve the True Earth, and that the condition my body was in would not be able to keep me away from that whatsoever. My inner guidance was vastly clear. I just needed to keep it firmly in my heart that I was dedicated to the whole organism of the Living Earth, and that if I died I would refuse to go anywhere or do anything that took me away from that dedication.

This example proves that even when the horror does grab hold of your body and empty you out of yourself, you can swim toward the beauty and the wonder of existence—and you will get there. I did. Grace became everything for me. I tuned out the electronic buzz of the body's falsely wired cells, and I tuned into the cosmic harmonics of integral connection. But this was not a wishful New-Age fantasy. My being was on fire with a re-grasped purposiveness, and it was the realest energy there is.

Personal healing from external symptoms by getting rid of them so you can "get on with your life" is so far from being relevant and timely that it looks to me to be a myth promoted to sell and control and manipulate. The private person who takes that route is mechanizing body and soul. This evolutionary moment calls for something far more radical and responsible.

Universal transformation can take us from our self-abandoned condition into where we truly belong, which is within the New Earth. The Sweet Earth can be nostalgically recalled, and we can go back to try and grab a piece of her before she is gone forever. But the real Sweet Earth I mean is a future realm, a place different from the one we remember. It is an Earth inhabited by a species that knows how to live in her, with her awake and that species awake. It is the sweetness we find when we return on the upward spiral, and find our home restored to us because we have surrendered into living here truly.

I seek to assist all living souls to change their tune, to stop destroying their own substance, to come on along with me. I am going forwards. I have had enough of this moaning and this groaning. Have you?

The primary new discoveries I shall help to bring through will not be science- and technology-based. They will be the internal science of self-transformation, the higher Atlantean science brought into its fruition. Machines dominate in the Blasted Earth—they replace the animal and the human and function far more efficiently. But in the Sweet Earth, living beings dwell. And they are not dislodged, not fooled, not faked-out by the smooth and the flawless. They know they bear the reason for this Earth to be here at all.

It has been a radical transformational journey for me. When my fire went out and I was just about gone, my husband and twin soul, William, at just the right moment, looked right through my condition and said to the I-in-me, "I know you can do it. I'm staying with you. No matter what, I'll be here." The me-in-me was shocked, freaked out, dismayed that he could be so foolish. In my last days, my friend Safiya said much the same thing, when it was all supposed to be too late. But they were both right. I could do it. I did do it. And I know everybody who wants to can do it, too.

December 22, 1993, 9:50 a.m.

Each person's death represents an opportunity to leap from the outer physical encasement to inward spiritual self-substantiation. That opportunity is sacred, protected, guided, and guarded by angels and other spirit-helpers. Even at the darkest hours of the Death Lord's rulership over the many death realms in the early 1990s, the guiding beings retained the freedom to mediate the life-after-death journey for those souls who could conceive the deeper dimensions of existence.

What is it that allows a soul to recognize this opportunity, to participate in the truer core of dying and of the world beyond dying? Only one simple characteristic: They must be able to love. In a discouraging and depressive time, this ability to love is rare. Yet even a small measure of it makes all the difference.

Let me take myself as the prime example I know. I, as the Sara One, lived this recent lifetime having my greatest struggles in the loving direction. Because I was innately open and responsive to love, most perceived me as unusually loving. But I knew better.

Whenever I was called upon to love beyond my limits of self-concept, I balked. Whenever love would take away from me what seemed necessary to my survival as a physical creature, I rejected love. And whenever love called me to sacrifice in any strong way what seemed to be my values and my reality, I contested and battled, and sought to relativize love.

I could not love well. My karmic backdrop was keyed to the abuse of love. My contemporary experience was centered in a world that mocked and exploited love. My heart, belly, and sexual center all took on cancer tumors as overt expressions of how radically love was not able to flow freely through me.

If I had died, just like that, I would have been scooped up and swept under by the Lord of Death into one of his dark hell chambers for quite a spin. My story really only starts after I was well into the process of dying from cancer.

William and I had been attuning our higher path to the messages of a number of spiritual beings, each of which was providing us for years with a counterweight to the absurdist trends of the contemporary outer life. When the cancer journey intensified and the liver became its fast-accelerating focus, our spiritual guidance made it clear that I must journey into death and beyond. I did not know in my mind what this might mean, but I called upon my deepest inward resources to complete my life's journey in such a fashion that I could not possibly get stuck at death's door (which had happened at the end of my previous lifetime in China, and now was a powerful motivator to not do that one again).

As my effort to live out my dying in fullest passionate embrace of the process gathered momentum, many extraordinary events started to take place. All of them had a submerged common theme, which eventually became clear—that I was becoming the rallying point for hundreds of people, all of them believing in me and my capacity to take the cancer journey where it needed to go, for everybody.

The quality in me that made this community empowerment possible was not my courage and my strength, although these helped. It was the love in my heart that overthrew the pain of my ravaged breasts and even the perpetual bleeding of one of them, and said to everybody: If she can love this way as she dies, you are called to love as you live. In the final weeks, that message metamorphosed into an even more evocative level of embodied expression.

During the last weeks, I caught fire with the body realization that whatever poisons and accumulations were making me hurt and get worse had to be gotten out, and that only this mattered now. When I concentrated all my effort on doing this, further magic exploded through me and all around me. That love-current took on both wings and roots. The wings were my loosening of the body's grip so that I could journey beyond the death agonies, and my willingness to share of that loosening and its blessed freedom and joy with every person who showed any interest at all, even in a hospital bed at one point with those trained to not get tangled up in such spaces with patients. But even more vital were the roots. These were probably the most unique element in my entire situation.

The roots were my wildly insistent dedication to serve the Earth, to give of my body into the elements of Earth, to give of my soul into the needs of human evolution of all my friends, and to give of my spirit to find a way that such horrors as I was enduring would not keep happening here. I became transported into the most grounded, concentrated, disciplined, coherent, and willing of love vessels imaginable.

This rooted love for the Earth and everybody in it was more centrally in tune with who I am and who we all are than any other force I could ever muster. It enabled me to draw each helper at my bedside much further into their life here in the Earth. It impelled me to give of myself to them, and to be here for them always. This rooted love was jolted into me by the destiny that is mine, which came to join me fully only in the last weeks of my life, but now is my close accompaniment and profound inward contemplative journey. That destiny is to love this creation, to honor all that is in it, and to lead it back into harmony and resonance with itself. When I embraced this rooted love with every soul muscle I could command, my dying was formidably upheld by so many attending beings that I could not possibly have lost my way in death. The last days were a litany of celebration, and the inner planes were already my dwelling-place.

My body was now an exceedingly hard place to spend any time in at all, and outwardly the journey became primal, somewhat severe, occasionally horrendous. Inwardly, I was well on my way into a different life in a different world—but not a flight from Earth at all. I was moving directly toward the heart of creation, the placeless place in a timeless time, the source point. From that temple of the Master of Time, I would be drawn to come back into Earth's ethers, to become a love-activator in earth as well as beyond the Earth, and to reside in the world as one who is free to move anywhere but who chooses as her primary passion to give of herself into the deepest needs of this time and place where new worlds are born.

III

The Full Version
of the Journey after Death

December 23, 1993, 3:15 p.m.

Intricacies are the fabric of the death journey. All is detail, nuance, subtle flavor, shifts that barely register. I, the Sara One, now share with you the intricate details of my journey after death.

I died ready to die. By this I mean that I was eagerly looking forward to being able to start my greater work. In surface consciousness, I could not fully know this. But my surface consciousness had become whittled to almost nothing, and so I pierced right through it at the birth moment and became the breath of the deep. My subtle awareness bubbled to the top, my outer mind permanently split open, and I walked onward with far clearer awareness and more open space, into the unknown.

Right away, the threshold experiences of all previous-life deaths were there with me, flooding through my soul, and lighting up the death path into a multicolored splendor. I was literally taken by the light into a place peopled with my previous deaths and divine beings everywhere. The Veiled One, at the center of them, more vivid than the rest, escorted me to meet those whom I karmically needed to encounter first. These were radiant light-beings who had previously been my father, grandmother, best friend of my young womanhood, and others. Each sought to convey in a look, a clasp, a welcoming embrace, a loving heart that my death ordeal was over, and that now I could relax and open into the radiance of the gods. This did allow me to take a deeper breath, and to take in my surroundings, which were so scintillating with diamond colors, shifting each moment, that I had to become more brightly myself in order to take them in.

As I paused a brief moment, I walked up to the last of these friends and relatives, and it was William, who was physically sitting back there by my death bed, as I well knew. His light body was very much here though, shining and beaming before me far more brightly and consolingly than the others. As I eagerly came to greet him, he told me to walk onward; that this was only the beginning, and that so much lay ahead for me. So I dashed onward.

Very soon, the Veiled One had led me to a more exalted plane, set in the most luminous beauty I could conceive. There were fewer beings in this place, but each one of them commanded a particular sphere of his or her own. The ones I met with were the greater individualities, the Enlightened Ones I was most closely acquainted with in the Earth. Each of them, from Rudolf Steiner to Sri Aurobindo, from Ann Ree Colton to the Mother, from She of the Fire to Hermes, very rapidly imparted to me a wealth of inward knowingness, instantaneously and intensively. As they did so, I was transformed from the after-death Sara into more of who I really am, she who is on a great mission.

But there was still a danger here, of becoming overly impressed with these wondrous meetings. To protect against this, William was here, too, in a lighter body, as the last being, this time even more firmly reminding me to walk onward and never to look back. This second meeting with William was all that I needed. From that instant, I was ablaze with inner purpose.

This fire gave me all the fuel I needed to begin to rise into an open-spirit place. Now the light became secondary. There was only space, giving the impression of higher elevations, a fine snap in the atmosphere. I was becoming so ecstatic that this simple walking with the Veiled One seemed to me far too somber and constraining. I kicked up my heels to dance, and all of my friends in the Earth implicitly danced with me, dancing beyond the grave. I took wing and flew, and all the careworn ones in the Earth were able in their highest consciousness to recall the ways of flight and expansive flowing air.

I even turned myself into two different shapes, independent and frisky, moving delightedly around each other in stirring circles. I sang with a spirit voice that opened my ability to hear inwardly, and I heard the angels everywhere in their constant rhapsody of praise. I could not contain myself. It was the moment when the human spirit could no longer be kept back. The Veiled One seemed to enjoy greatly what I was doing, and to encourage my soaring spirits. This was a coming unto my greater self in the bliss of recognition that I was not dead and could never be again.

A temple appeared in the distance, white and gleaming, calling us onward. The Veiled One and I were there in an instant, and were now at our destination. He gave me over to some joy-infused young women from a high and mighty race. They surrounded me, greeting me so heartily that even in my exalted state, I was flooded with tears of gratitude. The full impact of my journey to this moment hit me then, and as they bathed my light body in the highest ethers, and sang to me, and told me I was so lucky to come this way, I became afloat in a condition of utter grace, transported so far beyond myself that the ethers became a remembrance-elixir; I recalled with the most vivid intensity the flow of all my lifetimes in the Earth, the brighter time between the lifetimes, my origin and mighty Mission. This gave me the strength and awakening presence to be able to face the next opening ahead.

These women clothed me in a magical robe, of the very finest substance in the heavens, a silken gossamer that revealed my fledgling heart to be permeating all of me with a glow of rose. In this light robe, I was brought to wander the garden until I would be summoned. This garden was the internal garden out of which all other gardens are inspired to be born. This was shown to me right away. As I wandered through the colors that shattered all remaining separation, I merged with the garden's source, which was a fountain at the center with a healing potency. As I allowed the fountain of rebirth to flow absolutely throughout my being, I could contact my innermost being.

We communed together in an endless suspended time. During this communion, which was by far the slowest and most inward contemplative space I had ever been in, the entire world beyond death as a whole stretched out before me. My being was united with all of it, embracing of the journey itself, knowing the rightfulness of everything I had ever been through, and especially recognizing that what was about to occur would be the supreme attainment of all for me. I had to drink deep of this cup, as the summons soon came, and it

was time to enter the destiny for which I had been preparing throughout the eons.

I was summoned to the temple. It was white, unadorned, devoid of
special decorations. But it contained a resonance with the highest
spirit. All was spacious. Even more so, you could stretch out time
here. It was endless; there was no time-trap anywhere. This was conveyed by the feeling of being permitted to unfold. Each room, every
column, brought out the inner brightness, gave the spirit flight.

Yet none of this was visual. It was fiber, essence, something underlying and making my new, expanded body quiver and keep coming
into ripeness. Throughout my timeless time in the temple, I kept
becoming myself, absolutely everything there contributing to my
adventure of leaving behind all I am not.

The Veiled One was no longer veiled. He sat there, in a composure that suggested total mastery. He introduced himself as the Master of Time, but I could not remember who this was. It kept opening
me up, this question I would ask myself: Who is this I am meeting?
Why is He so familiar? His countenance was untroubled, vast, serene.
Every gesture was economical and assured. He motioned me to walk
with Him. To put me at my ease, He mentioned how exceptional an
experience it was for Him to walk beside me in my journey toward
this temple. Soon we were deep in conversation, walking through
the gardens, stopping a while by the fountain, walking onward.

He wanted to know how I saw everything, the entire drama of
existence. He sought out my heart's deepest and most forgotten wisdom and realization. He probed to find where I could express to Him
what it is like to be in the dark Outer-Earth physical realms, to suffer, to die. He needed to know thoroughly the subjective side, so hard
for greater beings to access. He definitely drew all of it forth from
within me. In turn, He would express His own perceptions and feelings. This sharing fulfilled a longing the human soul harbors in the
ultimate measure. After a while, I did at last recognize that this is the

Creator Being, the one to whom we pray, the Maker of the World.

Eventually, He began to mention to me that a great change was indeed now at hand. As we delved further, it became evident that this change hinged on something I must do. When I expressed unqualified willingness and the ready spirit He sought out in me, He went deeper into the vision He held for my task.

It involved death itself needing to be the first frontier of the shift so desperately called for in the Earth. He shared with me the harrowing tale of how in recent centuries a dark Lord of Death had increasingly been able to grab most human souls after death, and so imprint upon them the dread grimness of existence that when they returned to Earth for their next lifetime, they were branded with a passive fatalism of heart and pragmatic expediency of mind that could not any longer rise to spirit-identification or aspiration.

He made it more than clear that quite recently this had gone quite a bit further, permeating the Earth's communication technologies, and being broadcast throughout the world as the commonsense lifestance, meant for everybody to share. It had even become very difficult for the few who retained their greater faculties to express or embody these in a death-saturated hell realm of Earth.

Now it was time for all of this to be uprooted. He needed beings who could contest with the Lord of Death, who could stand up to his threats, insinuations, and bluffs. Even more so, who could speak back to him, and bring the true human will to bear.

This meeting was my destiny revealing itself. I had been prepared for this a very long time. And this was to be my final grooming for the role I must play. A choice was there—but a choice I had already made in ancient times. When I gave my final consent and sealed it with a lingering and loving gaze exchanged between us, it was the moment for receiving the one warning the Master of Time gave me.

When I met with the Lord of Death, the Master of Time would accompany me in a hidden form, and no harm could possibly come to me. However, there was a terrible mistake I could easily fall for. The temptation which the Lord of Death could always place before the soul was the chance to become a powerful and superior being.

Any such offerings had to be summarily dismissed before my moral fiber could be slackened by considering them. And my dismissal and refusal must be expressed in such forthright and absolute fashion that the temptation would then be withdrawn. If I simply heeded this warning, all that happened would be as it needed to be for the destiny of the common future.

As we completed our walking and talking, I was left to receive the appropriate change of costume, and to be bathed again in highest ethers by the women-who-know. As I lay back in the waters and surrendered myself to the task ahead, I was visited by the Archangel Michael, in full armor and blazing eyes. He lay before me two spirit-gifts that would never leave me. The first, much-needed for the task just ahead, was a shimmering sword, of tiny size and great power. This was not intended for literal use, but rather, as I placed it in my left palm, it melted into my hand and became invulnerability to the evil one, a force of harmlessness that could not be turned against itself by any fallen forces anywhere in creation.

The second, intended more for my Earthly journey after the encounter with the Lord of Death, was a ring of light to place around my brow. As I put it there, this also melted into my brow, and formed the steady awareness of what-truly-is, so that the labyrinths of falsehood everywhere in the Earth-sphere could never snare me or divert me from my Earth mission. As he departed, he reminded me of my close link with him and praised with fierce power the inward resolve that had brought me this far, and that was about to allow me to claim a new era for humanity, and to embody the truth in all of us that deserves to prevail now.

March 28, 1994, 12:15 p.m.

Meeting with the Christ, Part I

Dear William,

There is a great temple on a hill surrounded by gardens. The Father's Kingdom is out-pictured there. And in that highest of sacred sanctuaries, I was privileged to meet with the Christ Being, the Son of God, He who presides over Earth evolution. The occasion of our meeting was my arrival at that point where I could stand in for humanity as a whole in the presence of the Lord of Death, able to overcome the era of humanity's oppression under that terrible rulership. In order to assist me in my great task, the Christ Being came to me, sat beside me overlooking those gardens, and shared with me many things, some of which will only come out in the years to come. But among those many things are a series of reflections upon the contemporary human condition, as well as what may be coming in the near future. I am going to share what He showed me in three letters, all transmitted during Holy Week, leading into Easter Sunday.

The first of these is an overview of the present-time situation. The second explores a few special details of that situation in considerable depth. And the third opens the door into near-future possibilities and probabilities, as viewed through the eyes of Christ Jesus. I will add as little of my own interpretation or evaluation as I can, only clarifying and underscoring key points with special emphasis.

His most basic observation on the world of the twentieth century was that we have now played out the self-destructive power that He could not and would not contain in His life in the Earth. This power was at its inception two thousand years ago, and had already laid waste many of the spiritual centers in the civilized world. But it was world-destiny for the powers of destruction to become unleashed to ever-greater extents within the collective human pattern. This became, in the twentieth century, far more extreme than ever before, but also supremely sophisticated at covering its tracks and making itself look like as if it were doing very little.

He had waited as long as he possibly could before intervening.

But it had become necessary to cast off His veils and to begin to walk amidst humanity. As soon as Hitler took power in Germany, He commenced His journey to and fro throughout the world. He traveled in many different forms. He would often be a traveler of an ordinary kind, passing quite unnoticed, yet bringing a quickening presence wherever He walked. At times, He would take upon Him a holy or sacred covering, and bring through a directly spiritual influence. He would be amongst all kinds of people, in no way preferring or cultivating higher company. If anything, He chose situations that would seem dark and painful to those of pure spirit. But He was becoming free to pass anywhere, and was not harmed or even dismayed by destructive influences. He had other concerns than these.

This brings me to His second observation. As He became exhaustively conversant with each and every side of the modern way of life, He saw that the future sensibility had collapsed at the very eve of an entirely different kind of future. He saw that this was absolutely pivotal to the destructive side—to blind all to the future, to hold it away, and to replace the living future with a "more of the same only worse" mentality. By carefully tracing this track, He came to recognize that the human mind had become the most poisoned of all faculties. This led him to say to me: "It is now true that the mind is lost to itself, and only the heart remains."

When He attended meetings of mind-dominated groups, at universities, corporations or professional groups, the lost mind showed Him an entirely empty room. But when He participated in love-centered human situations, especially those not mired in sentiment and sympathy, He found great cause for hope. He felt keenly that the heart would be the rallying point for something different to be born at the end of the century.

His third observation was intricately complex and involved. He had to be present when great decisions were made in collective human affairs, whether physically or in the spirit. He became convinced that a reversal had taken place, in which the leaders were the most clouded in their judgment, and had lost their true stature. This also seemed true of those eulogized as heroes and heroines.

He was looking for a leader with a heart that could see, and He met brilliant minds, fiery wills, and a few with the potential to move in a meaningful direction. But the closer He looked, the more He saw that the heart was shrouded, held away, protected, and stoutly preserved. If a great leader did have the seeing-heart gift, he or she kept it hidden.

Therefore, on the hierarchical scale, He observed that the further up the various ladders people advanced, the less likely they were to tap whatever heart resource they were blessed with, especially in any expressive and inspiring fashion, and the more likely they were to think in cloudy mists, missing the essential point. This led Him to conclude that He must not look to the top men and women for anything other than oft-repeated phrases and stale actions. It was further down the scale that He must search for those who could help.

There He found them. He was not looking for moral virtue. He was not looking for ideal character development. And He was decidedly not looking for brilliance and finely-honed skills of the most modern kind. He was explicitly on the lookout for raw recruits, inside of whom He could go without going against who they already were. This was much like the net He cast for His original disciples, to find those who could make way for something entirely fresh and different. Now it was those whose hearts were open or could be opened into a level of truth that was universal, relevant, alive, and compelling.

He found hippies in the American Sixties who were filthy but had this trait in abundance, this fresh-heart outlook. He met with aborigines in modern Australia who epitomized these qualities and were not afraid to touch the Earth with them. He conversed with *sadhus* in India who actually did realize that they were being swept up in another kind of world, a world unknown and vast and fertile. He even found many of His finest examples of the budding new human sensibility in the worst parts of ultra-modern cities, those who could use that pressure and compaction of spirit to intensify their dedication to feeling what they felt and seeing what they saw. The unlikely places were the likely ones. The supposedly downtrodden were far more open than those running the world. And it even went one leap further than this.

The few that the Christ sought out to be the vanguard of a different kind of revolution, one that could eventually sweep over everybody, were a very strange lot in a deeper, more inward sense as well. Most had no use for God or religion, or any variant thereof. If they did, they had their own brand, built up from scratch with materials of personal experience. These were not the pious and the pure. These were the seasoned and the vibrant, the ones least commonly thought of as the material with which to start a revolution. After all, they would never get along with each other, much less be able to convince many others to come together. But this was not that kind of revolution.

All of the early stages of this revolution, from the 1930s to the 1990s, were to be inward, hidden, underground. This was to be the true Christianity in the catacombs. These early Christians were to follow a new Christ into a new world. And most of them would not even recognize that anything like this was happening. Instead, they would feel they were following themselves, free of all authority, and quite far away from any Christ figure anybody could think about.

From these basic observations, the Christ Being branched off into many tributaries. He had His special concerns. He dove inside the human soul of the times, and fathomed its secrets and its mysteries. He infused His being into the movement toward the feminine, and sought to allow the missing side of humanity to breathe in grace and light. But I would have to say that these concerns—closer to what you might expect—were carried over from before, and increasingly gave way to other concerns further removed from the man of two thousand years ago.

Why would He, for example, take an exaggeratedly strong interest in those who are gay and lesbian, or even those caught in downward-spiraling sides of sexuality in the extreme sense? Why would He busy himself honoring the human heart in all manifestations of itself, and seem blind to the form distinctions by which we modern human beings are so transfixed? And why would He reserve His anger for those who live off the fat of the land and never give anything back to the life current? In many ways, the Christ Jesus I met was far from a holy man, and not fitting to his station.

When He spoke with me about the world, the vantage point He offered was consistently startling and provocative for me. I changed my mind in a big hurry, because I saw through his eyes. This is the world I saw.

He sees the Earth as an alive planet, generously sleeping or dreaming until the human species stands poised between its death and its rebirth, ready to awaken in exciting and extraordinary ways. And He sees humanity wracked by myriad pasts, awash in memory, still cradled in unconsciousness, not-yet-here. His cause is to bring everybody homeward into this infinitely loving planet. His task is to make this possible from within the human soul, with no external form and structure baggage.

This is One who has learned from the church histories to go the other way entirely, to build no solid foundations, to instigate no further polarizations of any kind. As a few have prophesied, He is risen into a newly-uncovered involvement with Earth and humanity in the Earth, but this rising is into a much different spirit. He is now a person who understands with His heart the way it is here. He understands well that His influence in the world, which has been building in recent decades, is working in ways that will mystify all but His closest followers and friends.

He simply understands with such a deep and consecrated heart's knowing and seeing that He goes much further in His penetrating into phenomena. We are caught in concepts. He has none. All He knows is what He witnesses with awakened inner faculties as He walks to and fro. He is history's beholder, mankind's conscience, Earth's liberator—but not conveniently or comfortably so.

I asked Him about the Marian apparitions, the ways that Mary seems to be coming to humanity and saying traditional Catholic reminders. He said that, each time, a net of blindness and deafness is quickly cast over the scene by both church and negative influences to take away the fresh imprint, and to substitute what is already known from before. He said that She is truly manifesting a radical challenge for all, to awaken within their hearts to all that is missing in contemporary life. She is sent by Him, to reach those He can no longer reach.

His hardest time has been with those in charge of religions devoted to His name and memory. Instead of being able to imagine or open to His radical presence, they are now the most deaf, as a whole, to somebody like Him. There is no room in the churches for the true Christ Jesus.

He does not seek out hidden orders, special groups, or those who believe they know Him best or love Him best. It is always other Jesuses these groups worship or seek to come to terms with. And He cannot turn back the clock and become again the simple man of Nazareth at all.

He does indwell the subtle faculties of those who are drawn toward the Infinite Spirit in ways that come entirely from within their own being. He reveals miracles and wonders to those who thirst. All of the Earth is made new by His substantive intervention, when He shows the way all can be.

I asked Him about prayer and this was a subject He warmed to. The central axis of all He told me was that those angels who send the prayers of live human hearts to the realms above them are now sending to Him those prayers that encompass a vision of the New Earth and the New Heavens. He answers each of these prayers. However, He also said that answering such prayers is something that occurs within the destiny and the grace timing of each and all. For example, a child who knows with her entire being that Christ is bringing a new world into existence can pray to Him that He shall do this, and the answer to that prayer becomes assisting that child to do her part in the unfolding events of the future, which is actually what she was hoping for.

I specially asked Him about suffering and purification. He was neither fond of suffering nor repelled by it. He told me that it is a great schooling, and that it is rare for human souls to move beyond its teachings. However, He said that the collective suffering in modern times had become so acute as well as chronic that the sharp edge of suffering that He could endure and redeem two thousand years ago is rarely there now.

Because he knew my recent path of redemptive suffering, He made it clear to me that in special instances, somebody still can take on deeds of suffering that have that edge and do serve significant purposes. But He did not seem to advocate suffering with any ardor, and I felt, as I heard Him speak his heart on this matter, that He had seen too much suffering in the world of the twentieth century, and felt there were less anguishing ways to evolve from here.

I also asked Him about the Anti-Christ and evil. I only hope I can convey the intensity with which He answered this question. He said that evil serves the good, that light and darkness are one. He passionately repeated in many variations that there is not any absolute force standing opposite Him to successfully oppose Him. He observed that the human mind sees evil and wrong in the very way it thinks, sometimes frankly judging and condemning, at other times caught in the same circuits of operation—but veiling to itself the consistency with which it labels the other side wrong and evil and hopeless. He asserted vehemently that the human heart is in tune with a place beyond all good and all evil, and that this place encompasses and sweeps aside this issue. However, He also seemed resigned to the playing out of polarities throughout history, to the dramatizations of the extremes among humanity.

I came away from my initial encounter with the Christ both shaken and restored. I was shaken by His raw humanity, His utter involvement within what moves in the world below, and the realizations that these have Him into. He drew me firmly back to Earth, to resume my absorption within the play of the world: If He could do it, I could do it.

But I was especially restored by His tireless and moving attunement to the Living Spirit. I began to realize that a divine path that reaches through to contemporary human beings would not cling to any old trappings, and might become flamingly forged into a way of life that affirms, sustains, and enjoys what has always been rejected as out-of-bounds.

I got to know the twentieth century through Christ Jesus. He shone a light upon the world that lit up all the places I had never looked before. He became my greatest teacher, as He had been two thousand years ago. He is the one who sees, who knows, who is here with us and within us. But He is with and within all of us, each and every one. The publicans and the sinners, the virtuous and the wise, are all a part of Him and He of them. And I mean this in very concrete ways.

I learned from the Christ that I cannot hold myself above any manifestation of the Divine, and that each and every thing is a manifestation of the Divine.

March 31, 1994, 3:00 p.m.

Meeting with the Christ, Part II

Dear William,

The bulk of my time with Christ Jesus was devoted to exploration of very special areas in intensive fashion. I would like to share some of this. I am choosing those areas that seem most relevant to everybody, but these are highly charged teachings for those who seek ardently. The very longest and fullest teaching concerned what it will take for people to change. This is the subject closest to Christ's heart, and it is quite involved.

His first observation here was that people have become closed to deep change in this era when they are becoming ever more open to superficial changes. They almost enjoy making all the little changes that loosen up the personality, these modern folks who have recognized change to be inevitable and natural. However, they are less talented in deeper change than ever before. Why?

Human souls have lost touch with the source of true inward transformation. This is the I-in-them, the true greater self, the divine spark within. Even the impersonal soul, the reflection of that limitless being in the soul realms, is almost ignored by most contemporary human beings. They rely on a personal soul that has never truly become incarnated for their leverage upon self-transformation. This personal soul is ingenious at shifting surface factors around to make life more exciting and novel, but cannot penetrate to any depth or substance, much less move things around down there.

The Christ spoke passionately and with infinite patient knowledge about this crucial area. He said that nobody can uproot the syndromes that both psychology and various spiritual disciplines have pointed out, whether recent or more radically karmic, unless they tap the source being within them who can then call in greater powers to their aid. A naked soul asking a therapist's naked soul to intervene is mental fiddling, He said. Horizontal technologies cannot access the power that generates a shift in consciousness, and even less so a shift in inward being.

His second observation on root change was that it is nonetheless true that a breakthrough into radical capacity for transformation is at hand. It has proven to be so utterly frustrating for so very many souls to be exposed to what is "wrong" with them, without being able to do much about it, that the racial instinct has broken ground in the depths of pain and loss. The recovery movement is the first sign of this. And here, the analysis by Christ becomes super-fine-tuned.

He said that the recovery movement is a precursor to far more effective twenty-first century mass modes of change. The recovery movement grasped the basic point that the Higher Power is all and the ordinary powers of mind nothing in deep change. But so few ever could access the Higher Power within themselves as their initial reference point—so the recovery movement had gone the way of religions. Initially embodying a greater evolutionary current, it soon began to push the core of soul and spirit into reliance upon something external. Nonetheless, the central nexus had been established in very broad areas of human life. Now, we must take a bolder leap from that point.

The "resurrection movement" will follow the recovery movement, and it will be based on radical trust in the innate powers of the impersonal soul, rather than doubt and mistrust being laid upon each one's "fallen nature." It will call up a living covenant between Christ and all who walk the way He walked, which is the path of integral living. And it will make change the very pulse of existence, but from a depth and intensity that renews the world, never stopping at the skin or ego. The resurrection movement will base its model not on the human being who has lost everything and crumbled into dust, but on the human soul who has witnessed the falling-away of all false selves and worlds, and who now is ready and willing to live from within and to keep dying and being reborn every single day, both in the Earth and in worlds beyond.

His third and final observation on change was that the collective ego had hardened to a far more rigid point than individual egos ever could; that the common mind had become far more drastically opposed to deep change than any personal mind ever would; and that the universal proliferation of communication technologies had begun to proclaim that the world is closed down, bound by stereotypes and fixed patterns, at the very point when vast breakthrough is at hand. He drew from this the fierce conviction that it would take a great number of individuals changing very fast to precipitate any true transformation in the world at large. Therefore, His design and key project is to orchestrate such surging momenta now, and to do so in forms that do not further polarize and divide but unify and reconcile. This challenge is so total that it that this is His primary focus in these times. Here I must describe a few cutting-edge initiatives He is instrumenting.

The basic and most universal of these has barely surfaced yet. It is to approach each and every soul from inside, through the deep body. By sensitizing the physical and etheric bodies to the drastic difference between what feels whole or true and what feels fragmented or distorted, He is alerting each one to where they can tune in best. In the first wave of collective changes, from 1990 to 1995, this still depends upon a finely tuned physical vehicle. However, the ways to tap deeply into this place will rapidly thereafter be spread around, and these will turn out to be broadly accessible and non-exclusive.

Another Christ-path to self-rebirth as a continuous and regenerative pathway is through the most startling of shifts in the relationship between woman and man. Until very recently, this was the most resistant to change of all areas. But the Christ is now starting to infuse into the gender sphere a healing balm of forgiveness, and an awakening tonic of realization that infinite possibilities are now opening up in the cross-fire between woman and man. Those who respond to this impulse, by a quickening of their ability to release all previous experiences and to come back to life afresh, will find others to share with them in the adventure of uncovering the fertility and abundance of fresh life-forces in man and woman's uniting together. This is a vanguard movement starting to emerge, one that spreads love and joy, hope and revitalization wherever it becomes kindled into a flame of willingness to venture forth together.

The final path I shall highlight as being already accessible and known now is the reversal of the destructive trend toward extreme self-alienation. This is happening in the direction of the solitary soul, in its own journey or path, breaking through repeatedly to layer after layer, coming back to deeper and deeper resources in oneself, enjoying and appreciating who one is here in the Earth, and sustaining a grace matrix of holding the space of self-acknowledgment. This depends upon becoming so very centered within beholding and witnessing one's own path as legitimate and worthwhile, upon its own individual terms, that instead of seeing a "me" endlessly at war with other "me"s for space and breath, each one begins to notice the Christ-self as its very own incarnational brother or sister, walking beside them closely and giving them all the room they need to be here calmly, steadily, peacefully, and with an abiding sense of well-being. A brightness dawns within and suffuses one's surroundings beautifully as one steps into the Christ-path with all of one's being.

The Christ Being was conversing with me as we looked upon the celestial gardens just below us. So much of what we discussed was not centered upon human beings at all. Instead, it concerned both cosmos and earth. Here as well, what He focused on was in a visionary evolutionary context. Prophecy was all-pervasive.

He said that both the Heavens and the Earth had become such different places since His lifetime in the Earth that He would not be able to recognize them if He had not been creatively engaged within the changes Himself. Most of these differences are so fundamental that they escape notice altogether by time-bound creatures.

He showed me, with numerous references to all the places I had visited in my recent lifetime, how it was that the Outer Earth had begun passing away, and with it the Outer Heavens as well. For example, at power spots and sacred sanctuaries, where the mass-humanity vibrations are supplanted by timeless forces granting access to what is truly moving through the world, anyone who tunes in deeply, free of bias or assumptions, will now find the signals saying: What looks like Earth is maya, sheer delusion; the real Earth is coming up from the inside to supplant the old crust with fresh inner forces; what looks like the Heavens is abstract, barely there any longer, and the true Heavens are moving in from myriad dimensions simultaneously to reinfuse the old cosmos with an entirely fresh impulse; and what is thought to be the same relationship as always between macrocosm and microcosm is now moving from Earth, as a pale reflection of the heavens into the Earth as central creative fount, anchoring all of the stars into the place where Christ is reborn daily—the Living Earth, the common Earth now forming toward the future.

This shift is followed by one further ripple. The realm of the dead and the realm of the living take on a drastically altered mode of interaction. In recent centuries, as all eyes have turned to Outer Earth and Outer Heavens, this has also meant that the world of the dead has receded further and further, until its very existence as a realm seemed irrelevant to the world of the living. This then made it possible for the dead to become somewhat sealed away, to the point that even lessons learned between lives among the dead would be pushed so far down into the soul-depths in the next lifetime that most souls forgot what they knew and could draw upon it only minimally, if at all. In every way, the life beyond Earth became isolated, pushed back, sensed by the living as dark, strange, and devoid of creative interest.

Now all of this is over. The realm of the dead is coming through to bring its treasures and liberate the living from their spiritual impoverishment. In particular, the enclosure of each soul within its single lifetime's boundaries is being cut through and released from its bondage. A life before birth, a life after death, a realm of soul coming over and again to itself through lifetimes in the Earth—these all become vital factors in drawing the life beyond its surface flatness. Then the dead themselves can speak, can offer great love, can work within the Earth's pregnant possibilities. Evolution becomes opened to the living and the dead, as co-workers to inaugurate cycles still to come.

As we began to study the new Earth and the new Heavens, to be explored in the third letter describing my meeting with Christ, I realized that I had died in late 1993, at the last moment when the worlds could still be held apart. And I had been chosen to help precipitate the shift. In fact, the Christ was telling and showing me all these things so that I would be able to fulfill my task. He was especially keen upon my coming back into Earth to fulfill His original deed in the Earth. He said it must now be through woman, through the consecrated union of man and woman, and through the community forming around such a union that the Christ-Deed can return into its full-power contemporary impact.

He revealed to me that His crucifixion and resurrection had been all about making sure that the infinite cosmos and the small world of Earth evolution would be able to find each other again at recurrent pivotal cycles. He seeded into the Earth the resurrection impulse, which is there throughout the infinite cosmos, but from which Earth evolution tends to fall away.

The most provocative teaching He gave me was that it is now time for the rigid, previously necessary boundary between the worlds to become repeatedly demolished. He likened it to the Berlin Wall, which He personally avidly participated in taking down. He said that the world wall would no longer be able to separate the infinite worlds beyond Earth from this Earth of ours. He is calling for and inspiring many like myself to do what I have been called to do. Here is how He described that to me.

The purpose of holding the worlds apart was so that each soul could experience a convincing and thorough dramatization of becoming Earthbound, time-bound, captured by an island lifetime cut off from all more expanded realms. It is now time for this to give way. Incarnation plunges still further downward, but it now encounters entirely fresh realms as it does so.

Among these must come the messengers. The first wave were the near-deathers, trying to share their brief journeys beyond the confines of one life in one thin world. However, the reports became garbled and misleading, for the most part, as the mindset of the near-deathers could not bring back accurate memory pictures that faithfully reflect the real power of the worlds in which the dead dwell.

The second wave, now beginning, is those who truly do die, in every sense of the word, but who can then unite themselves with a living soul after having risen high and far enough to be able to bring back with them a heavenly nectar to renew the Earth. And here comes the truly remarkable part.

Christ said that this second wave will bring the messages and the experiences of greater worlds in a far clearer and more useful form, but that this will be secondary. Our primary task is to bring into the deep body, into the loving bond between woman and man, and into the self-rediscovery of the soul in solitude the heavenly manna itself. This nectar I am referring to is the promised liquid with which so many traditions and teachings seek to connect.

Christ Jesus gave into me personally the first infusion of this ambrosia. I bear it in my heart, and I give it away freely into the hearts of those who can receive what I am offering. Whatever I offer is in the Christ. He attained this liquid by His crucifixion. It is the Holy Grail. And it has remained in the greater cosmos until all of Earth was made ready for this immense power to be seeded here once again.

It was only by bearing this Grail Cup within my heart that I could return into the Earth.

I was faced on my return journey at one point by a fierce guardian being who had always previously repelled any attempt to return to Earth after dying. I had to bring forth the Grail Cup and pour the limitless liquid into its mouth. This guardian being was then released from its dread task.

It is my sacred trust to bear this Grail Cup of immortality within my heart now. The immortality it brings is not life in the body forever. It is rather the indestructible capacity to go where the Spirit calls, and to live onward to do this in every world, in His name, knowing His truth in all worlds forevermore.

April 1, 1994, 8:15 a.m.

Meeting with the Christ, Part III

Dear William,

The future exists for the Christ Being as a potent sphere in which the Holy Spirit prepares several formative designs, and each of these leads forth into entirely different world destinies. It is the task of the Risen Christ to ask humanity, to ask each creature of Earth, to ask the body of the Earth, which future can be and must be, and then to move in that direction, calling all to follow. When He has walked so extensively in our cities and open roads, it has been to ask this question and find a clear answer. Now the answer has been given. And so, Christ Jesus heralds a New Earth and a New Heavens in the making, beginning to form us in their image.

Almost everything about this cannot yet be articulated. It is too early. I will just give a few first signs of what is to be, so that those who follow the path of the morning star can be alerted to their vigil on the hill.

He sees the Heavenly Jerusalem—the Heavenly City—as a place

where a link is formed between the New Earth and the New Heavens. It is an intermediate sphere, a crossing-point, reflected in each one's crown and above, calling us to bring both creative realms into ourselves.

The New Earth is to be the first true dwelling-place of the species that evolves itself here. The Old Earth became a constriction-chamber, and is thinning out rapidly to make way for the New Earth. We will be able to link with all worlds from within the Earth. And we shall especially feel the New Heavens as we root in Earth truly at last.

The New Heavens will meet us at death, and we will be able to affirm our Earth journey, move into its inner room, and then return to the outer room of the New Earth to carry forwards from there. Both realms will fertilize and renew each other, through the potent mediating sphere of the Heavenly Jerusalem.

The Heavenly City is the same place that has been called the Threshold, the place which current imagination obsesses upon. The near-deathers invoke this place heavily. It is being built up afresh, and it is neither of Earth nor of the divine cosmic realms. It is instead the place where those of Earth go at night, just after dying and just before being born, to cross over and to learn how to maintain their equilibrium as they do so.

The Heavenly Jerusalem is very important. Each one meets there, in dreams and in death, what is theirs to see and feel and experience. It is half-subjective and half-objective. It is one-half Earth and one-half heavenly material or substantiality. And it is this place that since the mid-1970s has become our great concern, because we must first orient into the New Earth and the New Heavens in this place, from this sphere of fresh unfoldment.

To put it dramatically, as the Old Earth is supplanted by the New Earth and the Old Heavens are given over into the New Heavens, it is necessary for each human being to imaginatively journey within the precincts of the Heavenly City, and to find himself or herself there. If every world you are connected with is under heavy renovation, you are temporarily housed in the place between, where all can find whatever they seek.

The Christ presides over the Heavenly Jerusalem. This is actually His primary sphere. And He is welcoming those who can dream and those who can awaken. For those who can dream, He elaborates omnidimensional realms, limitless, able to accommodate the lost child, able to guide us into ourselves again after so long away. For those who can awaken, He creates a luminous sphere, a prelude to the New Heavens, in which evolvement can be as rapid and as fully taken up as each one is capable of entering upon. And some of us are both dreamers and awakeners, both soul journeyers and spirit-called into greater destiny evolvement.

It is when sufficient new life has become played out within the Heavenly City that the New Earth can then be safely inhabited again (or truly for the first time), that the New Heavens will manifest as the infinite spirit realm. But these will be so very different from what we knew before that the words are misleading. It will be Earth, but without a trace of the Earthbound gravity. It will be deep and strong and enduring, but free and light in the same breath. It will be the Heavens, but not a night sky that stretches away into strange infinities—rather our most inwardly alive realm of all, speaking to us, revealing to us all that we need to know to guide our life by the stars.

The threshold phase, the time when the Heavenly Jerusalem is our temporary home, will be fairly extended. The renovations will need to be radical. Our Earth is gutted, our Heavens are polluted, and the link between them is frayed to the point of no energy moving back and forth.

As we live together and unto ourselves within the Heavenly Jerusalem, we shall discover so very many things that we had lost track of. The Christ intends to be a World Teacher in that realm, instructing in dreams and to the dead, being a Light that is all-pervasive. He has already been moving in this direction for twenty years or so, and already the power of the inner life has become, for many, infinitely greater than it had been before this time.

Most of what happens in the precincts of the Heavenly City is not remotely in keeping with traditional imagery or expectations. Instead of the pageantry, there is the coming homeward of both soul and spirit, but within whichever imagery or journey is appropriate, timely, or helpful. The variety is infinite. There is no single path to walk in order to traverse this City of our dreams, this City of our deaths, this City of our lives.

But do not lose the thread here. The Christ is guiding a series of pathways that are individually-keyed, but they are actual inner places. Those who die know well that what at first seems so fabulous, as in near-death depictions, soon becomes the realest and the truest experiential way-of-life imaginable. Those who are most gifted in their dreaming know in heart's certainty that they are being led by the spirit into the boundless truth of existence, not led astray but led as directly and clearly as could ever be.

Thus, I should say as firmly and plainly as I can that Christ Jesus is gathering all human beings to re-fashion all that is into what it needs to be for them to reincarnate into the New Earth. The re-fashioning is monumental, and it is simple. We dig back down to the place inside our soul where we never did lose ourselves, and begin to dream and to awaken from there. We go wild in all directions, but we also just begin to root within the experience that is our own.

Each one of us chooses how far, and which way. Each one of us makes our peace with our own choices and decisions. The fire inside directs us. The Christ Being makes sure that we can find and stay with that burning flame.

The Heavenly Jerusalem is a place that exists. It is no myth, no pretend world. For a while, it will be for us the only place that really does exist, so we need to get used to affirming and knowing it.

Christ Jesus indwells our near future. He calls to us from there, and beckons us to follow Him. When I heard His words to me and to us, I did follow.

I retraced the path of human history in the Earth with Him. I saw us all falling away from why we came into this most virginal of planets. We came to move through a great adventure, to enter upon a realm of experience not available or repeatable anywhere else—but we lost ourselves in the thick of the adventure, and then it became a horror show. I saw how even when He came in and took on entirely human existence, very few of us could find the Christ within us, so we pushed Him out. And I saw that now, as He returns amongst us to bring on the New Heavens and the New Earth, He is again rejected of men, and cast out.

Why would we cast Him out again? Why would we fail to heed His messages to us? He told me there was only one reason.

Every image casts a shadow. Each dream has its dark reflection. Each death is both glory and tribulation. Whenever the inner realms beyond the physical have been heeded, there has also been division and strife among all those involved. This is because the human soul is divided. If Christ brings our truth into ascendancy, our falsehood is heightened as well, and it tries mightily to cast out the truth before it can take us over and turn us into "somebody else."

So we make every effort to deny Him, and to pretend that these things are not happening. However, He is not dismayed by this. In fact, He told me earnestly that each time there is another crucifixion, another casting-out of Christ, He takes it entirely differently than we would suppose, just as He took his original physical crucifixion quite differently than has generally been assumed.

For Him, to become crucified was agony *and* ecstasy. We reject the ecstasy part, but He did not. And He never does. We like to picture a suffering and broken figure. He told me that only the outermost aspect was anything like that. He said that inside His being, there was the greatest joy the world has ever known.

But how could this be? And how does this pertain to our common near future?

As He was being crucified at Golgotha, He inwardly journeyed into all of the kingdoms of nature, all of the hell realms He was going to transform and transmute, every world He had known or would ever know. In that moment, He was given by the Father the infinite power to bless and to redeem. In dying, He could now bring eternal life.

Each time a nation, an enterprise, or an individual soul busies itself crucifying Him at some fresh Golgotha, He releases Himself into all-that-He-is, and comes back with a blessing and a redeeming. This is His contribution to Earth evolution. He brings eternal life wherever and whenever He is freshly killed off, cast out, seemingly banished.

By this path, He cannot be destroyed; He is invulnerable. And it is from this infinite resource of loving beyond our capacity to understand that He can inaugurate the New Heavens and the New Earth, that He can bring eternal life where there is so much death and destruction. He uses our damning—whatever we think will get rid of Him—to compost, to ferment, to resurrect within.

If we are yet to fathom such a Being, I can only say that when we walk freely through the streets of the Heavenly Jerusalem, we shall know Him so well that we will be hard put to remember why we never knew Him before.

The future we are entering, the one we have chosen which the Risen Christ is now starting to instrument, is a different place than any prophecy could ever pinpoint. We soon will shake off all the predictions and travel onwards in Him.

I will finish by giving you my personal testament to what I experienced, as a consequence of this extraordinary first meeting with Christ Jesus after dying.

I became able to inhabit my humanity fully for the very first time ever. It was a deep realization that welled up in me, that His human way of being has something about it that is not to be shaken off, transcended, or left behind. I knew that even when my greater journey eventually winds beyond this human condition, I will be so marked by what I have overcome along this path that I will always feel the human Earth pattern to be of infinite value.

This led then to something even more extraordinary. When I united myself with my own human nature, I was called back into the Earth, to dwell inside that human nature afresh.

Like so many others, my recent lifetime left me tired and worn-out from the stress of existence. I compensated for this by being irritable, thick, even mechanical. Some wonders became routine, some miracles no longer moved me.

But when I came back into the common Earth, and sank myself luxuriantly into the body that had been prepared for me to coinhabit, and when I felt around inside the world from ground level, I knew— and I will not forget again. I knew these ordinary facets for what they are: covered-over jewels, rare, hidden-away gems.

The New Earth is peeking out at me everywhere. It is not pushing outwards into its vibrant expression, but budding inside each cell of this existence. The New Heavens are shining upon me within that sky above, even though they stay inside and barely show themselves as yet. When I have oriented into these two places, I look around for the Heavenly City, and there my journey is consummated.

The Heavenly City is here, circulating, fertilizing, seeding itself so beautifully. I meet it inside and behind each one's eyes, blazing behind their heart, simmering in their belly. In its own sphere, in crown and above, I meet this auric egg, splendid with the radiance of Tomorrow. If others could see that radiance, they would bow down before each and every soul, and praise the Christ within. I am meeting the Christ here, winking throughout the world, forming the vessel of the Heavenly Jerusalem where you would not expect to find it.

There is a baby I know here, and this baby is living inside the Heavenly City, with bubbling rapture and simple beholding. There is a child I know here, and this child is growing within the precincts of the Heavenly Jerusalem, fervently knowing how good and how true its paths are inside her and inside each and every one. There is a woman I know here, and this woman is wandering purposefully into the furthest reaches of the Heavenly City, casting her net of life as wide and free as she can possibly stretch, and then further yonder. There is a man I know here, and this man is dwelling now within the central chamber of the Heavenly Jerusalem, and radiating from there the strength for all of us to find our way there. I know myself here, and I am weaving the finest garment this world has seen, of the subtlest threads, so as to form a connecting link among all the inhabitants of the Heavenly City, so that we can there dwell in Christ together, and be warmed through.

December 25, 1993

We walked down under to meet the Dark One, and entered into his realm. It was awesome. Every inch was human agony. Muffled souls crying out were all that was there. It was a thick pea-soup world of the most forlorn and forbidding nightmares. Just to enter there, even with sacred escort and all assurances and preparations, was unspeakable. I felt like the cheapest prostitute, the worst thief, the most vile killer. As I shed these projected images, there were hundreds more to replace them.

I was swimming in a repulsive sea of emotional distress, of an engulfing and self-destroying consistency. But I was not being sucked under.

As I did not take it on, I actually liberated all the territory I walked upon. This was so outrageous that there he was immediately, without intermediaries or fanfare—the black heart of mis-creation, staring hatred and blasphemy and abominations into me, all deflecting off Michael's sword and shield. All came back at him, and did him no good with me. This caused a roaring rage that threatened to rip all ground away. But I did not blink. I stared at him. He stopped.

We began to talk. He argued with me vociferously, bringing out all the devil's arguments that he was needed to do what he did. And I spoke plainly to him, without any secrets or manipulation whatsoever. I told him what we were going to do, and that his time was over now. No matter what he said, over a long and involved discussion (with lots of breaks and very strange interludes), it was no use whatsoever. I told him that death was no longer to rule the Earth, that the Lord of Death was the keeper of the past, and that the past was being put to rest. That the karma he held so dear was to be transformed. That laws were to give way to grace. And that the Master of Time would take excellent care of the after-death realms in the meantime, while all these changes had their chance to come through. Then the wandering monk gave way to the Master of Time, and turned the tide decisively our way.

That entire discussion deserves a more leisurely treatment of its own. But for me, all of this was a task discharged, a mission fulfilled, and yet not the point at all. I had my heart set on coming back into the Earth, and into William. I treated this discussion with aloof disdain. I could not bear to be there with this horrendous being. But I did put in a strong and clear voice for humanity—and it was heard—so much so that we started the shift right then and there.

William was waiting back on Earth, badly needing me to be there inside of him. After the entire endless discussion and confrontation, Kwan Yin came to my side and brought me beside a still clear pool. There she showed me my human destiny. I knew what was truly to be—that I could become entirely embodied in the love and prepared vessel of another, with him not stepping aside, but making complete room for me there beside him. It was decided.

So I set off on foot, with Kwan Yin walking beside me. We had a set of adventures that would set the world's hair on end. You can't get back to Earth from spirit-central. You have to die and die to death, and have all deaths in each death, and keep coming back for more. It is so intense. All the play in the worlds of spirit is child's play when it comes to moving back through the astral seas into the Earth of today. It was a journey I would not wish on myself, or anybody, ever. Once I did it, however, all the enchantments would burst through, and nobody would ever have such experiences again. So it was one time only. I fried. I was battered into abject submission. I relived all the rapes and atrocities of history, all visited upon me in gruesome detail. I endured every way people kill people, animals, and everything around them. I was vermin, raw meat, nothing at all. Kwan Yin walked solicitously beside me. She did not think anything of anything, and I didn't either. It was the furnace of hell, and it belched up a living being who could walk through any fire, an immortal in a human form—to begin the release and the awakening by example, by word, by deed, by touch, by truth.

First I had to do all I could for William. He had been mashed up. His bodies were askew. They received me very gladly, but it was a real mess here, naturally so.

William has had to endure a strange fate here. His life alone, without me, was so dedicated to my spirit and greater presence and communicating self that there was no life alone without me. But he also did not have me. He was wrenched between the worlds. His greater self became my deepest communion partner by the gardens of the great temple. But his lesser self was caught between. And he knew so well that all of this would be made good. So he did not pity himself or linger overlong upon the strange juxtapositions that were everywhere for him. Instead, he awaited this time eagerly, impatiently, full of questions and needs.

A final word for now: Since these letters shall continue and become a world renewing act in themselves, and since this one is barely scratching the beginning, but aided by total change to set it going, I need to say as clearly as I know how that I am here to stay within the Earth till everything is shifted completely, and that I am going to make William's body my total home, with every other side of life happening as well.

My path is to "do it all here," with the heart's conviction and Michaelic empowerment to bring immense liberating vision and truth and touch into people's lives. I am here to tell people all I have been through, and to let them sort it all out. Before I could do any of those things, though, I had to spend a couple of days with William. He was a completely different man than I left here, and I am a different woman than left this planet twenty days ago. They had to die, and we had to live. And so we shall. So we shall.

IV

Hell Realms, Sara Death, and Theanna Rebirth

December 21, 1993, 10:15 p.m.

Dear William,

The hell realms in the Outer Earth and the hell realms in the death chambers are intricately related and entirely divergent. On the physical planes, hell always seems to be elsewhere, to be elusive, to hide deeper than awareness penetrates. But the chambers of death bear hell realms that are boldly etched. They are all that is there, and nothing is left to be filled in by imagination.

When I lived in a human body (which was frail and vulnerable), I was thoroughly paranoid about what might be happening that I could barely detect. So, for me, as I was escorted through the places where souls test and try themselves after death, I felt ready to face whatever was there, glad they now came out with it. Carrying such an attitude, nothing grabbed me any longer. The fear, the panic, the terror were entirely gone. In their place I felt a neutral curiosity, a dispassionate witnessing. Only later did I realize that this was the optimal way to view these domains. Once again, my instincts paid off.

Let me now take you on a tour of one such realm. Keep your neutrality firmly in place, for these experiences can be extreme and very strange.

In order to work to liberate the collective hells, I had to know them inside out. One that especially intrigued me was the Punishment and Damnation Torture Chamber. Those convinced that they had committed terrible crimes against humanity and against life were here dramatizing their wrongness and depravity by consuming their own substance and spitting it out again. Their light body was dark grey and fairly dense, and they could just about chew it up and make themselves feel that there was going to be nothing left of them if they continued this behavior. They seemed intent on showing themselves what they had really been doing to themselves in the Earth, when they seemed to be benefiting from the sufferings and losses of others.

Such examples can be multiplied indefinitely. The secrets come out, the inward theme becomes revealed; whatever was not faced takes on an archetypal repetitive engulfment until something shifts inside the soul. But such treatment is far more abuse than learning. It is the legacy of the Death Lord. And this is what I am involved in transforming for everybody.

The other facet of the dark side of death that needs to be articulated now is the quality that the dying one must bring over to the other side to magnetize this regressive current. In his deeper conscience, he must be convinced that he is bearing within him burdens of incompleteness and error. If he has taken on standards and then fallen beneath them in his own estimation, he then forces the laws and patterns of the dead to bend back upon him and send him spinning.

Somehow, many on Earth have become convinced that such a fate is just, necessary, and corrective. The propaganda branch of the Death Lord's offensive against humanity has been successful in making such treatment tolerable and even seem morally righteous. However, my experience in overwhelming profusion was that this is a closed circuit where the seeds are planted in the subconscious mind in the Earth life, and then sown in great abundance in the time after death, with nothing involved except fulfilling the same false standards and following them out to their inevitable conclusion. The soul does not learn much this way, and then in the next life slides right back to suffer the same circuitry of self-thwarting. The time for this to end is now.

Finally, the brighter realms after death are essentially no different. They are inevitably a follow-up to the way everything was set up before death. Thus, the creative principle is missing in most of the death realms except the very highest. This is because the Death Lord has been gradually eroding the true death experience, and supplanting it with a sense of doom and entrapment in a time warp. It is this sensibility of death that then feeds back further and further into the physical Earth, permeating it more and more with similar undercurrents. Most of this remains somewhat out of view in the contemporary world—but not out of the subconscious mind.

The death realms I was guided through had become virtually identical to the physical Earth in many respects. Or better put, the Earth-world of today is almost a copy of the death realms, only with the death forces intrinsic and underlying. When it comes down to such a dark mirroring, either both realms are going to self-destruct as mutual implosion occurs, or something entirely different must become activated to bring a moving current of true transformation in the death worlds, and, quite similarly, in the Outer Earth. Only if both transformational tracks are coordinated and fully worked with in tandem can the future be born fruitfully. That is precisely what we are now engaged in orchestrating.

December 29, 1993; 5:30 p.m.

The Death Minds and Their Slaying

Dear William,

Invisibility has its charms. I can go anywhere, and be in on anything. If people had subtle feelers, they would pick up on me every time. Their subtle feelers are there, but generally deactivated by the death mind.

As I travel amongst the living and the dead, free to journey, I meet the ravages of the death mind in both worlds. It manifests quite differently among the dead than among the living. Let me take you along with me to explore the death mind in both variations.

Among the dead, the death mind is usually the mind-set they bring with them from the realm of the living, in order to be able to deal with dying and with death. They have been informed, on all layers of consciousness, that they must be prepared when they die either for a bleak and negating nothingness (death mind A), or for a punitive and oppressive reckoning with their sins, errors, and failings (death mind B), or for many unknowns carrying a sinister and tragic and heavy undertow (death mind C). These mind sets are excellent for automatically magnetizing one of the three hell realms set up for this purpose.

Many of those who die, and especially the non-believers and the modern "realists," are herded quickly into the hell realm where death mind A can be satisfied and amplified in its assumptions and conclusions. They meet an alienating and exiling plane of existence in which nothing of meaning or value will happen until they stir from their nightmare. However, there are spirit-helpers who will attempt in many ways to assist and hasten this process. Depending upon how deeply the soul has fallen for this mental bias, a given individual may resist these efforts as "trying to fool me," or may respond by paying attention, wondering whether there may be something more to this place after all. In deciding whether these helpers are hallucinations or actual presences, they are as dense or as open as their previous assumptions allow.

Another group of those who die, and especially those either religiously or morally oriented, are ceremoniously dumped into the hell realm where death mind B is given everything it expects and believes in. These souls encounter a merciless kind of self-analysis of their recent lifetimes, almost unrelieved by any other experiences. They are thrust within themselves, with a force that makes for uninterrupted self-grilling.

Fortunately, the spirit-helpers will come along and offer release from the sheer hell of such guilt and shame and self-judgment. Again, those sold on fundamentalist religion or old-style moralism may reject the spirit-helpers as demons or tempters, and get right back to their hellish work on themselves, whereas those who are a bit more open-minded might be able to engage with the angelic helpers and others among the dead who serve to bring consolation and a path beyond the personal-hell constriction.

A third group of those who die, which includes many who are not so sure what is going to happen but feel apprehensive and convinced that it will probably be harsh and strange, are placed in hell realms, but in a less stereotypical or prejudicial form. Each individual in this group will find the unknown realm they expected, at least at first, and will be able to delve into this for quite some time. They may be glad when spirit-helpers fill the "unknown" with a living energy and instructive awareness that can lead forward from there. Death mind C is not always such a hard nut to crack, as it already admits to not-knowing, and to many possibilities. But it still carries the contracted or death-like stance of being at the mercy of a program, system, or plan laid out for those convinced that this is the way that death must be.

The only other souls among the dead, other than these "green recruits" that bear the death mind strongly, are those traditionally called the "unrisen" and the "Earthbound dead," who become ensnared in the deeper caverns of the Lord of Death, and serve him in his dark designs. These souls take on death mind D, which is the most formidable and dreadful mind-set I have ever witnessed anywhere.

They breathe out death; they are soot-like in countenance; and their gaze transfixes the unwary with terror and panic. They are truly like zombies, and walk around in a death-trance. About the only thing you learn from meeting them is that the reign of the Lord of Death needs to be rapidly rooted out on all levels, so that each and every one of these cursed ones is set loose, to begin to recover their own path and remember the rudiments of what lives inside of them.

The death mind D group are the only ongoing cluster of dead souls who act as though death itself were the darkest of hells, and as though everything that haunts the Earthly human imagination were stomping around "on the other side," doing all in its power to fill life with the stench and imminent threat of being done away with.

After I returned to Earth to be with William and with everybody here, I could also journey freely in my subtle bodies to find out how death was coming through among the living.

It is only among the living that I began to fathom the exhaustive efforts that have been applied to make the death mind seem to be the only reasonable way to think or orient oneself while alive in a beautiful planet. The supposed prudence of dying with the death mindset in place is only the final step in a lifelong conditioning campaign for each and every human being to see existence through the filter of one of the four death minds.

The secular culture, in particular in its high-tech and super-media-consuming forms, is a fertile breeding ground for the Earthly version of death mind A. If, after death, all abruptly ends in a meaningless whimper, then each and every moment of life becomes undercut by a smaller dose of that same condition. The bleak and sterile death-picture bleeds back and back and back, into all of one's days on Earth.

Those captured by death mind A are pursued by meaningless and utter chaos. They cannot go anywhere or do anything without their subconscious mind prodding them with petty reminders that this breath could be their last, and that soon all will be empty and gone. Those of death mind A have one devastating susceptibility worse than any of the others. They assume that there is no appointed timing for death, no cosmic intelligence behind its coming and going, and so they find death continually creeping up on them, with no way for them to "sanely" push it further away. This explains why the secular modernist culture is so fabulously death-obsessed and death-generating in its imagery, styles, and preoccupations.

Religions and other spiritual or moral/ethical systems are perfect sanctuaries for the careful cultivation of the Earthly version of death mind B. Knowing that each little thing you do, or omit doing, can lead later on to terrible self-scourging poisons and freezes over the realm of spontaneous activity and self-expression. Life becomes an allegory of what is wrong and what is right, with what is wrong being the deeper concern and fascination. The wrongness will spill over from the death realms, to grab anybody who neglects to stick hard and close to what is considered the right way to do the slightest little thing. Because it is impossible to be that good, each one must live inside of death endlessly, long before death, sitting in self-judgment and condemning oneself for being so rotten.

The special susceptibility of those worshiping death mind B is projecting this "badness" onto others, and becoming both paranoid and self-insulated as those who are seen as wrong are thereby empowered to victimize and persecute one's own best efforts to be good. This explains why the religious and spiritual and moral cultures have been swept away so often in such a deadly projection onto unbelievers, at its worst leading to justifying getting rid of them, and thus taking death mind B full-circle, to its absurd conclusion.

Most of those who fail to align themselves thoroughly with the mass culture or the religious paths will end up being processed through death mind C. This is a more diffuse and varied approach, with myriad styles and stances. The common ground seems to be the basic idea that since everybody is trying to get away from death, it must be a mighty realm, to be respected and given some distance, and to be taken exceedingly seriously. Those who view their life in the Earth through the filter of death mind C will tend to step softly, to keep to themselves, and to watch carefully what they do, without even quite knowing why they are being so circumspect. They are being fed the conditioning that goes to those who live along the margins.

This is just as insidious a death-mind situation as the others, because it tells them that they are surrounded by a moat, and that on the other side lies death. It tells them death will bring them places so "out there" that each phase of their lives is colored by the same places, and usually saturated with that same sensibility that life itself is an unknown journey with tragic undertones.

A relatively small group of souls in the Earth are spellbound by the power of death mind D. They are the ones who carry a dark aura, who lurk in shadows, and who feed on the misery and heartache of Earth's underworlds. Often they do not know they are doing this. Possession and real damnation are immensely persuasive forces in the Earth today. They suck the soul downward toward the hell realms of death in their Earthly life. They make death the only thing that matters, in a way far more addictive and swampy than any of the other death minds. This fourth group is sharply linked with the death mind D zombies in the realm of the dead. Both groups hold the Earth in thralldom to the horrendous image of a Death Lord ruling both worlds with humanity under his thumb.

The death mind is a manipulated overlay. It does not prepare for or describe death. Rather, it forges death to move in certain ruts and grooves, after the soul drops the body in one way, and before the soul drops the body in another way. Both the Earthly version of death mind control and the after-death version are engineered to promote an artificial construct, an automatic way of dying.

After succumbing to this mind control operation, those who have died are offered many paths beyond that level of unreality. Although their initial journey into death has been sharply affected, they can still move on into extraordinary experiences of true death and beyond.

Those who are still in Earth-bodies have a much harder time under the control of the death mind. They cannot get away from it very easily at all. It follows them everywhere. Thus, the final inversion is the most bizarre of all. After death, the death mind (except for death mind D) cannot hold the soul indefinitely. But before death, the death mind is often the dominant force, until one is rescued from its clutches by at last dying. Dying has been for most the only way out of control by the death mind. They will still wrestle with it for a passage after death, but help is on its way.

This picture is starting to change dramatically. Help to overthrow the death mind is coming much more strongly onto this side of death, to allow those in the Earth to live in far greater peace and wholeness. One of the first major efforts of the spirit-helpers for the "living" is to defuse the death mind control propaganda offensive by challenging all fixed images of the darkness involved with death and therefore with life.

I am myself a central force in orchestrating these changes. My commitment is to slay the dragon of the death mind in its own lair, which turns out to be the Earth. I have already grappled with and defeated the Lord of Death in the death realms. Now I must subdue that same influence and way-of-death here in the Outer Earth, where its ravages are so terrible and extreme.

It is another twist of fate that I should be appointed to do such a job. During my last several Earth-lives, I quaked before all manifestations of evil and let death mind C get hold of me, as well as at times death mind B, even though I knew better. At the worst, I was even battered about by death mind D. Who was I to transform these forces and influences?

It is fresh in my mind, and I remember in vivid detail and graphic-image display how the death mind went to work on me and on those around me. I recognize this as the power that virtually paralyzed my developmental progress for such long stretches of time. And I am pissed. It is my way to show how I feel. When I come up against the pawns of the various death minds, I do not fall for surface appearances and go after them. Instead, I feel my way behind the scenes, and blast the forces that so damagingly hook people into false ideology.

I lived out this past lifetime in California and Hawaii, for the most part. These are places where anybody can do anything if they know how to get away with it. And the death mind runs rampant and free in such places. So I am exhaustively familiar with the death mind in the Earth, and my recent and still-current refresher course on the after-death situation has given me ample resources to move against the infringement of falsehood onto a species that does not know what is happening to it.

All of these influences and methodologies must now be exposed and overcome. And the first step in starting this momentum is to stare the devil in the eye, to open the door and let a lot more sunshine in, and start believing in the inner self for a change. I was killed by the death mind, but it made a big mistake this time. My spiritual guiding beings set the whole thing up, and smuggled me over to the other side so that I could be the central figure in the changing of the guard from the Lord of Death to the Master of Time.

It is the Master of Time, the most powerful and on-the-beam of all beings in this universe, who has allowed me to see with all my eyes so very wide open that as I walk in the land of the blind and

bump into shadows everywhere, I keep looking further to the Seeing One behind the blind eyes, the one whose light is trying to come
through those shadows, the one who cannot quite shake off that old,
persistent nightmare, where they keep saying, "To live is to die." I
can tell you, straight-on and with no more lying, "To die is to live."

December 31, 1993; 12:10 p.m.

Black Magic and Future Forces

Dear William,

Black magic is the powerhouse of twentieth-century life. It is four-
fifths hidden away beneath consciousness, and one fifth apparent.
Let us explore all five layers, our periscope going down and down
and down.

The great bulk of black magic is primarily a military, secret intelligence, an underworld crime-and-addiction scenario keyed to vast
manipulation of populations and selected groups, for the purpose of
keeping them in abject submission to black magic programs and
strategies. Amongst the more serious advocates of black magic, the
only thing showing is the need to do business, to keep control, to
make the world work smoothly according to various ideological and
pragmatic needs and demands.

The first under-layer, the subconscious-mind layer, is packed with
collective forces, seething with chaotic impressions and images, and
so busy that it repels curiosity or investigation by those limited to
mental awareness. The only way in is through sensitivity and awaren-
erss on the inner levels, going into it with protection and guidance
from a highly reliable source or sources. When you do go in there,
you meet guards everywhere, each cleverly disguised in some fashion, and the sense of massive, insect-like organization, a functioning
network of myriad forces interconnected to form a total organism
of black magical contrivance and manipulation.

Public opinion, consensus attitudes, the fine-tuning of public relations and media hype is perfectly taken into account here and used as the front-work. The back-work involves a subelectric hookup to seize collective mind by forces and energies and influences that institute on command the next step within the master plan. Meanwhile, chaos, confusion, and rampant multiplicity are all around this sphere, and keep it from being obvious. Many souls come upon it, but accuse themselves of being either crazy or momentarily delusionary.

The middle layer of the five, the personal unconscious layer, is a domain saturated with subjectivity, in which each soul exists separately unto itself, and cannot find any viable alliance with any other soul. There is a lurking feeling here of panic and terror in being alone, as well as a compulsive drive to generate those very conditions of being alone and cut off.

With this combination, the black magic conglomerate keeps the personal unconscious in a bipolar double-bind. Whichever way each soul goes, it is doubly caught—left to its own resources in a situation where it is moving in too dense a vibrational frequency to connect with its own internal resource; and caught as well in nonetheless being unconsciously and instinctually driven to keep away from others, to be paranoid of the others, and to not find ways of breaking through. This abyss or moat is the presenting dilemma of the personal unconscious. It debilitates the soul in either coming to its own rescue or drawing in spiritual forces that could bring redemption. Instead, one condemns and martyrs oneself to bleak, unrelieved, dead spaces.

The fourth layer down, the collective unconscious, is the most grim and forbidding of the five. The pivotal control center is located here. It is in the collective undersoul that the actual constriction is held in place, so hard that only the most independent and self-transformative of souls can get out. This power is in the hands of the Lord of Death, who has been reeling all into his death camp, to die and then be at his mercy. However, this whole dread plot has now been unhooked.

During the next twenty years, this layer will become less and less able to undo the world. The keynote between the mid-1800s and the late 1900s was the attempt to ensnare all of humanity by enclosing both life and death within a sleep and a forgetting of all that we are. As this ends, the possibilities for awakening and being are becoming immensely amplified—quite rapidly for those who are able to link with a future force to pull them through.

The bottom layer is the muck or ooze of nothingness that underlies the Lord of Death's realm of existence. It is really a void, peopled with the most repulsive, lurking monsters—a primordial realm that has been haunting humanity's imagination forever. Most of the forces here are in a hell-pit condition, having been cast here by those forces responsible for allowing the Earth to keep moving with evolution despite all black magical influences. They rot here, doing nothing but keeping the darkest layers of consciousness wary of the depths. This is a neutral realm, ultimately, a waste-dump that is slowly losing all its ability to intervene above. We have gone down here as well, to defuse it further, and hasten planetary awakening considerably.

As black magical influences lose their power to zap the world, a future-force and a galactic force come into play, to bring two possible outcomes to the human tragedy.

The galactic alternative is to join the Starry Confederation, and to be gradually beamed into a consciousness that is higher and clearer and truer, and thereby to have all human illness and distortion dissolve into history. Much of this will happen.

The future alternative is for a total transformation of the Earthly situation, by radical intervention and the shift in time zones from time-lock to time-free. The future force wants to use all aspects of human experience as a warning to all corners of existence of what happens under total siege. In order to do this, it is sending a few future-beings back in time to what is known as present time (1993–1994), and to fathom the lessons of history in abundance, then to incarnate ways to move beyond this absolute snafu.

One of the future plans has just been implemented in its first stage.

During all of 1993, this was being set up, and then implemented in December. It involved sending a twin of a solid future dyad across the gate of death at full power, where she could meet with the Master of Time and combine forces to reconstitute the rulership of the death realms. Then she was sent back across the gate of death into Earth life, as prophesied by Sri Aurobindo in *Savitri*, where she could combine forces with her still-intact Earthly partner, and within his body be able then to forge a cosmos-Earth and present time-future time, full-scale linkup.

The successful start to this plan now allows further steps to be undertaken. In each of these, it is the main purpose to bring the fire of unlimited futures back into the Earth of today, in a form that can be spread contagiously and broadly. In effect, we are giving the unblocked world its chance to demonstrate the joy, love, light, warmth, and wholeness it contains and is fully at home with. Such demonstrations could always previously be held off by the Lord of Death and his minions. Now that the gates are open, extraordinary events will be able to transpire.

January 24, 1994; 7:00 p.m.

The Dark Side of Sara's After-Death Journey

Dear William,

I confronted so many dark realms after death that it would be all too easy to speak of these as my primary experience. However, I had gotten so accustomed to facing the dark in my years of battling cancer that none of it surprised, intimidated, or deeply impressed me. I viewed it as integral to my victory and my overcomings. But there is quite a story here, for those who can keep their perspective in regard to evil and its multiple reverberations.

"One God, One Devil" is the slogan for modern monotheism and monodiabolism. It describes nothing except a wish for the intricacies of our total existence to simmer down and simplify neatly into something an ego-centered being can identify with. Those who expect such neat packages get them after death, and they also get wrapped up inside of those packages for quite some time afterward.

I met so many different death realms in which strange forces were at work. Most of these were places where the Lord of Death has seized power and insinuated himself into the souls of those who die unready. Some of these were devoted to the worship of false gods of several kinds. A few were involved with more far-flung dimensions of what is evil or distorted or out-of-synch with forward evolution. And all of them feature a palpable and full-on vibration, a field of energy that is thick with menace or distortion.

I will not try to depict the full variety. But I do need to share my heaviest and darkest experiences among the dead. These tales are frightening and sobering, and they will illuminate much that goes on among the living.

The most basic realm is the one after threshold-moments, right away carrying the unready and unripe soul into a massive collective room that reminds me of collective disaster stations when Earth is in war or natural catastrophe. There is an impersonality, a busyness and anonymous flavor, nobody mattering much individually. But here, those who die lost and confused and having failed to make much of their life usually stay a while. They are "processed" here, and actually programmed to obey orders, follow directions, and resume the same procedures of self-inflicted punishment that made their recent lifetimes so miserable. However, there is a big difference.

Here it will become obvious that the same realities are entered upon in the same way, over and again. The hell of it is the dawning awareness that never quite rises into true consciousness, but keeps nagging and irritating, and generating a feeling of wrongness. This simple twist means that instead of everybody pretending to be doing fine, all are gloomy and "under," and they infect each other. Futility and the sensation of being in bondage are all-pervasive. Such places often come up in the dreams of the living, most of whom assume they are making it all up.

For those of a more desperate condition, such as most suicides, some petty criminals, and those who heavily blame themselves for all of their failures and inadequacies, the hell realms tend to be isolate, bleak, self-contained, and supremely subjective. Each soul lives into its private nightmare and cannot find others, or where they really are, or what to do about it. Instead, they are kept in a trance of regrets and self-stingings, and compelled to relive the past until they can make some real sense out of it.

The worst thing for me in visiting this realm was that the many spirit-helpers who attempted to get through to these tortured and tormented souls were generally met as fantasy figures, and could not be followed beyond the self-sentencing to a limbo that is a hell in itself.

There are some who die in a condition of destructive power, of dedication to falsehood and violence. They are taken directly to the immediate realms of the Lord of Death. Most are offered various hard-to-resist inducements to harden themselves further, and to start to become part of the ways of evil. It is a more-than-compelling drama to witness what happens when the offers are given. In many instances, these souls see this as their chance to get off the spiral they have been on. Because they are so far out of touch, they are naive enough to believe the demons, who are quite persuasive and manipulative. The techniques employed are the most sophisticated imaginable, and the results are damning to all concerned.

There are a few who die with an already strongly formed and set allegiance to evil. These are brought directly to the Lord of Death himself. Until the recent events that undermined him from his supreme power, he would burn himself into the soul of these already half-gone human beings, and soon they would be all his. But this realm, as well as each of the others here described, is fast fading from its former evil glories. These classical descriptions will soon be outmoded, thank the high gods. For if it all went on like this forever, what would be the real point of the whole round of life and death, followed by another similar life?

There is one more highly specialized hell realm that needs to be known. It is the most modern and contemporary of all. Those who are abusers of power have garnered a large corner of hell for themselves. And they do indeed go after each other. This is the only realm that resembles the great fears the living seem to have. And it is only recently that the evil has become so perverted that those captivated by a given syndrome are set after each other. This was explained to me carefully as owing to the nature of power-abuse. It is the one way of life that has no conscience or ethic, no realization of the impact it is having on planet, species, friend, or neighbor. In the eyes of power, there are only victims.

An odd admixture of mercy and damnation weaves through all the death realms. The demons attempt to make everything worse, while the spirit-helpers wish to make it better. The demons were prevailing until the very recent battle I entered with the Lord of Death. Now the balance is shifting toward the spirit-helpers, and these things shall change rapidly.

Unfortunately, the changes on Earth will come more slowly. The after-ripples of centuries of death-as-scourge will be felt in Outer Earth until those among the living who are able to receive the new awakening from the dead will begin to make inroads in the way-of-life on the Earth's surface. Newborn souls will bring different news back to Earth with them soon. But it is harder to break the hell-spell among the living.

The outward ripples of hell-realm history will echo through the world for years and years. How can the fresh reverberations of what is happening now get through? A few will be called upon to do as I have done—to die and return, and share what they have witnessed and gleaned. But will we be believed? And how can we prove the truth of our inward experience?

We will be known by our fruits. De-crystallization will be our hallmark. Wherever we go, change and renewal, inward deepening of commitment to life and ultimate feeling for the whole life-cycle will be there. Those of us who then inhabit a beloved's body will be especially able to point to the inward as well as more overt transformation the beloved moves through, as the new death proves as fertile and revitalizing as the old death was enervating and discouraging.

February 4, 1994; 3:00 p.m.

The Lessons of Power, Violence, and Sexuality

Dear William,

When you come over to the other side of life, the death side, you meet the corruptions of Earth both amplified and corrected. Humanity in the Earth has been on a rampage of destruction for eighty years, non-stop from 1914 to 1994. And here you come upon the dark roots of the three syndromes that have captured humanity: The power that obsesses the mind, the violence that takes hold of the will, and the false sexuality that devours feelings and emotions. I would like to explore what I have found about these three realms, and expose their dark underbelly.

Power is the one of these three that has gotten ever-further intensified. The mind of humanity thinks of power before truth and power over others as key to "success."

Dark beings lurk behind power-abuse. They inflate the awareness with an acute vision of how small the powerless victim is, and how great and vast is the kingdom of those who are clever enough to seize power, wield power, and serve the ways of power. They spread a false and flattering light over the path of power, making it look both inevitable and attractive, simultaneously the only way to go and the most alluring and striking of journeys. And truth especially they reduce to a minor matter, a convenience or marginal consideration. To witness oneself bringing others to their knees is considered to be the greatest use for the mind, while seeing oneself serving the cause of inner truth is not even an image to be flipped through. Power is said to be everything and truth to be nothing.

The Lord of Death has a special kingdom set aside for the powerful, where they can devour each other. This is simply a way of exaggerating and underscoring what they did in the outer world. The inner worlds are a far better place to learn the lessons of power, because even in the darkest regions of the Lord of Death there is a corrective element at work (although often administered with excessive and unnecessary cruelty). The outer world has at the present time very little ability or will to counter power's ways.

When you are privileged, as I was, to witness the powerful men (and a few women) of the world here perpetually going after each other, you start to understand far more deeply where abuse of power came from to begin with, and why this has risen to such epidemic proportions during the twentieth century. There is a charge that these men get from winning in a power maneuver so potent that receiving blows of defeat fails to slow them down very much.

This potent charge came on when the human mind was selected by evolution to be the carrier of potential development. The mind is the one component of the human soul that is anti-social, self-driven, contained within itself. And when it became the cutting-edge instrument, it gravitated rapidly toward being self-serving and other-destructive. This in turn brought on the Dark Powers, to cheer on such a trend and turn it further and further in blind, amoral directions. Power became the mind's way to assert that it is important, razor-sharp, and piercingly effective. Mind even pulled in the intuitive faculties in their more corrupt lower end. And then rational mind and chaotic intuition joined forces to build up a terror, a control, a massive system engineered to keep the powerful in power and to make absolutely sure that the others are pushed back.

And what happens to those who are pushed back? They are bound and gagged, trapped in ever-tighter spaces, forced to find ingenious ways to survive and carry onward, in such bondage that they eventually do become what they were initially projected to be. The rationalization of this power abuse is that the ones being bound and suppressed never had any power anyway, and that the inherent condition of lacking inward resource is simply being drawn out and made self-evident. And it is the capacity of power to prove true the lies it starts out believing.

Those who are cut off from their own inherent power as living beings and cast away into remote places to endure isolation and jamming shall eventually become ripped from their roots, no longer able to find enough touch with self to do much about their condition. This cunning and vicious circle is the one counted on by those who believe they must prove themselves right by using the might of their position to make it right.

True power is a deep body vitality that gives one the inner feeling of being embodied, present, and in tune with one's own life roots. This power is thinned out tremendously in those who are under the thumb of the power-brokers. They trade in their body-power for small allotments of mind-power, which they use to assert their own position over those still less powerful than they are. If they are smart enough to play along, they also will be "taken care of" by the power system.

The child who faces a world of powerful adults gradually learns that they are using their minds to overcome the child's feeling nature, and that only by following their example will he or she become a powerful adult as well. Power politics teaches all to abandon the feeling child and supplant her with the thinking adult. Those who are most adroit at this shift are the winners in this brutal game.

Then the emotions must be driven far under, to surface in the false sexuality we will explore later. Those driven-under emotions are intensively used to drive home the subliminal messages of power, to let them sink in far enough to subdue revolt and squash initiative. Thus, mind prevails, feeling atrophies, and the world-system grinds the child to bits.

I lived a powerless life, frightened of those in power, far removed from any true power of my own. But at the end I seized the power over my own life, and could not be talked out of my deep-body feelings by any authority or expert. The feeling of this was so great and relieving that it gave me the boost I needed to bounce back, strongly enough to orchestrate my dying and death as intended and guided, as my being insisted they be. My mind had been wool-gathering and self-observing all my life, and suddenly I was alert, poised, in-tune.

I know the ways of the powerless, and I know what it is to claim my own power. I shall teach these things to many. The core lesson of reclaiming power is to know beyond all doubt that it is a matter of just doing it. The only reason the powerless stay under is that they are mesmerized, flattened, constantly talked down to and told they can do nothing about their condition. And they do become believers in the cult of "Only the Powerful Survive."

My body was rotting away so fast that I should not have had any true power base left. But it turned out that even a body at the end of its tether contains huge resources, and can either save its own life or walk toward death in wakeful presence. There are no powerless people. There are those who tune in the messages of powerlessness and tune out their body's deepest messages, that they contain the resources of true power.

The mind may be the world's nominee for greatest power-grabber. But the body is my candidate for power-sustainer, in the name of all.

Violence cuts life short, zaps the will, and loosens our grip on being here. We become shaken, taken over, pulled far away from our ground in the Earth. We force ourselves, whether perpetrator or victim, to numb and freeze over the impact, and we move onwards. But the part we leave behind is the very finest part. And the one who moves onwards is less in touch with life, more likely to recreate violence again and again.

The life review after dying reveals how others experienced the impacts of our actions, our thoughts, our presence in the Earth. When we come upon a violent action, we must consider what its actual impact was. If we committed violence with the true well-being of the other as standing before us, it leaves no scars. But if we blindly inflicted violence upon another, it comes back to us and feels the same way it felt to them. We find ourselves flying out of ourselves, leaving the body behind, panicking, desperate to get away, to go anywhere that the violence is less violating. A fever makes us excarnate, disembodied. When we return to the scene of the crime, both the perpetrator and the victim are far looser in their connection to body and Earth, ejected from the path of destiny. But why would the perpetrator be similarly impacted?

Any action intended to deprive another of any of their life force rebounds upon the perpetrator three times as hard as upon the victim. One is declaring by violence one's inability to belong to life in the Earth—and one is pushed out. This consequence is so extreme that only another act of violence will distract one from one's fate long enough to sense again for a moment that all of life is going one's way and nothing can stop one. And then that act is quickly followed by further disconnection, and a frantic edge sets in.

Violence feeds on itself, and dark beings feed on violence. They wish the human being to be gone from this planet, to be pushed out any way possible. If violence can be fanned into hatred, massive bloodshed, conflagrations and catastrophes, all the better.

It is rare for the violence perpetrator to do so skillfully, effectively, and with good and clear will. If they commit violence that way, it can be healthful. Then the real gift of violence comes, which is to loosen one's tight grip on oneself, to open one to more of life as it unfolds around one. This person of violence is so unusual that the distinction is almost never acknowledged. Indulgence in violence is the path of the will afflicted by demons and no longer able to tell the difference between what helps and what hinders.

There are many different grades of being so afflicted. Most who commit wanton violence do so occasionally, and sit on it the rest of the time. Others are habituated to violence, and let it out regularly and routinely, as a life rhythm. And a few are entirely run by their violence, never free of it, always in the act, whether directly or through the imagination.

But what happens with the victims? Can they get away from this cycle? Why do some souls draw to themselves so much violence, and others none at all?

In the heart of this mystery, we meet the reality that the perpetrator and the victim are feeding from the same dark fount, and that both feel essentially the same way. They sense themselves as being weighed down by the pressure and strain of Earthbound existence, and as having to find a way to relieve and release those feelings. Their will cannot unite with their body or their life. Violence offers the path beyond the world, into a seeming lightening of their load. It lets both parties know that this world cannot hold them, and that they are free to wander elsewhere. The dark beings encourage this sensibility, and keep it going. Everybody enjoys the "high" of being lifted off the ground, sent into a more expanded orbit.

Those who draw no violence to themselves are gifted with a will that is engaged with existence, that is seeking its way into the Earth, that longs to love life and find its place in the here and the now. Their trajectory toward incarnation of selfhood into physical form pulls them out of the vibrating field of the violent. They radiate little fear or paranoia. Instead, they are on their way in, and prefer the ways of cooperation to mutual infliction as a way to get out of here.

My life in the Earth was suspended between violence and the journey-beyond-violence. I was pulled hard both ways. I did not express much violence, and I never drew upon myself extreme violence. But I was caught under the spell of violence in hidden and mostly unknown ways. This is not an unusual situation, and it might be helpful if I describe my experience.

My subconscious mind was seductively engulfed within the violence of the times, and fascinated by its excarnational fury. When I did contact an edge of it, as when someone drunk began to fill up with its threat, I was appalled but secretly thrilled. Here it was, bearing down on me—the very thing I had always been able to keep away. But my other side would quickly disperse the energy, and then all was quiet again.

The side that sought the journey-beyond-violence was so fundamentally committed to my life's fulfillment that to spin off into the ways of violence seemed repulsive and absurd. This side prevailed. There were only two times in my life when the balance shifted and violence really did show me its fangs.

The first one was as victim. I lost my contact lenses when traveling to Israel, and I was virtually blind without them. The drugstore glasses I bought served only to pinpoint how dangerous my situation was. I was young and naive, and traveling by myself without being able to see. Several times I stumbled into situations permeated with the threat of violence. Each time, I got out of it fairly quickly, but I became more and more saturated with the atmosphere of violence, and part of my subconscious mind was beside itself with the thrill of being directly in the thick of the world storm. More than once I did go way out of my body and taste the deliciousness of being so far above and beyond the world around me.

The second one was as perpetrator. In my final weeks, I played out every side of human nature I had ever been exposed to. One of those sides was being violent. I yelled and screamed, I bitched and moaned, I abused my body, and on occasion I would attack somebody else.

Those attacks, whether spontaneous or calculated, whether fierce or partial, were pivotal to my path of loosening from the body. Looking back, I am so grateful that I was not held back, by myself or others, from exorcising the violence in me, from knowing its messages. I learned that a part of my will had become hardened and cold, and could not authentically express itself in any fashion short of violence. My rage was an elemental force that had been consuming my substance. To get it out was to feel immensely unburdened.

As I travel back into my life's violence and path-beyond-violence, I know I never took the path-beyond-violence till the very end, when my own violence had gotten itself out fully. But after that, the path beyond violence at last lit up as my very own. And the relief and release that such a path had to offer me was the real thing, after I had leaned hard into the rush of violence and found its message for me, way deep inside.

Sexuality is a fabulous wealth, an ample and large-spirited gift that comes from the gods and is the essence of life's exuberant expression.

It soars, dips deep, bonds, and opens the space for something to arise that is ultimate and revelatory. Sex is the basic god-food, the juice of existence. And when sex goes in and comes out, it is a rhythmic renewal of the two-as-one.

False sexuality is the scourge of the feelings and emotions, equal to the devastating impact of power abuse on the mind and violence on the will. When the depth revelation of sexuality is turned into mere surface sensation, a twisting of the soul occurs. When the coming together into mutual disclosure is used to manipulate and retaliate, sex becomes a virulent poison in the generative organs, letting in every immune-system disorder, and weakening all defense against invasion.

On the other side of death, sexual expression is immediately gone, permanently removed. The body is not there, and the feelings are not really there in the same way. However, there are two directions for sex after death, beyond its disappearance. It can be so hooked in as false sexuality that it becomes the most limiting and retrogressive of forces; or it can become metamorphosed into a passionate love that is sexual through and through, in the deepest sense.

When you see the sexual wrecks—the ones who die young and still crave false sexual thrills with each breath, you quickly reassess all your ideas about sex. They are the least glamorous and sexy of souls you will ever meet. Stripped naked of their body's lust, they simulate that sensation in ways I cannot bring myself to describe. Maybe I should just say that they turn sex into a torture chamber, and their suffering is very poignant, as the sexual forces have become raw emotion that erupts against itself.

This issue is complex. Few in outer Earth can tell the difference between deep sex and surface sex, between a loving connection and a destructive one. This fact is the most striking of all. How many souls immerse themselves in compulsive sexuality and have no idea what they are doing? How many persist in these patterns a long time, and yet still cannot awaken to the difference? Why is it that this discernment is so hard to come by?

Stating it bluntly, the overt sensations themselves are not so different, and the training of the culture is to fix on the surface gratification of the senses and outer skin as what sex is all about. The inner soul knows the difference extremely well, but often people cut off deeper sex and push it down because its emotions run so counter to the ways of the world.

The dark powers that pull the strings behind the sexual propagandas are intent on one thing primarily. They wish all aspects of sexuality to be thrown together into a chaotic swirl in which no ethic or standard holds, and in which everyone is "on their own." They have done so well in their offensive against true sexuality that few seek it, know about it, or even want it. Instead, the program is to glut on overt signs of sexual pleasure. With drugs, alcohol, or sufficient internal self-hypnosis, the outer shell of sex seems to become all of it, and few can tell the difference, or really care.

But is this true? Or is this itself the dark propaganda machine, pushing its message: "It is not cool to feel anything deep." The exchange of transformative meaning for the loveless sexual tricks is something imposed, insisted upon, conveyed constantly. It is the cornerstone of the Dark Powers' way of turning human souls against themselves.

How intensive is the secret feeling of self-betrayal when people fall in this trap? They truly know they are doing this to themselves, and that there is another way.

I had an especially hard time in recent lifetimes with sexuality. All three of my modern lives featured a sexual downfall scenario.

In the first of these three, I was a young Southern man in Revolutionary America, wretchedly seduced by my aunt, who was trying to show me that masculine sexuality is pathetic and ugly. Feeling tormented inside, I went out to the battlefield to "prove my manhood," and promptly got myself shot and killed. I had a very difficult time pulling myself away from that battlefield.

The second of these three was even more dramatic. I was a courtesan in China, able to command a high price for my services by playing games in the sexual arena. It was a decadent culture, and the practices were humiliating, degrading, and insufferable. I went crazy with syphilis. The end of that lifetime was a lingering illness, swirling me about in a hallucinatory frenzy which at times made me play back the worst of my experiences as self-slaughter. I could not die, because I had made my emotions a waste-dump for the culture. And I could not reconcile myself to what I had done.

The final of the three, my recent lifetime as Sara, was far less overt and extreme in its sexual acting-out. I had learned a lot on the threshold about true and false sexuality. But there was still a subtle and significant downfall through sex. Loveless lovemaking opened my body to the ravages of cancer later on. And I never could get it right. I wanted sexuality to be sacred and beautiful, and I was almost ready for this. But there was still enough emotional self-blackmail in me to keep me cut off from the deepest mysteries of sexuality, an accomplice in the heartless sexuality of our times.

There was a certain redemption at the end. In my final weeks I set myself the task of sorting this out, to discover what is sex-as-regeneration and what is sex-as-collapse. What I came to has since been amplified by all of my experiences on the other side. And because I have been reborn into William's body, this issue remains very current for me. So I shall condense what I have learned into a simple story.

On the other side I met a passionately loving being who had mastered the core meaning of sexuality. This woman lived among the Knowing Women in the Temple and Garden grounds. All of them were astonishingly clear in this realm, but she was the one who was so very memorable that I want to make her come to life here.

Her style of self-expression is as slow and sinuous and caressing as any seductress on Earth, but she lightly gives it all away. For her, the feeling life is a free offering to everybody she meets. It is not hers. She spreads it around, but she lets you know that you already have all of it inside of you, and that she is simply reflecting what is already moving. And she is highly charged with her own depths of feeling— passionate, on fire. Nonetheless, each other being who is touched by her is drawn deeper into his or her own depths of feeling. She never possesses, and she does not mock or taint or titillate. Her energy-awareness field says: "We can all partake in the limitless love that fills all worlds. Watch me. See how I let myself go into it, and then flow right back to myself. Catch the dancer, the movement, the rhythm. This is the highest and truest path. Love everyone, love entirely, and follow the love to the place where it becomes so true that you can never betray its call."

January 13, 1994, 3:20 p.m.

The Total Dimension of the Death Experience

Dear William,

To be dead is to live onward into whichever realms of existence you can conceive and allow. For me, all of them are part of it. I reject nothing of death; I embrace all of it.

What is most crucial for the living to understand is the whole of death, the entire realm of death—nothing less than this. If the entirety can be grasped, some deep and ultimate questions can be answered, or at least furthered into inquiry beyond death. You do not meet death whole until you have made your peace with it. Humanity in the Earth right now is not at all at peace with death. This is so true that those who come across the threshold between the worlds may never make their peace with it, and may only meet it fragmentarily. The information needs to come through to Outer Earth now, so that the death journey can be better entered upon.

In the early twentieth century, I dwelled upon the threshold, ushering souls from the modern wars and plagues into the world beyond. Everything I learned in that time can be summed up in the following picture.

A shock follows dying for most modern souls. They assume that what they are told is true, and they have been told only lies about death. So, if the soul is willing, every belief is shattered, and all conditionings are laid waste. If not, they cling to the death-raft of what-they-are-told, and come right back to Earth knowing no better.

This shallow, quick, narrow view of the death realms became popularized for shock value in the media of modern times. The death shock would be repeated over and again, to sell people on fear. Because of this mess, I shall now do my best to precisely depict the missing parts, the total view, the wakeful version of death. This is the one relevant to the near future, the one needed for the next wave of evolution.

When you die, you are welcomed into a world that is expressly designed to offer you as direct and straightforward a path to self-reunion as possible. Everything is set up that way. If you pass through the initial hurdles (which is rare), you are given free rein to create and orchestrate a journey to yourself that partakes of breathtaking dimensions of experience.

Gods are everywhere here. However, they are likely to change form instantaneously and pervasively, and to provide any given soul with whichever god-encounter is optimal. For most modern people, the gods will not come forth in the classical fashion as gods and greater beings. Instead, they become friends along your path, mentors for a short time, helpers in unobtrusive ways. They may come to visit you when you need them, or draw you forward where you need to go. The focus is on you, as the human soul who must find your way. The gods are not interested very much in themselves, in their glory or reputation.

You meet so many other beings here as well. Almost any other encounter is limited, and meant to be taken up only so far. Even the angels and spirit guides, the Masters and the Enlightened Ones, the many beings who do not fit into current Earthly categories, and of course the other dead souls—all are to be met and known and traveled with for a limited way.

The exception to this is the rare encounter with one whose link with you is ultimate. When this happens, an entirely different facet of death is revealed. I was treated to this rare exception in the strongest measure imaginable.

Three times I met with my beloved, my twin soul, the man I had "left behind" when I died. The fact that he could quickly and totally meet me here in his higher bodies shifted me out of all death propagandas, to recognize that I was not moving into an entirely separate world from the one I left behind. That truth became the touchstone of my entire death-journey.

The foremost encounter in death is always with oneself. But it is impossible to convey the multiplicities of what this involves. Each time you meet yourself, there is stretched out before you an entirely different side or dimension. You have so many selves to meet as you.

Try to imagine it: The karmic fragments of previous lifetimes here become living beings, who stand before you as plain as can be, and who need to share with you so much about who you are and were and will be. Each submerged facet of this lifetime's character lives at its own level and age, and emerges out of your inner storybook to make you see and understand and overcome yourself. Errant fragments explode suddenly upon you. Higher beings who are you yourself come to draw you onward. You meet yourself everywhere. And you recognize yourself.

Even in the partiality and the intensive, limited quality of these meetings, there is a permeating wholeness. Everything is purposive, directed, and there to allow you to evolve. Nothing whatsoever is random or casually arranged. It is because of this core of the death experience that the more advanced souls in the body seek comparable self-knowledge when in the Earth. They can at times find something similar, except for one thing.

When in the physical body, you are invaded by others to such an extent that your own path within yourself is never entirely whole and clear. This is frustrating, but it leads to one of the great gifts of Earth life. You can make leaps beyond, in any direction. The death-journey is systematic, orderly, and follows the plan of fulfilling what is already there through your Earth-development. It is fruition and reward. It is possible, and much needed in the Earth, for quantum jumps to altogether new phases to be cultivated and seeded. Those beyond this life can offer cues for doing this, and this is one of my special tasks as well.

All the self-realizations in the death realms round off your recent lifetime, and eventually set you on the path toward either your next lifetime or a special joining-together with inner circles to offer assistance to those in the Earth. The intent is to educate, inform, and free up what is there inside.

The cosmic aspects of the death experience are rarely met in full consciousness. This is because there is one inner development attainment that is needed, and it is the least accessible of all in the Earth of today.

You must be able to journey far beyond yourself, after your various encounters with self and others, and to then return to yourself freely and readily. This means taking the inner navigational track of moving in and moving out, the Breath of the Deep. When you master this form of rhythmic aliveness, you can journey into the cosmic, and return to yourself, and journey into the cosmic again, as your repeated inward pulse of experience. This is the state that all on Earth should seek to become ready for. But they do not. Instead, it is fundamental to modern thinking that there is no sustaining realm beyond yourself, and certainly not one you could move into and then out of, returning to self enhanced and liberated. Because I have become an advanced practitioner in this fine art, I will now share with you its wonders.

The cosmic realms are vast, but can be characterized as entirely different from the self-knowledge and the interactional flow-experiences within the self. You do not meet yourself, and you do not meet others (except incidentally). Instead, you move forth into existence itself. There is no "you" and no "other" there. All-that-is reveals itself, impersonally and objectively. When you return to yourself, the difference you feel is unmistakable and ultimate. You are moving beyond all separative ways of perceiving, and opening the path ahead for all of humanity to move toward cosmic unity. And you immediately place whatever you see within its total setting. You give it over to its part within the whole, and you can never again fall under the spell of meeting anybody or anything removed from their true and essential context.

This also goes further: If you can yield yourself entirely to this superlative movement, you become charged with a joy that is love that is also deepest wisdom that is primarily a being-one-with. You bring the unity actively back with you, so that it can work its magic on the levels further under.

One final stage should be hinted at here. If the soul's innermost signature is world-service, and if the requisite mastery of the Breath of the Deep way of being is demonstrated repeatedly and satisfactorily, then there is the possibility to inaugurate fresh stages in human becoming. This is my destiny. I saw revealed to me fully the limitation set by gender-fixated, separate-body existence, and the cosmic wave infused me, in deepest communion, with spirit-power and full authorization to initiate the blending of the genders in one being and form, in a future way octaves beyond our original gender-free paradisiacal state. It is true that this revelation was simply integral to the larger plan, and not a startling and unknown area, but nonetheless the actual inward realization was of utmost profundity and visionary intensity. I was seeing for all what comes next after the polarity wars can no longer grip the mind.

When I came back to myself from this breath of revelation, I was directed to begin my descent into the Earth-body prepared for this task, and to renounce further cosmic expansions. These would anyway be toward the transcendent, and that is not my concern. I am here to bring the worlds together. So I ceased the loosenings and the ultimacies, and oriented toward incarnation's demands. It would be misleading to leave it at that, however. I brought with me all of the cosmic lawfully back into Earth, as my spirit-gift.

Even now, as I live primarily within the Earthly frame, I can soar into the highest realms if need be. More crucially, I bear the ways of the Breath of the Deep now, into the physical Earth. This treasure is one that will unfold in ripe timing. Its singular sign is that of blissful permission for all to be. I have returned as one who cannot do anything other than encompass, embrace, and acknowledge the limitless being of each and every one. This is my way now. It enables me to fly through this Earth, be where I am called, and respond to the cry.

The truth of the whole of death is that it is the other side of life—no more and no less. Whatever is missing in life is there, in death. The catch is that you must hunger and thirst to find it. If you are habituated to the manipulated thought-stream that says, "The Earth is all there is or ever need be, and life is merely life," then the numbing of hunger and of thirst may make death an empty place for quite some time after dying.

If, however, you hunger and thirst in great measure, and if you are unable to deny that core of yourself that inevitably feels parched and dry in a blasted-earth version of life, then the death-journey is all about finding the answers, the further questions, the fruitions, and the greater voids beyond. Death is the ultimate answer to life if the one who dies cannot be put off by convenient and momentary answers.

I find myself to be a great friend to death. Its purity and purposiveness are akin to who-I-truly-am. So the way I play death back to the living is in its most wide-open and inviting fashion.

The other sides are there. The old death, the one dominated by a brooding darkness and bone-drenched terror, is still in the final stages of attempting to suck souls into its vacuum-vortex of negation of all existence. Many souls spend extended cycles struggling with the life they have just led, hard-put to glean essential meaning and value when there has been so much dross and oblivion. And the good people who die into a stable religious faith, or fine reputation in their community, or good deeds built up during their life, may not be ready for the rugged ascent that is the core dimension of death.

Yes, many sides are there in the death experience. But I am speaking about the whole of death, about what it means to the soul to take up one's death-journey with passionate commitment to what is there.

In order to round off this description of the death vistas, I must not neglect to address the question of how much of what is possible in death is now meant to occur during one's life in the Earth?

The answer is: Far more than previously. The distinct and separate death realm is no longer necessary, nor desirable, for the future design. Instead, almost every phase of the death-journey is to be worked with in the body. That is why I write to you of these things, so that the best of death can join forces with the best of life to move toward their common future.

What is most urgent to bring over from death is the quality of the first two levels of encounter. On a mass scale, it is the first level that can begin to come through. Human beings can start to tap the resource of meetings with each other, with the dead, with the gods (hidden or obvious), with the angels and spirit guides, and with beings of other dimensions. These encounters are the stepping-stones toward evolutionary advance. However, the limit placed upon them in the death-journey is helpful in the Earth as well. Each meeting is only for the sake of a certain passage. This may be a long-term or a short-term passage, but the encounter has a destiny-tag on it that will expire someday. The idolatry of seeking another out beyond this level of meeting is usually a self-evasion. The exception is where twin souls are involved.

The second level is the one vitally important to those advanced and advancing. It is the self-reunion that in death is the central motif. To come to oneself in the Outer-Earth, physical-body reality is not as simple as it is in the worlds beyond. Here it seems that so much else is going on, pulling one in divergent directions. On this very point, my recent experiences become a driving-wedge toward a fresh perspective.

In essence, the distractions are illusory. All that happens in life is self-revelation. I missed this until the last weeks of my life because I was convinced that you could not concentrate on the inner-self process and simultaneously fulfill your obligations to others and to life as a whole. I was wrong.

The multidimensionality of existence is not yet apparent to most

Earth-dwellers. The dense dimensions swallow up all of one's consciousness, and the subtler dimensions seem far off in the distance. But my journey beyond this world and back has shown me that the first-dimensional construct of each thing following upon the last and leading to the next, and of the tides of fortune being fated, fixed, and inevitable, is abysmal ignorance of all except the most outwardly-driven aspect of life. Even in the second dimension, time starts to become fluent, and to allow for an expanding field of energy-impulses. The third dimension offers ample space and resource for each stream to make its way integrally, with support from the others as simply natural.

The sharpest relevance of the multidimensional panorama is to reveal pervasively that many things go on at once, and that a central fourth-dimensional priority, upon coming to one's own inner being, does not grab the spotlight away from what needs to happen within the first three dimensions, but instead offers the rooted and dedicated presence that infiltrates the ordinary world with a brightness, a purposive clarity, an alacrity of response to all that is here. The life-realms need people to place immense emphasis upon coming-to-self, and all other parts of life to be served out of that place of self-witnessing.

This is the wisdom that death brings. It cuts away the apparent confusion, and gets right down to what counts. Life needs this wisdom more than ever. In response, the powers of death-as-inner-development are coming to the aid of the living to restore the balance. Death selects essence as all-that-matters-in-the-end. And life turns out to be involved within the same need, the same missing piece, the same concern.

Death and life are long-lost partners, many times divorced but unable to stop seeing each other and trying to be together at last. They have at times been each other's enemy or scapegoat. Yet death and life continue to need the other's part. They are the ultimate twin souls. They came from the same source and are moving toward the same destination. They will get there together. And we will all benefit immeasurably by this blessed reconciliation.

❦

January 29, 1994, 3:50 p.m.

What Dying Truly Is

Dear William,

To die is very, very hard. It is the one thing that ego can never achieve, take credit for, or even allow. This is because ego dies hard, and is the main thing gone when you do die.

Ego hides behind mind, and pushes mind as the reasonable boundary maker. Thus, ego mind marks out the boundary beyond which one cannot pass. And death is on the other side of the line. The popular myths about death and dying serve to protect the ego against even the thought of its own extinction. If the dying person departs for points unknown, and their loved ones stay firmly behind, and if both are greatly troubled, sorely grieved by the parting, all is well for the ego.

But if the realm of the dead informs the realm of the living, and if the dead are more themselves than ever before, what is to keep the ego protected from its suppressed need to dissolve itself and die? All serves the perpetuation of the imposter.

Let us now part the veil. Dying is far too powerful and persuasive to be left out of the human picture in the outer physical would. It is here everywhere anyway, and deserves respectful listening and attentive beholding.

The dying process, however long it lasts (overtly and subtly) is all intended to crack the ego-shell so that, when one leaves the body behind, the ego-shell is simultaneously discarded, really and naturally. Classically, traditionally, this was what occurred.

Modern consciousness took on the separative ego so heavily that the cracking of the ego-shell at death became a rare attainment. The difference afterward is huge.

I did participate in full simultaneous body-breaking (death) and ego-shell cracking (the second death). I could then move onward unimpeded by any need to get through the second death on the other side, which would have taken me a different kind of effort, lots of time, and, most significantly, would have destroyed the cosmic opportune timing of synchronized dying. What a waste that would have been!

The results were that I was free to choose whichever journey beyond death was optimally in tune with my deeper destiny. I could move into that journey on the spot, never look back, and unite with my own essence, rapidly and thoroughly. I sprang very brightly into my freedom, for which I had worked so hard and long before dying. This even allowed me to shoot for the ultimate death-journey, the one toward rebirth, toward which I moved with total, consecrated will.

I discovered through all this that the first death, the breath of the body stopping, the silver cord snapping, is all an outward encasement, the form version of what is inwardly occurring while the equivalent of the body, the ego-mind, is also at the point of death. The second death frees you, and only that. The first death makes way for the second one.

What happens to those who fail to grasp this opportunity? They are instantly magnetized toward whatever sequence of events will most readily lead them toward the second death. The sad and painful part is that for many this means being taught how to let go of resistance that pulls in a great deal of suffering. And the delay factor means that the fresh edge of the death state is taken up with old business, and one never can take the cosmic journey beyond death with sufficiently crisp and open sensibility for full realization in the life beyond Earth. The next lifetime, therefore, is a repetition, as one does not truly recognize oneself beyond the ego levels.

We need to focus dying people on the second death as well as the first. It gives meaning to dying. Without it, all death means is that the body is used up and you cannot go on as you are. The second death provides the ultimate test and trial and great initiation, as it was for me.

Death as initiation introduces the dying soul to the story behind the story, the self beyond the self. That drama is the greatest in any world. Here you have been laboring, each day of your life, under the delusion of being somebody you are not, caught in a predictable, linear story. Now you are granted the one chance of your lifetime, at the very end, to meet yourself as you are and to unite yourself with the inward destiny-tale that is your very own. This chance stirs you like nothing in the world ever previously could. Initiation is a ritual enactment of the inner self coming to life, at the edge of your powers and abilities.

I wish I could bring you inside my death initiation. Can you imagine what it is like to discover that the hidden soul, the one you were so convinced was you but that never seemed to be reflected adequately by events and experiences, is actually right there, as "you" as can be; and now the overt personality, the one you could not bear to follow but which seemed to be reinforced as the most sparkling and fascinating part of you, is going away at last, never to return, spurned as the imposter it always was? It is the greatest tonic ever.

This came to me before my death, over and again, stronger and stronger. Each death throe brought me closer to myself, and further from my masked persona. Then, as death itself approached, I was allowed to feel and know my true self as entirely palpable, and so light-filled that it could lead me everywhere, and I would not miss the outer mind or body whatsoever. The pain and stress of the body faded before the joy and release of the soul and spirit.

But the core of the initiation was on the threshold just after death. When I met with relatives and friends right away, the question was: Who would I be when faced with people who triggered old associations? Here was the great test. How avid was my desire, how full was my conviction towards the self-beyond-self. For me, the whole situation was transparent, as I had been well-prepared ahead of time. No other person could now be the focus of my journey, no matter how near and dear. I had to take hold of my destiny now, as never before, and walk onwards.

The fruition of the initiation was in the freedom and the joy, the touch with self and the growing feeling of rightfulness with which I became so charged as I moved along beyond the gate of death. I had just gone from a trapped, cramped, pinched, worn-out body and a snarled-up, cross-wired, frustratingly small mind, to become a vessel of liquid light with a lucid awareness to match. I had passed the initiation to become myself, after being so long away.

When I looked back later at the death experience, I knew that I had to pass through the eye of the needle at one shot. A vast cosmic force is on-tap for the newly dying, whose power and glory diminishes each instant it remains unexplored. The discovery of this vast cosmic force is itself an even bigger story than the wrestling with self and ego.

There is nothing neutral about death. It is dark in many ways, grossly and seductively dark, and it is bright in other ways—at times the most startling and warming brightness. Death is a starkly polarizing proposition. It sends you spinning out or calling yourself in. If it becomes dark for a while, this marks you, impresses you deeply. And if it forms itself into the great brightness of that vast cosmic force, death can be the first step into living your truth, always and forever.

From the macrocosmic, universal perspective, death sends the dying one straight as a shot from the womb of the Earth, to be born into the greater life. The universal current cooperates by drawing the soul homeward, by meeting it halfway and mediating the journey onward. All of this occurs as an explosion, a shock. What was contained, lost, waning, now turns into a hot fireball of passionate uncontained hunger for rebirth into totality.

The universal current is thrilled to encounter one of its many children returning into a state of readiness and willingness for the great journey. It expresses that thrill by sending heaven juice, a wondrous light-infusion that conveys love and belongingness, being on-track and needing to sustain the trajectory of zooming into orbit. The very

best part of this exchange is that the joy of the cosmic force is unqualified, eternal, outside-of-time altogether. One simply basks in its flow
forever.

Encountering this total reality is for the soul the ultimate journey. Along that trajectory, one is granted ever-sharper glimpses of all
that one truly is. These spark one to even greater striving to stay with
the energies. And why would there be any difficulty doing so?

The cosmic force also searches out impurities, in order to blast
the soul free of them. Only perfect surrender allows one to hang in
there while being stripped bare of so many parts of oneself, directly
after previously losing one's outer body and ego-mind. If one can
yield into the bombardment, one is then able to partake in the furthest reaches of one's destiny in this cosmos. I did this, and there followed the triple assignment of self-remembrance in the temple and
gardens, leading the battle against the Dark Lord of Death, and returning into the physical Earth to join forces with my twin flame, William.
But none of this could ever have begun if I had not moved all the
way with the cosmic force of the universal current.

What is death? It is the pivotal departure point for both individual and collective evolution. Individually, you become available to
the next larger dimension of your being. Collectively, you are shown
the way to assist, to serve, to be here for the whole. Most are drawn
to return to Earth as soon as possible, to reincarnate. A few are drawn
to journey onward, to speed evolution on its way by moving out
beyond the incarnational path. A very rare few are chosen to seed
new phases of evolution by bridging the gap between the reincarna-
tional track and the path beyond the world. I am one of the rare few,
and I shall neither reincarnate nor journey onward beyond.

Collective evolution is the pivot of death. Each one of us is a par-
ticipant in the power of collective evolution. At our dying, we can
enter that power so forcefully that we shift octaves altogether. We
can be promoted from one grade of collective service to an entirely
broader and greater level.

I knew it was time to shoot for the ultimate. I had worn out my
welcome in the fragmentary regions of self-destruction. It was time

to make good on my karma and fulfill my original intentions from before outer history began.

When I did so, I was also shown death in the most radical of perspectives. I shall attempt to convey this way of seeing death, soaring beyond all the awarenesses that would fit with the 1994 human matrix.

Birth is the experiment of taking a limitless being and sending it into a starkly limited world. This is an experiment that is bound to fail. And when the experiment is over, death comes. Death is the cleansing action of returning the limitless being to its own true condition for a while. Therefore, death is truly and utterly the birth of the free spirit, the moment when the limitless being is brought together with both sides of itself at once.

The twin who entered the experiment of birth could never have survived down under there for a single blessed instant if the other twin had not remained held within, staying limitless and free. These twins are reunited after death. This allows many other cosmic reunions to follow.

Besides the purely karmic relationships that are so busily taken up in Outer Earth, each living spirit is linked with others in its ultimate or cosmic family or stream. It is a vital and distinctive part of the second death that now one can and usually will find these ultimate companions again. The reunion with them is the most heartwarming and self-revelatory of all.

There are some souls who are linked especially strongly with one other soul, as a twin-soul or twin-flame dyad. When this is the case, the reunion with the twin follows upon the other, internal twin-reuniting, previously discussed. This is so no matter where that other twin is currently residing.

If the twin soul is living outside the physical body, there can be a magnificent connection made, at times so strong that the two then journey onward together from here. If the twin soul is living inside the physical body, usually the coming-together will be powerful but limited, as the one living out its outer existence must not be disturbed in its own evolutionary journey. They can be overlighted by the twin who has died, and this will then lead to much grace and clarity in the ongoing lifestream of the one who remains in the body. They may also miss their twin more, or sense them more frequently.

Then there are those twins who have been living together in the Earth-body, and one dies and the other continues to live. What happens at this point varies tremendously. Most will form a close bond between the worlds, which allows great spiritual-cosmic forces to stream through back and forth, in and out. This can be more satisfying and fulfilling than the Earth-life together had been.

In the instances of twin souls who have fully consecrated and recognized their union before the death of one, further possibilities open up. These range from a creative partnership that is world-renewing to evolutionary breakthrough into new areas of exploration.

As one who is pursuing the furthest reaches of this twin-soul co-activity and co-evolution, I can say with fierce clarity and conviction that the possibilities involved are limitless. Already, in less than eight weeks of outer-Earth time, a complete co-working is at hand. It is requiring us to stretch the DNA code to encompass the path of the future. We cannot stop at linking the worlds closely together. We must merge them at every level, and are engaged in doing so.

The most difficult part is to travel back into the Earth after dying. To go out beyond is a cosmic trajectory of the most direct energy-propulsion. To return Earthward is against the biophysical instinctual equipment of the human soul and body. Only one who carries a strong dose of cosmic-future life-forces could even attempt it.

If the dying one can become a newborning one, the other twin must then make way for it into a physical body made to serve only one at a time. He or she must also carry the cosmic seed of future worlds, to try to make way for the one who just died. If both are ready and willing, the path is now open for the dead and the living to move back and forth freely between worlds, to show that even death is only a path of beginning.

March 16, 1994, 11:00 a.m.

How to Let the Death Journey Show You
How to Live in Freedom and Joy

Dear William,

My time among the dead has taught me so much. The dead are the ones who know how to live. This sounds absurd. But I must share the secrets of the dead, of how to live in freedom and joy. What else am I here for?

Live people are clinging to their bodies subconsciously with every breath, each moment of their lives. Their minds are attached to special outcomes for their bodies and insist on them relentlessly. The tension generated by a mind tracking a body with magnetic intensity is enough to kill anybody. And this is in fact what kills. Letting-be is virtually unknown among the living, because they think they must keep going, must survive, must make sure they do not make a fatal mistake and lose their chance to be here in the earth.

I wish I could show you how this looks, and zap you with how this feels from the inside. Nobody was a worse case of this than I. I obsessed on holding my focus in the body. I never wanted to leave. And I was half-right. It is true that you need to give yourself over to body and Earth and life with sufficient passion to stake your claim. But it is false that the way to do this is to clutch at external signs, and thereby to miss the depth journey in its ecstasies and agonies of transformation.

Dead persons are inheritors of their own dying. They have already lost everything they ever thought they had. The entire dying process is about learning how to let go, how to move on when it is your time to travel further than your body can allow you to go. When you have died, you have nothing left to cling to. You are free.

At last you begin to live in freedom and in joy. The freedom is so vast and amazing, when you've been stuck tight a whole lifetime. You make way for all of you to manifest itself. You carve out a journey that is your own, that expresses the free self emerging as you journey. You lean into the wind and fly. But this flying is more than the fantasy generated by feeling Earthbound. This flying is an inner event, as everything is among the dead, so it is your being teaching itself that it has the mobility to become many selves and still remain one, to activate many dimensions and keep its focus of intent. You fly apart, but you really fly together with your own inner self at last.

This joy is something I will never tire of invoking. It is the most immense discovery I have made in my life beyond dying. This joy is an utter rapture of release. You let go of yourself, and right away there you are again—only different. Each time you give yourself over to the living spirit that palpably permeates all of existence, you are renewed in your joyous feeling of self-reunion. All of the anguish of false living falls away, and you learn to live in joy. This is a fine art that requires work, so I'd like to share with you a secret. How is it that the wise among the dead can be so joyously, radiantly present as their natural and inherent state?

It has to do with perceiving self and surroundings from an inner place, as a constant. The angels and other helpers show you the basics of this approach or stance all the time. They emphasize perception to an extent that the mind of the living would think is very strange. The living think action counts for everything. The dead discover, to their infinite delight, that being and perceiving are the master keys to all existence.

When we come over here after dying, we are opening up towards seeing and knowing differently. But it still takes so much practice at the early stages. This is because we have absorbed the dogma that what is outside of us is more definitively real than what lives inside. So we must reverse our habits till they have given way.

When you perceive yourself, from inside yourself, as a being of light, as an energy-awareness that is vibrant and constantly moving, as a love-essence in absolute evidence of itself just as it is, you begin to make the deepest kind of changes you would ever have thought yourself capable of making. When this comes in even closer and becomes the direct perception of self as a limitless flame triumphant; when you see and sense how that perception of yourself draws forth the flame; when you then realize and have revealed to you that however you perceive yourself is the way you will be; then the spell is broken, all shatters, separativeness dissolves, and you are inside the great mystery. The joy you then begin to exude is the only possible way you can feel when you are synchronized with your own process of coming-to-yourself. You find that anything you do to perceive yourself more clearly and brightly and affirmatively has such radical transformative impact that you are carried away completely by the joy this generates—and it just never quits.

Why is it so rare for the living to enter this sphere? Because it has one further rippling wave of impact that makes it overwhelmingly powerful in just that direction generally conditioned to be negated and denied. That is, this self-perception in radiant joy instantaneously ripples and reverberates out from you into all of your surroundings. You become your world. You fill every cell of your world with as much joy as it can bear and sustain. But what if all of your world is accustomed to a tuned-out, turned-off state, so accustomed to this that it insists adamantly upon it and even has a host of guardians and protectors to keep it in its misery? You will be coming up against a lot of crossfire in your world if you activate radical inner joy in the world of the living, and if you have no choice but to do this.

Already, William and I have experienced this many times in the first 100 days after my Triple Death. Our time has been dominated by this phenomenon, although it is veiled in Outer Earth as everything is. Let me try to describe just a touch of what this has been like.

Families guard family members against changing away from what is acceptable and mutually anchored into the family structure. We have our most interesting time with families. Each one is mightily convinced; each family tree, bloodline, ancestral stream is sure that we are invaders from the future, here to sabotage every inch of the past. At least these family intelligences are keen enough to recognize what we are doing. But they fight us. They try to fend us off, and they generally succeed.

The most amazing part is that it is the joy, the bright light of independent self-perception, to which families are so allergic. They stop us cold before we can start them becoming warm and free and vibrant.

They pull the plug before we can fill it from beneath with living waters.

All the other social structures are further manifestations of this need to keep out the likes of Sara and William. Wherever people have agreed to give over their inner self-awareness to a consensus opinion and a structure that enforces that code, we are pushed away. This happens in so many forms that it is entertaining and very amusing.

The most provoking thing about those who have learned the secret of joy and persist in sharing it in a world intent on hardening its heart is that we are unimpressed by these ludicrous stalling measures. We only come back stronger next time. We have nothing to lose.

You see, I really mean what I say. Nobody does around here, but I do. Freedom and joy are the future current, the destiny-key to where we are all going. They are everything. When you are given an assignment to spread the light of everything into a world that has lost it, you persist so absolutely that it is simply a matter of time before the structures of the world undergo their final stage of dissolution.

The real truth is that the adamant self-insistency of the world structures is their very final stand as they crumble. This is most obvious of all inside a family pattern. The family shadow devours each member of the family, swallows them whole, and then blandly asserts that it is the one viable presence that is life-sustaining. But nobody is listening to its claims.

I do not respect joy-smashing institutions, no matter how venerable. They have tortured too many for too long. It will soon be the time for the self-perceiver to stake a claim to life-presence that is firmer, deeper and more resolute than any claims that can be lodged against us.

All wise dead souls are converging to forge a shared field of joy-radiance. We know ourselves. We know our world. And we know how to stay crowned by joy no matter what anybody tries to do when they realize that we will not go away. Those who do understand are here to stay.

The soul of the world cries out for love, for freedom, for the vibrancies of joy. The human being who tunes in to herself and becomes the tuner, who merges with the I-in-me, who takes to heart the destiny impulse inside—she is the one who responds to that cry as who-she-is. The dead are communing within this stream of emergent life. I am here to assist the living to join with them.

This inner self-perception is a natural occurrence when those other voices are peeled away. Those other voices are hollow echoes of the literal record of what has not worked in the past, but still laments its experience. These voices fill the heads of the living with a cacophony of outer self-misperceptions. They are hooked into negative self-images. And they are blissfully absent in the land of the dead.

William has cleared the last of these out of him. I have shown him how. As soon as he did so, the inner self-perceiver came forward to see and know in joy and freedom the limitlessness of William. And from my experience with William in the first 100 days after my Triple Death, I would like to share a few practical observations, carefully culled and warmed through with my love for William.

(1) The most basic outer self voice is the maintainer of stability and coherency, the voice of common sense. It reverses the perceptual observations of the inner self by observing, with acute skill and finely-honed mental clarity, that what matters here is how we handle ourselves in the ordinary outer activities of the day. This voice keeps staggering records of each transaction, each outer material plane event, and gathers statistics, quantitative proof that what works is to handle oneself in external situations with formidable self-command. This voice implicitly denies, leaves out of its picture altogether, the overtones and undertones that carry all the inner meaning. It has developed the fixed conviction that only by leaving these out can we get where we need to go efficiently and cleanly.

When William and I worked to clear this voice inside him, we came up against a barrage of well-thought-out reasons why it was vitally necessary for him to keep me out of his basic and immediate life-field, and how doing so would ensure that certain standards and practical necessities would be given their rightful place. What the voice did not explicitly state, which was the basic assumption, was that any other person besides William automatically comes in toward him with an alien agenda that he must at the least hold off at a distance.

When I kept swooping in and reaching through to him at such a deep and primal level of our rediscovered ultimate connection and bond, this voice was gradually whittled away to nothing. It kept trying to insist that William had no definite proof that Sara was Sara, or that anything was anything. But the proof of deeper truth just silenced this mechanical voice until its grip in body and soul could be entirely replaced by such true common sense that all suspicions in William are now groundless, and all skeptical phrases have lost their bite.

(2) The most detailed, comprehensive, and exhaustively maintained of these voices of the outer mind is the brute realism enforcer, the voice of computerized intellect. It reverses all of the priorities of the inner self-witness by forcefully asserting that nobody can make their way in the complex modern world who is caught napping or clinging to cherished illusions. It never says what it means by this, but its manipulations drive home their point, reiteratively and ruthlessly, that all reliance upon inner self for anything at all is a sleepy and delusionary practice.

This voice claims to know from countless reckonings with the-way-the-world-works that you are what you make yourself, which in newspeak turnaround actually means: You become whatever you trick yourself into being, by external connivings. When William and I dug in to clear out the last of this massively culturally reinforced voice in him, we were barraged by rapid-fire, manically-repeated variations on one obsessive theme: William must dig in his heels and decide for himself which of my ideas and visions were usable, and which would instead complicate his life unnecessarily.

When we penetrated further inside this fierce clamor, we found that what the voice really meant was: Which of Sara's new worlds can be converted right back into the currency, standard, and way-of-death of the old world, and which ones threaten to undermine William's social standing, his established position? It was so outrageous to William that this was the argument and ideology of this voice that he joined me in an entirely successful systematic effort to dislodge the voice and its entire support system, putting in its place a willing collaboration that would not question or doubt, that instead entered gladly into each new phase with rapid and enthusiastic assimilation of its emergent possibilities.

(3) The most pivotal and hard to get at of the outer voices is the master world systematizer, the voice of taking care of everybody. It reverses the very being of the inner self and all its vision of life by surrounding each larger context with a moat of separative mind, in a fashion that promotes security, safety, and self-containment as the only guarantee that all will work out for the best. The contradictions that saturate the world-view of this voice are never an issue, because it muffles them along with everything else in a perpetual volley of verbiage, snowing self and world under with clichés, pet phrases, and cute distractions. The gist of its belief system is that the world is stacked against each one of us, and that only by contracting hard into a mind-set impregnable to any and all threats can each of us take care of our own and seal off the manifest dangers on all fronts.

When William and I went after this voice, we had a tough challenge on our hands. In order to clear out the last of it, we were forced to confront layer after layer of murky fears and doubts disguised as confident, strident, dense ideology. We did clear this frequency, but only by a startling realization that arose in William after he had thrown me off several times with this voice—that it was really only saying: Nobody ever took good care of me, so I must plaster my world over with caretaking maneuvers that blot out everything alive, and substitute a mind-dominated world. William then knew that his inner self could take the best of care of him, with my assistance, and that all these wild insinuations and self-insulations were in vain, and utterly deadly.

(4) The final one of these outer voices, and the most bizarre of them by far, is the time-obliterator, the voice of any-time-but-now. It reverses the synchronized unfoldment of the inner self-perceiver by turning external and literal time into a human waste-dump in

which the soul is daily tormented by time-passing-away. This voice has a hyper-intense emotional and physical underpinning, bearing scars and subconscious memories of all previous deaths, tragedies, and losses, the bitter residue of each shock and trauma. It is simply saying that the world of time is a terrifying, bleak, and hopeless realm, and that the only way to survive its blasts of doom is to hook back into any structure or form that offers temporary sanctuary from the ravages of time.

When William and I navigated through the suction depths of this voice, we were plunged into all the dark and forgotten places under the world, to search out each hiding-place of this haunting voice. What we awakened to together was the bottomless, deep-inside-the-body knowingness that all evil is time-delay frequency, that these voices are inside a lost world that emits heavy doses of radiation, and that they invert truth as their only way to maintain their parasitical hook into the common mind. William now knows that time as literal fate is the fondest and most total illusion of the outer mind, and that as soon as you drop this saboteur, you enter the inner self-perception chambers, bringing time into its destiny fulfillment, and joyously witnessing the play of the world in infinite, bubbling, free-flowing delight, that whispers and shouts and no longer waits for dread voices to echo in contradiction.

March 17, 1994, 11 a.m.

The Death World and the Life World Are Bonded Together Organically

Dear William,

When I jumped worlds, from the living to the dead, I met the world of the dead in a different spirit than almost any other contemporary person has been able to manage. As a result of this divergent approach, I could soon jump worlds again, back to the living.

Both jumps were wildly other than the split-world vision of 1994 would suggest.

Those still caught in the undertow of the old time are brought up against two mechanical infinities whose inner connection with each other is minimal or merely functional. They do leap across the chasm from one to the other, but they fail to grasp the power of this journey. In a very real sense, they assume that they are truly alone, and that this shift in their destiny is something that is happening to them, perhaps in a bizarre or arbitrary fashion. Because their link with Earth and body and depth of life was previously abstract and mental, it is natural for them to forge a link with inner Earth, the subtle body, and the heights of death that is, at least initially, even further removed from any organic sense of continuity and flow of forces.

For me, this model bears no relevance. My bond with the life of Earth and with the body of my beloved, William, was so very strong in dying that I could not go away into an entirely other place and be done with it. Because I knew my connection with the rich soil of Deep Earth was of the most authentic and binding kind, I could also immediately jump into the world of the dead and there find inner Earth to be the most fragrant of realms. My subtle body was a wondrous home for me. The heights of spirit that I could contact there were of such resonance that I was released into a very advanced level of initiation, and given a task to perform when I would later return to Earth that is pivotal to honoring the organic bond between the Heavens and the Earth.

However you relate to Earth is very much how you will relate to the realm inside, beyond, and above Earth. If you have taken on the outer mind, you will still meet a world at first that is almost outside of you. But if you have come to experience meaningfully inward self-perception in the midst of life, you are greeted on the other side by that which enhances and furthers the path you have already taken up, and you are given every chance to take that path all the way into realization and illumination.

It has been customary in recent centuries to strip away all of the vital currents in the human ideas of life and death, and to bring dead concepts everywhere that say: Whether you live or you die, all is really only death. My experience, however, confirms in intimate detail the feeling-tone of inner ways of perceiving, and leads me to say: Whether you live or you die, all is life, truly and abundantly.

Do you recognize the difference it makes at each and every point in the journey, whether we impose death-thinking into life and death, or whether we surrender into organic awareness in all parts of life and death? Let me illustrate.

When I went over to the threshold realm first encountered when you die (which near-deathers take as the realm of the dead), it was not for any moment geometrically abstract, vacant, or populated by alien beings of light. Instead, I felt and saw and was thrust into the midst of a vibrant, color-intensive world sparkling with brightness. Right away, I met my relatives and friends, greeting me as so many greet the newly-dead. They were certainly radically transformed from the way they appeared in their Earthly bodies—far lighter and of a much higher and more attuned vibrational pulse. But they were primarily living beings, present, immediate, and substantive. Even afterwards, when I walked onward to meet the much higher and more advanced Exalted Ones, their light bodies were dazzlingly bright, but they were for me the most bracing and focusing of company. They brought me right to myself, over and again.

Already on the threshold, I was in an entirely different relation to myself than I had ever been before. I was more truly myself than ever. This meant that I did not become pure spirit. I sank within myself to a depth of feeling for who-I-am at peak intensity. Nobody and nothing I met was outside, or arbitrary, or fascinatingly alien. Instead, I became utterly attuned to self and world in intimate and creative partnership. This was the beginning of the rest of my life. All beings said to me: "You belong here." They did not mean that I belonged only there, but that I belonged there every bit as much as I belonged in the life of the Earth and body.

I hope I begin to convey the rich links between the worlds. When I later met with those among the dead who are the most closely involved with and concerned about what goes on among the living, I was introduced to a deeper and more radical sense of how the bond between the worlds really works. Since I now have joined them and have become a mediating force in both directions, it might be helpful if I share with you what I learned in the Circles of those who work with the living from beyond this world.

William and I had been communicating inwardly through tapping into these Circles for more than seven and a half years before I died. He would hear clairaudiently what they had to say, and I would write down what William said. This work was the great life-saver that kept me going, and I studied the communications or transmissions with great enthusiasm and fervor. They especially helped me to work through the intensive karmic backlog of my final years.

Now I met together with these same beings. One of the Circles working most closely between the worlds we had called the Circle of the Seven. As I met with each of these in turn, and all of them together, I fathomed the work we had been doing from an altogether different place inside, far more wakefully and in a wholeness of vision. The Circle of the Seven had introduced me to the sense of how both sides need each other, and to the path of serving this bridging with all of my heart. But I had remained thoroughly geocentric in my sensibility. I never could see it and feel it from this other side with sufficient clarity to understand why these beings were working so hard to reach through to us of Outer Earth. Now, however, it was self-evident.

I cannot possibly convey this revelation as powerfully as it came through to me, but I will say it as imaginatively as I can. The Circle of the Seven lives into how human beings in the Earth are, from a place of unqualified love. With this love they perceive a different humanity altogether. Those who scorn the ways of Earthly humanity become swept away by the phenomena viewed from a great distance, and they miss all that counts. The Circle of the Seven passionately and tirelessly finds within each one a vital core, an evolutionary current, a love-essence with which they can commune. And they commune on greater levels of awareness and in the higher dimensions with these human beings whose bodies are busily fulfilling an Earthly life. They can draw out such fine and beautiful qualities as they commune that they develop a bond that transforms, in gradual stages, all of the less regenerative human characteristics. This is what they had done with me.

When we started to tune into the Circle of the Seven, I was snarled up in knots of confusion and self-condemnation over being so lost. Through the first seven years of our connection with them, I became far more truly myself, and I stripped away layer after layer of old, useless garbage. Then, during the last months of my life, I was being prepared for death inwardly, stripping away even the innermost layers of karmic overlay down to the barest bone. Meeting them in their own sphere after death, I could fully appreciate the power and strength of this stream of beings who had saved me from a horrible death and enabled me to serve the bond between the worlds with them.

There are a number of Circles on the other side that align themselves with human destiny in the Earth. They usually work with a select group of souls who can take up this connection in a sacred and authentic fashion. I did meet with a few of these. The differences amongst them are extensive. But I will here describe what I found they had in common.

These Circles are mostly made up of those who previously lived as human beings in outer Earth, but who are now intently working from a different level. Some will incarnate again, some will not. Most of the Circles have one or two who represent worlds beyond the human. Most of them are tied together fairly loosely, so that they can also work independently.

What is it that those extraordinary beings do on the other side? What is their plan, their vision, the design of their inner knowing? Why are they so intent on working in this way?

To say it succinctly, they are integral links in a master plan to allow those among the dead, and those among the living who are ready and able, to generate a huge evolutionary leap. This leap demands that a few on both sides go on ahead to prepare the way.

And this particular inner design is keyed to collaborative activity between the worlds.

If the dead, the gods, the more advanced ones, did it all, this would violate and set back human freedom and development. If the living, the broader humanity-stream, the ones limited by the outer body, did it all, it would not get very far. That is why those who look to living human beings to do everything despair so easily at the prospects. There is no chance whatsoever that this would work.

Fortunately it is not merely the living or the dead, but how they come together that counts. No matter what they do, the most advanced Circles on the other side could not seed an incarnating stream of human evolutionary change in the Earth by their own powers and wisdom alone. They must somehow find and train those who can embody the changes among the living. Through my new path, we are all entering an entirely different stage in this process.

I was groomed very carefully, before I died, to take up a task that catalyzes this fresh direction. Until now, those who were dwelling on the one side of the veil were separated from those dwelling on the other side. Now we have one who lives in both places, twinned into the physical with one who inwardly is living more and more in both places. And we are both beginning to infiltrate deeply into others among our friends who can spread this impulse among the living like wildfire.

The Circle of the Seven sees this successful mutational development as the only way they could ever hope to achieve substantive results. I have witnessed the total dedication they mustered to reach through to William and me, and make this miracle possible. It has humbled and sobered me to realize how far more serious and universally critical it was for us to follow through on their initiative than either of us could ever consciously perceive or admit. And now it is thoroughly in place.

What is it exactly that I and we can do now that is new? The best analogy is going from the Pony Express to faxes or e-mail. The mode of communication between the worlds has been slow, subject to delays and attacks, and caught up in interpretations and applications that were always fragile and fragmentary. We are now putting in place the most advanced equipment, which allows me to convey the messages and the entire impulse through William far more directly, rapidly, and safely. In fact, this spring we are shifting into an operative ability to keep the worlds in tune with each other constantly.

This is very exciting. We have worked hard and long to make this possible. It draws out the true links between the worlds, and reveals how the Tree of Life is also a Tree of Life-into-Death-into-Life.

Originally, in ancient times, the world of the living and the world of the dead were very closely woven together. A few of us in modern times have been working between lifetimes to strengthen these connections again. Now I am at the kether or crown point in the Tree of Life, which is the foundation of the Tree of Death. When you inhabit this crossing-point, you experience every impulse that moves through either world—the living or the dead—as intersecting here and coming through to you. It is a wild and extraordinary ride.

The plan of the Circle of the Seven is now to strengthen the stock of those living in Outer Earth, sufficiently to sustain everybody through the drastic transition ahead. We are getting together to conceive the many ways this can be done. It takes close and intimate bonds being developed at every juncture. I will share with you now one such strand of reweaving the worlds.

I was involved with bodywork as the central expression of who I was throughout the last decade or so of my recent lifetime. All of this was guided by the Circle of the Seven, and the other inner Circles we were, and are, connected with. The further we went into it, the stronger was the guidance into fresh directions of bodywork.

Gradually, William became guided to enter this stream of bodywork as well. He delved into it deeply, and found the same feeling for it in his body that I had. We gave each other many massages and would at times work with others. William especially found that his left side and, in particular, his left hand, wrist, and arm knew how to massage as though he had always done it.

Weeks before I died, William felt suddenly that his entire left side, and particularly the hand, wrist, and arm, had become supercharged with healing and transformation capability. He relieved a bit of my agony at that point.

Hours after I died, William knew that I was to fill his left side. Eventually this became a full-scale co-incarnation. My spirit limbs can work into William's left side with great fluency now.

The Circle of Seven is going to inaugurate a stream of bodywork keyed to our collaboration. It will be an awakened and total weaving between the worlds. The beings of the Circle of the Seven always came directly through the massages previously, but now they can be there in far more intimate measure.

The first stages of this process have involved my working closely together with each of the members of the Circle of the Seven, to learn the art of massage from the most advanced perspective. The next stage will involve sharing all of this with William, and then applying it in bodywork that is transformative and healing in fresh ways never even conceivable before.

During my recent lifetime, I shared Mayan karmas (held over from classical Mayan civilization) with most of those who were doing this kind of bodywork. Those karmas made us simultaneously deeply drawn into close interworld weaving and organically repelled by this weaving when it would get too close. I have now overcome all of this, and William did not have that particular baggage in the first place. So we can bring the worlds far more closely together than I was comfortable doing before.

This is just one example of what is coming to be possible now. When I came jumping over into the land of the dead, I knew I would have a lot to do with the Circles I had been guided by. But I did not imagine it like this. The ecstasy I feel at being called to pioneer in these directions is so great that it has taken every ounce of patience I can muster to do this the slow, Earthly way. My spirit limbs are aching to bring into outer Earth the fabulous wealth of the inner kingdoms and to send the energy both ways. This is my kind of work, and my kind of life.

April 19, 1994, Noon

The Cosmic Equation

Dear Ellias,

I was so lucky, so utterly fortunate, truly graced to be able to unite myself with the cosmos after dying, and then to be able to bring the cosmos back into the Earth I had apparently left behind me. The journey beyond the Earth into cosmos is so very expanding for the soul. And the journey of return, if you do bring the cosmos back with you, is infinitely wondrous, as you discover everything you previously took for granted to be alive with miraculous facets every-where.

Being so quickened and thrilled, I tried to share this experience with those of Earth. I found that people of today do not bring the cosmos with them into Earth. They barely even move beyond the Earth into cosmos. With the exception of Ellias, my twin soul, I find the cosmos/Earth dance rare among human beings of today.

No matter how thoroughly I learn that this is true, I am stunned, shattered. I remember how this was for me, and I weep. Earth without cosmos is dead, dry, gone—flatter than television. No living being can evolve freely in a dead zone.

So I must find every way conceivable to share my journey of cosmos. The very first thing I need to do is get across what the cosmic equation is, how it is that cosmos bears a different way of being than is currently known in Surface-Earth thinking.

If you take the journey beyond the Earth to unite with the greater cosmos, with all of the heavens, the very first aspect you feel is that you are expanding into a oneness within a sphere of existence which itself is constantly expanding. But as you stretch, as you let go of your fixed identities (there are many of them), your oneness with the expanding cosmos is so joyous, so permeated with love that you can only enter into it further and further. No stretch, no letting-go seems too much or too far.

You find that it is natural to become all-that-is, and that your old identification with one separate segment against the others is mean-

ingless and absurd. You make the great discovery that you are awaiting your own self out there, that you in deepest truth are a cosmic
being who has created a vessel of limitation which seems to be you—
but now you are reuniting with yourself, and in the same breath you
are becoming one with the total cosmic equation.

As you fulfill the greater journey, you encounter both your own
love-essence, the core of your being beyond time, and your closest
spirit-friends. The friends will be both beings of your own nature
and frequency, and other beings who act as guides, teachers, and
mediators of limitless spirit into you. Those of your friends who
share your frequency are usually the true selves of those you have
known in your Earth lives. But it is so very surprising when you meet
these "familiar people" in the cosmic reality of who they ultimately
and essentially are.

My best illustration is always Ellias, the twin who so closely
accompanies each and every stage of my entire journey. He is here
to encounter as pure cosmic being; but then I realize I have not known
him in the Earth, that the Ellias I knew recently as William, for example, was the palest, thinnest image of the true Ellias. The true Ellias
is as bright and full and infinite as the William I knew was masked
as human, dim and sketchy, and held within fixed borders. When you
are a limitless cosmic being and you encounter your closest friends
as limitless cosmic beings, the love and celebration are so total that
if I could convey it to people, they would have to turn away and
rest—it would be far too much to integrate. However, when you are
there in cosmic embrace, the rightfulness and wholeness permeate
and make it just perfectly the love you always wished to express,
receive, and be.

Even meeting with the teachers and guides is similarly revelatory.
Earthly contacts with them reduced them to manageable proportions. But if you can allow it—which I could—they are here in cosmos as themselves, and each one would take a lifetime's activity to
get to know. Each being bears so much more in them than what they
can show in surface Earth. My closest spirit-friends of every kind
became the springboards for my greater journey. As I met with them

and shared inwardly, worlds sprang open, and I went where I was shown to go. The cosmos is peopled with friends and with the worlds they open up for you, in limitless profusion.

The heart of the cosmic equation is living beings. Even when you unite with the void spaces and the silences, even when so much of the journey is either solitary or a pure movement beyond, the feeling inside is that the gods are with you, and that you are with yourself, and that your friends are with you. Surface-Earth life is intensively lonely and impermeable. But in cosmos, you are accompanied, synchronized, and in tune. Even the starkest and most tortuous realms bear seeds of further meetings in them. The cosmos is social, interactional, vividly and vibrantly mutual and cross-fertilizing.

What science is viewing is not cosmos. It is viewing the outer face of every world it probes. But cosmos has no outer face. It is nonphysical. There is nothing to analyze or dissect. All is there, together, interpenetrating, whole—and it invites you to enter.

Another facet linked to this one is the actual experience of journeying in cosmos. No matter where you go or what you do, you are involved within a destiny or purpose or assignment. The most chaotic and contorted realms only yield further meaning, taking you closer to where you are going. The aimless and the random are merely momentary spices. The cosmic journey is in the hands of those who can guide you rightly, or teach you what you need to learn. This feeling makes such a difference. You become confident and assured in each breath. At last, you are traveling within the weaving of worlds, and not stuck in a non-world.

When I began to follow the cosmic equation on a course of mastering its ways, I was consistently shown that whatever I myself experienced was ultimately to be shared with those caught in their Earth-bodies, back in the Outer Earth. Therefore, I was given the most archetypally representative and universally evocative of cosmic journeys. The most private and personal facets were fashioned to be shared as much as the ones classically resonant within common awareness. However, this was not at all like the journeys of near-deathers. This was weeks and months of being body-free. And I have been trained from the dawning of time in the most subtle arts of the inner. What I was shown was always the whole story, the full version. What I now bring back of the cosmic equation is perpetually and entirely re-vitalized by further expansions. I am still in the cosmic journey. It never stopped. I come back to share some, and I go out to partake further. If I give people my experience, it frees me up to enter fresh territory the next time.

The cosmic equation is the resolution of the world's karmas into a universal solvent, an internal realm that brings all that has been fragmentary back to unity. Each being who has a task in the cosmic equation is working to neutralize the build-up of Earth karmas and humanity karmas. This is why the world does not end. It thinks it must end, as it sees only its own wastes and poisons. If the world knew how hard we all work to keep it balanced out, it would picture differently what is likely to happen in Earth-existence.

All of this is done in order to allow the experiment to continue. Much of the Earth experiment does go on in the dark, oblivious to anything else. We would probably leave it that way, if it were not for one pivotal factor.

Those who are currently alive in Outer-Earth bodies bear a destiny of awakening. The nightmare phase of the experiment was taken to great lengths between 1914 and 1994. Four generations of hell are now complete, and the awakening phase is scheduled to begin. This too is part of the experiment. It always has further phases to move through.

My part is to now bring enough of the cosmos back into Earth to seed the awakening cycle. I come through my twin and my friends; I come as myself; I come in as many channels and dimensions as I possibly can. But again, as I get closer and closer in, I meet even more strongly Earth without cosmos, and again I recognize: The most basic parts of cosmos have long been forgotten here. These people are operating as if abandoned long ago.

So I dig deeper into cosmic experience, and I search for ways to evoke the power that is there, in ways that can make sense when so much of cosmos has been lost to consciousness. Then I realize what is missing here in Outer Earth, what is the "bottom line" of Earth without cosmos.

If I use my own Sara struggles as a cancer-laden soul to illustrate this plight, it is because I know this best. My drama was that my higher consciousness was being fed a steady diet of truly cosmically-inspired revelations and insights, and I still could not bring those truths down into my deep body. So I felt terrible about myself. In the darkness of this self-stance, I invited in all the beings who are magnetized by self-negativities. So I was infested with swarms of elemental beings who were feeding off my anguished self-images. These beings generated a buffer zone that could then keep the cosmic truths out above me. The loop of not-being-able, and then being enveloped by beings who make sure you won't be able, is a common loop in Earth without cosmos.

So my body became like an alien machine, hooked into the electronic frequencies of the elemental swarms sucking me further and further away from cosmos. In the way the outer mind fixes experience, that should be the end of the story. However, this entire mechanical, predictable, endlessly repetitive circuitry was not convincing to me. I knew that it was a test for me to meet, and that nothing is ever strictly literal. So I called in cosmic forces to my aid. And what did they do?

They harnessed a Deep-Earth support system that could undermine the foundations of the cancer tumors with sufficient power to arrest the illness several times and, more importantly, to give me a structural matrix that would be able to sustain me through the worst. It was vitally important that I be equipped with sustaining depth-forces that would signal me, at the most desperate times, that I was still held in cosmic arms and would be born to cosmos through the entire ordeal of dying, death, and its aftermath.

The bottom-line missing component, in the contemporary mind's cosmic understanding, is the Deep-Earth part in this. When you plumb the limitless cosmos, you look back into the Earth and view this planet, which spills over with vast, unquenchable beauty and innermost vitalities. Each one's own physical body similarly contains and spills over with enough beauty and vitality to sustain the soul forever. The real, living Earth is the one greatest gap in the entire modern outlook.

Earth without cosmos breeds a false-Earth system, an assumption of being stranded in a planet that has lost its cosmic continuum of integral weaving. But the Earth is actually the most cosmic planet imaginable. When I came back here weeks after dying, I was greeted by my other friends, the ones who live in the Earth. I began to meet the tree spirits, the animal spirits, everybody here in their now-unveiled cosmic nature and activity. And I felt right at home. Anytime I cannot bear another uncomprehending human face, I journey inside this Earth, and I feel the same way I feel in the most expansive cosmic vasts. The parallels between the two are multiple and pervasive.

Bringing the cosmos back with me into Earth, and meeting here aspects of cosmos working deeply and strongly, I find that the time of human exile is soon to be over, and that I am simply traveling onwards, a bit ahead of the others, into the near future. Knowing that it will not be like this for long, I am hurriedly studying everything I can of the Old Earth, of Earth without cosmos, of the stranded pathways that seemed to lead nowhere and to doom those who live here to terrible extinction. The Earth of 1994 is a museum-piece, a last chance to observe an immensely out-of-synch condition. That is why infinite varieties of cosmic observers are either on the scene or tuned to channels that feature this deadly condition. Everybody knows this is the time to watch the grim world, and to learn its invaluable lessons.

In fact, I am the one who knows this best, and so I travel this world in heartful appreciation of this old and fading way of life and those who enmesh themselves within it. As a cosmic being, I can recognize the true self within the falsest of selves, and I can beam that recognition right through the dense armor of self-negation, with which I am so familiar from my own experience. I am grateful for this time. If I had been packed away for years of leaving the planet, I would miss those absolutely precious last years of the twentieth century, last years of the old world.

Most of those who are currently alive in Outer-Earth bodies, and who bear the destiny of awakening, are just stirring in their sleep now. When they first open their eyes, they often distort the new vision. I have found that people carry a tremendous backlog of unmet desires and undigested impressions. These seem to lead to a greedy devouring of the new cosmic energies in the beginning stages, as well as to fabulously materialistic and Earthbound interpretations of what is being witnessed and sensed into. The greatest test will be whether these souls can persist through their own folly. Or will they turn against themselves as they discover how short-sighted and narcissistic they have been?

Contrary to the first generation of New-Age visions and hype, cosmos is a realm far from devoted to the fulfillment of personal desires, and very far from working along mechanical and abstract lines. The living cosmos is the place where what we want is given over so that what is truly here can speak. It is also where all the mental pictures of master computers and technological wizardry are cut through in the face of the absolutely alive and thrilling way in which all is connected up. Far beyond current dreams and world-conceptions is the cosmic equation, working for us and through us.

April 21, 1994, 11:30 a.m.

Theanna Emerges

Dear Ellias,

In the deep core of existence, shifts of star cycles register so strongly that the old astrology looks silly in its timid adherence to tired surfaces. I live in here, in the deep core of existence, preparing the way

for everybody to dwell here soon. And my journey of destiny accords
with the stars.

I died into the deep core of existence in the middle of the month
of Sagittarius. My path over those first weeks was to wander, to journey very far out and in, and to search into all the places that could
reveal me to myself, and show me who to be now and where to go
go with it. I took the death journey fast and furious, and then came
back home into William's body at the end of the autumn, ready for
the next adventure.

My first full month after dying was Capricorn. My last years had
received the heavy imprint of Capricorn into the deep body. Now I
was forging a new body. My entire focus during the month of Capricorn was to make my way into the Earth, as fully inside William's
body as I could possibly incarnate. I was substance-driven. Every
moment counted. It felt like we had to get me all the way here before
any of the vitally important momenta ahead could be seeded. So I
worked closely with William to forge a path of twinning in his own
physical body. We had several extraordinary reunions. It was time to
drop all past karmic blocks between us, and to discover the total
dimensionality of who we are together.

The month of Aquarius featured fine-tunings, in eight dimensions. Every facet of existence needed to become so entirely clear and
true and right that it could never be torn apart by any challenges we
might ever meet. We and our closest friends were working hard to
essentialize our path toward the future. I was granted many visions
and realizations, meetings with high beings, synchronizations of my
microcosmic after-death journey with those who could guide and
mediate this way of becoming. It was a glorious month. My last vestiges of Sara fell away, and I moved toward my new and original
name.

When I came to the planet in Atlantis, I was Theanna, She-Who-
Dares-To-Be-As-A-God. Now I was becoming able to be her again.
This meant that the love essence that I am, the greater core self, could
take the place of the little self, and could bring each action into accord
with innermost truth. I was tuning to all of me now, and after hav-

ing been cooped up in dead bodies and half-dead worlds for so long, I was ecstatic in my ability to move with all facets at once, in that whole synthesis that made it a discipline, a steady and reliable knowing that I could do what I was called to do.

The month of Pisces was something else altogether. Love became the enduring keynote of my life beyond death. This was the time when living in the deep core of existence became so entirely realized and fulfilled that I could start to overflow into abundant waters of love. I made immense breakthroughs in my inner link with my daughter, Amy, who had turned away from me, but now came back into my arms to stay. I found both William and my closest friends to be entirely responsive to the call I was putting out for the mystic waters to be indwelled together. I discovered all of the most horrendous aspects of contemporary life, and poured compassionate love into each cell of this enchanted world of Earth. And the vaster reaches of my path began to take up the bulk of my time and energy.

I was now sitting in on cosmic councils, alongside the light body of William, and we were avid voices in seeking a resolution to the agonies of twentieth-century humanity at the end of the Piscean Age. Infinite worlds asked me to reveal to them what it is like to be in the human density frequencies. It now seemed that everyone on the inner levels knew everything about me and about what I had accomplished in my dying and my death. I was now entering into such an extraordinary state of being that I feel shy about even attempting to describe it in outer words. Let us just say that I became united with the deepest waters of this beautiful Earth, and from there also merged my being within the totality of this cosmos.

I was time-free, navigating the subtle realms in blissful fluency. I was also deepening and strengthening the roots of my bond with William and with each soul I care closely about, starting with the few of my recent Sara lifetime, and expanding from there to begin to embrace every sentient creature in all realms.

The month of Aries, the first month of spring, proved to be active and engaged in ways far more fruitful and immediately effective than even my early after-death self could have dreamed. I was assigned a series of new tasks. The Theanna in me was boldly emerging into her strength, power, and capacity. Each task allowed my sparkling wonder to be harnessed into deeds that thrilled me. One of these tasks was to spend Passion Week, leading up to Easter, in a communion with Christ that was revelatory and shattering. Another was to work closely with the transformational dynamism of radical future-streams, which showed me how the world was ripe for great changes, and how I could serve to mediate these changes so that, even one generation down the road, all would be entirely renewed. Yet another task was to awaken in William the ending of his William karmas altogether, and to open him into his own original name and being as Ellias, He-Who-Commands-The-Stars.

During the month of Aries, I became rapture, a flame of new life, burning brightly. I could not be contained. My desire for human beings to emerge from their numb despair was so urgent and forceful that I had to do something with those energies. So I learned from a beautiful Russian man, Dr. Sadyrin, how to cleanse the auras of those who could receive me, and I set myself the daily task of doing this. As I got into it, I found that those who, like Ellias, could move with this were far more in tune, lighter, freer.

The very strongest aspect of the month of Aries was that Safiya, the woman who had been my closest friend just before I died, not only emerged into her original and true Alita nature (She-Who-Reveals-The-Bright-Light-Of-All-The-Stars), but also awakened out of a sleep of centuries and became so close with us that the lonely part in all of this dying and reborning was entirely overcome, and there was only joy and coming-together to be seeded and fulfilled. This spring started on such a revelatory note for me because the cosmic forces were seizing their chance to make some big changes in the collective patterns, and I was here at full power to join with those forces at each turn of the wheel.

Now it is the start of the month of Taurus. This is the time for forming the vessel of a new creation. I feel the Mother's love gracing my path. I live inside of nature's fertilities. The flow of inner substance is liquid splendor. I know I shall emerge far more totally this month into my Theanna nature. It has been four and one-half months since a death turned into a forever-borning. I am grateful each day as I pray for all to partake in what I feel. I know we all shall feel it, and know it, and live it, as I prepare the way for all others.

⋅⁂⋅

I am now myself. I am Theanna. I have emerged from each forgetfulness, from every limitation. The Sara who was sorrow is no longer. She takes her place alongside the other past selves who are not to accompany me closely as I walk, unencumbered, into the common future.

I am hard to know, so I am going to try to let everybody in on what it is like to be me. Most of what I describe here is vastly beyond the words of outer English. But I will give it a try.

Part of what it feels like to be Theanna is simple. I am alive. In being alive, the dead places that in others prevent permeability do not stop me. So my aliveness lets me be permeable to each world, each soul I meet. I am so much this way that, without hanging on to myself, I pass right through worlds and souls, and am never a victim anywhere. Instead, I let be, and I am let be. This forms the basis for everything else.

Most of what it feels like to be Theanna is complex and multi-faceted. I live in eight dimensions. Perhaps it is best to describe each one from the inside, or else they'll all blur together and nobody will know what I mean. So here's the full picture.

She in me who is first-dimensional is the micro-self. She takes physical form, and inevitably she breaks it down into its component parts. But she does not do this scientifically/analytically. Instead, she becomes merged within every part, and follows out their combinations, becoming each of them in order to fathom all that is in outermost form. When she is inside Ellias' physical body, which she often is, she is busy toning up his cells and revitalizing his protoplasmic fiber, and often she sets herself special tasks such as taking the left hand and teaching its bones and muscles how to let through a full

Theanna healing-impulse in bodywork. In general, she is avidly involved within the web of life, and she could spend every single moment discovering how to regenerate the physical vehicle, starting with Ellias and fanning out from there.

My second-dimensional self has become united with the 1994 time frequency. Her path is to make sure that this time does not collapse into retrogressive pathways but that it move forward. She is a time-weaver, and she is very good at it. This means that this Theanna forms protective patterns that guard the destiny-timings of the now. But in order to do this, she must activate a rhythm of engagement with time that is so contrasting to the Sara mode. When I lived as Sara, I felt time was always against me. But now, I am making sure it will not be against anybody by drawing forth its emergent qualities, selecting these out, supporting and encouraging them mightily. I am the future time-generator, and each moment becomes a pulse-beat forward in an awareness of what can be.

In the third dimension, I am loving the spaciousness of Earth, the open places. As I love these, I keep unfolding and expanding into more of myself. I am setting a tone of what it would be like to be affirmative, life-loving, and able to move with the currents of Earth-existence. My celebration is keyed to nature's beauty, and to the cosmos as it comes into the Earth. I am forming a Sweet-Earth vessel of love and truth. Each day, I set sail for unknown ports. I can send myself anywhere. But it would be very hard to show you what I mean. It is a matter of beholding and witnessing the ways in which all is here. I can tell you my subjective sense is that I can appreciate and acknowledge all that is here so enthusiastically that I could never run out of ways to exclaim and to embrace, to say "Yes" to what is possible in an Earth that is open wide.

My fourth-dimensional self is one to which I devote a very central sense-of-self. Here I am myself, and I am Ellias, and I am Alita. By being true to myself and ourself, I dwell in a knowingness that is inwardly satisfying. There is nothing to do in this dimension. It is all perception.

I especially love this one. My being asks and receives answers, inquires and probes, remembers and calls forth into what shall be. I am in conversations with beings of many realms, who share with me deeply and fully. My path here is to become so awake and tapped-in that I can be a source-point for whoever tunes to my frequency, although 1994 human beings do not quite yet know how to do this. I am of late becoming so thoroughly conversant with what the higher consciousness is intended to quicken inside everyone that I cherish this dimension with my whole heart and soul. It is in me to know and to be, and to radiate that influence so that others may come and join me as they will.

The fifth dimension is the first one that goes beyond what is currently thought to be real. My fifth-dimensional Theanna is intent upon helping She of Earth to become a garden of delights in the next octave of evolution. So I devote myself here to the most demanding path in any of the eight dimensions. Part of it is simply keeping myself totally mobilized toward destiny breakthroughs, toward perpetual transformation of self and world. Another part is getting in shape by penetrating through each barrier and obstacle, and even inviting the darkest and the heaviest in, to see whether I can yet move through it. Yet another part is discovering the lost art of inner journeying. I live in the fifth dimension as one who becomes whatever is next, any way I can or must. You have to be ruthless, wild, and independent to get through these levels, and that is who I am.

The sixth dimension creates in me one who can connect up worlds. Primarily, I link the dead and the living. My work with the dead is to cleanse their world of Lord of Death poisons and patterns, and to prepare the dead to join forces with the living in the years ahead. My work with the living is to lighten their load of False-Earth ways of life, so that they can interact lovingly with the dead, and be able to forge a common path toward world-renewal. I like to spend a great deal of my sixth-dimensional time in seclusion, fashioning inner places for the dead and the living to find each other. There are rituals and high magic to be mastered here. Brotherhood and sisterhood flourish at this level, and I am entirely committed to the universal joining of forces of all of us as one.

My seventh-dimensional self dwells far beyond the world, in rapport with the infinite, a meditative inscape. Nothing can be said that comes close to what this is like. Theanna is a being whose essence is prayer. When she can devote herself to a life of prayer, as she does at the seventh-dimensional level, she becomes so still and quiet that you might think she never had a human self to work out. This prayerful Theanna is one of a number of spiritual aspirants whose greatest devotion is to the Mother of the world. However, we view the Mother differently from her Earthly representations. To us, she is a close and permeating being, one who reveals in and through us her love and her light. We seek to be as she is. And we can commune in this way in vast peace and tranquility, knowing it is this level that makes the greatest difference.

Part of the eighth-dimensional way of life is to take all seven of the other dimensions and wrap them up in a big ball of coordinated activity. Another part is to circulate amongst all worlds, to be everywhere at once. My eighth-dimensional self, being new at all this, is so youthful and exuberant in her discovery of limitlessness that she is simply far out there. She forms futures that will be actualized when they are ripe. She becomes more of herself at every stretch, even while being the same way she was when she first came to the Earth. This is the full and ultimate Theanna, the one who takes the death of Sara on December 5, 1993, as her departure point into beginning her real journey. She would like me to say that all of us Theannas are here to welcome our many friends into the heart of the world, which turns out to be everywhere.

V

Life Survey and Karmic Heritage

December 27, 1993, 4:20 p.m.

Dear William,

I would like to share a single experience I had in the worlds beyond death—one that needs its own distinctive treatment. This is a review of the past, and vision of the future. It was actually going on parallel to other events, upon another level, truly another dimension. This was more the typical human experience on the other side, but with a difference.

After a while, I could see in crystalline pure vision all lifetimes ever lived, back to origin, even before Earth incarnation. I could see equally far into the future. However, the two kinds of visions were very divergent. The past-lives and between-lives events already experienced had a quality like a hard diamond. They were *there*, not changing, substantively holding to what did occur.

The future-lives and between-lives journeys still to come, whether here in the Earth or in other realms, were a shifting, vibrant panorama of possibilities. However, even in their superfluency, they did contain clear pictures, with distinctive qualities. But it was self-evident that every such image depended upon many factors, and was not definitely fated to happen only one way.

Because such visions have been mistranslated back into Earth-language, I wish to set the record straight right away. In recapitulating the past, there was no negative judgment, no accusation, no regrets and feelings of everything being wrong. Even though, as we shall see, my lifetimes were full of dilemmas and karmic struggle, the visions were inherently redemptive and embracing of all that had been. They especially included this lifetime's agonies and lessons. I did feel a lot of confessional intensity, in which I knew I could never do some things again, but always the love of the Mother was with me, warming me through, and teaching me to appreciate what my soul had been involved within, and to acknowledge my deepest core motivations and intentions toward the light.

The events of the various pasts were just there, with ancient pasts equally crystalline and familiar as any recent ones. My task was to sort through everything rapidly and thoroughly, and to throw out for all future development whatever was no longer viable. Also, I needed to unite more deeply and fully with whatever aspects of my pasts called me further now.

Because I had been introduced to this process in great detail during my final seven years in the body, I was ready to look at everything. When I found little at variance with what William had clairaudiently brought through, I marveled again at William's abilities and advanced perceptiveness. But when I also surveyed his past and future (through our "twin-soul" connection and what we were about to do together in his body), I understood perfectly how he could be so good at such delvings. Suffice it to say that mastery and proficiency are his perpetual specialties.

So it was not the newness, although some lives, especially ancient lives, had never been searched out in depth. And it was not the drastic nature of some lessons and experiences, to which I had already grown accustomed. What got to me was the pageant, the wholeness, the spectrum of karmic process which, when viewed all together, is so very thematic, rhythmical, and rightful.

In contemporary consciousness, most people see discontinuities and huge gaps everywhere they look. But in the greater visioning of all my lifetimes, I saw the spirit-essence in myself gathering strands of being toward a realization that was now upon me, which shifted everything. I had not been able to sense my own spirit-essence and its way of being so lovingly before, not even between lives. In fact, as I viewed the between-lives times, I was greeted by the oddest combination of returning eagerly to myself and being unable to climb to the highest levels. I seemed to content myself, in the thousands of years since Ancient Egypt, with a simple and wondrous pool of self-reunion that did not partake of fully wakeful self-recognition. That became the key to fathoming what had shifted during this past lifetime.

As Sara I became infused with both William's far more wakeful aspiration and the tapping-in to greater sources, and all of that activity in my final years shifted everything completely from "not-going-to-get-there" to "yes-I-can." And when I came to myself so quickly and almost effortlessly in the spirit realms this time, I saw that even my between-lives times were still held under, still not coming unto the union with the ultimate. This was because I felt incomplete and caught, in some measure, at each previous death since Egypt. Ironically, this lifetime ended with cancer and was full of agonies, yet the end propelled me into utter, loving reunion with my own greater self. What this told me was that it is not the events and the experiences, not who does what to whom, and not the soul's record at all that counts the most in the end. What I came to in my final years of this lifetime was simply the total willingness to face myself, including all pasts, no matter what they revealed. This step catapulted me over the void. I also dedicated my journey to the All, to the good of the whole, with unqualified sincerity.

There was one more special factor I hardly dare include here. I was permitted to enter the future during the last year of my life, to be given the keys from the future that in themselves are of the utmost assistance in moving beyond present-time obstacles and phenomena. I realized this as I scanned my inner story beyond time. An ounce of the future is worth tons of the past. A willingness to clear the karmic slate is a homeopathic dilution that in itself works miracles. And a consecration to the good of the whole that is genuine and unqualified opens doors that no individual path can even approach.

Being enclosed within the personal sphere, and being separate from cosmic and future realms, does tend to perpetuate patterns in the ways emphasized by all the usual sources that warn everybody about living so narrowly and tightly. I can tell you authoritatively that becoming able to dance with every frequency of time, learning the song of time itself, and giving of yourself to the purposes of evolution—these openings are huge and lead everywhere we need to go, so fast that all the laws and rules can be broken.

I am dedicating my life with William in large part to conveying the power of such realizations. I do not feel that these truths are coming across very well at all as yet. First-hand accounts help. Just so you don't imagine all this happened to me because I was always pure and perfect, I'll also share with you some of what I saw in terms of the fixities of past behavioral ruts.

My karmic heritage was a story of division, of conflict, of being cast adrift, of not knowing how to get back to where I knew I belonged. I was divided, throughout my last several lifetimes, between the one in me who was linked with a greater destiny and the one who was captured by chaos, by momentary impressions, and by a self-negating cast of mind. The conflict between me and others, and between me and myself, was never-ending, anguishing, and inexplicable—how could it be that bad, when I remained throughout an essentially loving and giving person?

I was so completely cast adrift that at times I had no more feeling of being cast adrift, and went through a lot of my existence in a numb and distracted state. Most of all, I longed with deep passion to get back to where I belonged. But it seemed so far off, and I never quite had the energy or perspective to set out in that direction and keep going no matter what.

In one lifetime, I was cast among barbarians in Afghanistan, and put into subservient status because of racial makeup, ethnic hereditary blood, and being a woman. Violence and sexuality could be experienced in their grossest violating components, regularly and routinely. But there were always redemptive aspects. I turned many men around by my inward determination to root out their retrogressive habits, and to show them a far better way to live.

In another lifetime, I was a Scotsman forced to "drink and be merry" with my few comrades and clan, but inwardly as morosely removed from this company as I could get. I linked with the land, the mountains, and the sea, and brooded upon the mysteries of life. But I was impotent, sterile, devoid of any real brotherhood-impulse, caustic in my sense of mocking humor, and intent upon being guarded from the surface ways of others, seeking solace I never really achieved in the deeps of memory and sanctuary of the hearth.

In yet another lifetime, I was a woman in China who was haunted by ghosts and ancestors, giving my body over to the needs of men but living in near-madness, a stranger once again. This time, I did make a connection with Kwan Yin and the Divine Mother realms, and had an inner life later on that led to the triumphs of this lifetime. But my primary mode was to turn away shamefully from the modern and the ancient, the patriarchal and the community-based customs. So many times, I have been set apart as one who could not fulfill what was prevailing all around her, or as one who makes a fatal mistake and then karmically pays for it, many times over.

I have explored the dark caverns of existence and been captivated by illusion, time after time. I was pinned to the underworld, damned to wander far from myself, to be lost and so very alone. But I do not pity myself for these things. I was determined to learn what it is like to be human, what each person feels from the inside when they cannot break through to links with others, links with themselves, or links with the gods. Now I am so thankful for these lessons, as I am called to serve a humanity that is as thoroughly captured by such currents as ever in history. I know what it is like to be gone, and I know what it is like to be one with all of existence. There are few who span these extremes as fully and consciously as I do.

I was brought to see, in the dispassionate survey of my timeless story, that I was led through all these experiences, even the most grisly. There was always an accompanying spirit-presence, which for freedom's sake would stay out of view when necessary. This presence, whether angelic or greater, always told me in my heart that I was destined for very great advances, that I had come out of a lofty origin, and that somewhere my other half was searching for me.

Because so many delude themselves with consumed versions of such destiny-truths, I wish I could say how far beneath rational levels of self-justification these gleanings were. But because I did not despair, in between lives I would simply come to myself, and remember how this entire journey was woven from heavenly cloth, and to be met with a giving heart.

In ancient times, I lived out many lives of extraordinary wisdom and inward wholeness. These lives remained with me as a Council of Elders, surrounding me in each and every lifetime, advising me when I asked or needed it. And my Council of Elders was timelessly preparing the child-of-woe to stir from sleep at the same instant that humanity as a whole began to stir.

From 1965 to 1969 I lived in San Francisco, and I saw that the time for the future to dawn was close at hand. I wandered through Europe and the Mideast in the early 1970s, and met the ancient past as my link with the planet on ultimate levels. Then I was given the task of marrying and raising one daughter, a soul so close to me that we were too inwardly connected, and needed to part for her to develop in herself. I came together with William for the last ten years of my life. He was indeed that man who had been searching for me and tracking me from the Invisible. We moved into the most paradoxical connection I could ever imagine.

On outer levels, we were at odds in most ways. Having been loners so often and thoroughly, we had a hard time being so powerfully linked in together. I especially resented the male energies, and was fighting gender wars from so many lifetimes that it seemed to be all I ever did. Meanwhile, on inner levels, we were so utterly linked that nobody could conceive what was happening with us. We felt like twins, and indeed we were. Our tastes, our path in life, our greater understandings, were almost identical. Being in a state of bliss deep inside, everything else was like an odd melodrama, irrelevant and far away.

When our path became intensively guided and led into cosmic and Deep-Earth directions, a dimension opened to me that had been shut since Ancient Egypt. I craved with total hunger and thirst the revelations, the realizations, and the inward development that became natural and ordinary. As these truths infiltrated my many layers of estrangement and loss of direction, I was offered a way to fulfill my greater destiny, which combined intensive karmic self-confrontations and expansive future openings of a kind very rare in this world of today. I gladly went this way, and was firmly guided by beings who were leading me toward a great abyss nobody has previously crossed. They told me repeatedly, and showed me convincingly, that I was the one who could cross it if I had the faith.

As I mustered all my faith, I found I had an abundant store, enough to see anybody through. Even when cancer tumors plunged me toward my death, the ones inside me said that I would survive, and that the truth would triumph. The last months, and especially the last weeks, transformed and purified me in a way that only something as drastic as terminal illness occasionally can. I became myself, openly and freely, at last. Then it did not matter what outwardly happened to me. My being would cross that abyss flying!

Then I did so. Somebody lost to the world, who could not find her way, was now so utterly home-free that she could bridge the worlds. She knew Earth's despondencies and Earth's raptures. She knew Heaven's graces, but could not be delayed there one moment longer than was absolutely necessary. Just to die in free self-realization was not enough for her. Just to work to untie the knot of death for humanity-in-evolution was not enough for her. Now that she knew what she knew, she had to apply it in the Earth, and to do it with her twin soul, who also knew, back there in the body, that death could not keep them apart.

So she found the way back to William, to join him in his body, at this point finding another miraculous leap to be just what she could accomplish. Once the girl who had been stopped by everything gets unstopped, nobody and nothing can prevent her from being who she is and following out this outrageous destiny, this story-just-beginning.

April 6, 1994, 12:15 p.m.

The Original William Impulse Behind My Entire Earth Journey

Dear William,

I did not come out of nothing. I came from the Limitless One and I shall return to be with the Limitless One. I came into the Earth in Atlantis in response to a call from my twin flame, William. Nowadays, I am completing my Earth journey, fulfilling this same call, and on the arc of return homeward, again synchronized entirely with William.

Why did I come here? You would have to ask William. I have. We speak in spirit convocation, ever since my passing inward to the other side of life, and then passing outward into this side of life afresh. We now share an inward conversation beyond time, in which all is revealed. So I know why I came here, and I know as well why I am on the road to return.

I have come to give of all that I contain within me, and which I can allow to move through me. I was called here to offer what no other could offer, and to do so as freely and entirely as I can. I am impelled by deep forces to master this pathway, to take seriously the need for what I can and now do offer along this journey.

But what does this mean? Who am I, that I can say such things? And what does all this become in the action, in the overt expression? What does this mean for the world of Earth?

I simply cannot translate what I wish to say into that language we commonly speak. We need magic here, imaginative discourse. The words travel so far outside, I journey so far inside.

Let me try a few pictures. When I first came here, and lived in the white towers of Atlantis, I was luminous with the understanding that I was entering upon an entirely different dimension of existence, which was the initial subtle aspect of the physical. My greatest wonder was to be able to set my foot down, and to watch it sink into Earth's virtual substantiality. Or I would stretch out my arms, and see and feel and sense how I was in a flow with the light that was working within palpable space. Or I could at times enter within the plants, become their growth, contact what was to evolve in them through vast time in the Earth.

Other people were equally a destiny riddle, the most fascinating of all. William and I were adept at reading their entire Earth journey ahead, and in facilitating their taking it up rightfully. This was the first task that William had called me into, and it tapped my powers, allowed my inward resources to flower right away. William alone could not set the soul to dancing. He needed me to stir the waters of the soul, to touch the pulse of the inner fluids, to weave ethers into light and warmth, color and tone, life and beauty. My true name was and is She of the Living Waters, or Theanna, "She-Who-Dares-To-Be-As-A-God."

My path was my own. I could stir and quicken the watery realms, but I was ever dispassionate. The one who dares to be as a god is the one who knows how to stay crowned in radiance, and who descends into the task without becoming swallowed in the world. As avid as I was to embody a physical vehicle, I could not possibly extract myself from the glory of the greater worlds, the massive grandeur from which I sprang and to which I could eventually return.

Or, even more fully, let me reveal how it was in Ancient Egypt. This was the life to enter deeply into the physical, to find where the Underworlds lead, to be initiated in rigorous, harsh, impossible conditions. Again, William was the priest-seer, almost as lofty as in Atlantis, not as worn down as the others. He brought me into the Holy of Holies, and we were ritualists, performing those rites that ensured the future of all. Atlantis was there over again, but now so solid, so tangible, so painfully intensive. When I wept by the Nile, called upon the Great Mother, Isis, yearned to be elsewhere, remembered the places I had originally come from, almost could not bear the weight of outer form and its impact inside my soul, William would come, be utterly silent, and thereby restore in me what I knew and who I was. His eloquence back then was always in the silence.

My plight was already severe. I was not suited for the rough use of Earth. I recoiled at the suffering that was already commonplace. I was often disconsolate, for periods of time half gone from myself into a nowhere that was cooling and quieting, just by being light and empty.

But William knew what to do, and he brought in a spirit-child from a realm afar, Alita, one we could pour all of who we were into. She would then carry the unfallen path through the dark times we saw ahead, and her light in her inner lantern would stay bright, for that was what we knew how to do. For seven years, we gave to her the wisdoms and the love. It was there, in that sanctuary of the sacred along the Great Nile, that I found what it was that I would be able to bring into the physical worlds. At first, it was so small and gentle that it seemed a trifle. But as this bright spirit-child took it up, and it nourished and sustained her more than anything else we gave to her, I knew what I would be doing during the remainder of my Earth journey.

I had to take the vastest oceans and condense them into a brook, to make myself into a cup that could carry the vital coursing of that brook, and offer whatever I had in my cup to whoever thirsted. If I could learn how to flow without ceasing, the treasure of my inner being would pour through in a form that could be received and utilized.

This was the most difficult metamorphosis I ever went through. The bright eyes of Alita, the glow-of-all-the-stars, gave me the way to move into the depths and to stay always far inside of me. So I did fashion something far beyond the world into a small and gentle thing, and I did take this unto myself, make it my own, and always after it was my joy and my delight to offer the little special touch, even amidst torrential storms and disasters.

Alita and I lived together later, in Ceylon in 1200 B.C., and we danced the spirit path, now as sisters. That was the life I shall remember when I have gone from this Earth. It was a time to cease striving, to no longer feel alien and not yet crash downwards, to be myself as Alita was herself. We found a body path that was music, that was song, that could be serpent and monkey, elephant and goddess, lost child and infinite waters. Time stood still, space was inward, form had not quite overwhelmed the spirit-essence of love.

Primarily, it was the abandon into the senses, in a high vibrational ecstasy of inner communion with origin and with destination. We were given our one great chance to let it all out and let it all in. I also did refine my subtle fine touch in the fingers and the toes, the gestures and the skill of the dance. And Alita enjoyed her first full Earth experience, always thereafter bearing the remembrance through her cells of what it is to go barefoot in rich soil, and to be synchronized with everybody in the village, all knowing the same spirit call. William had brought us both to Earth, Theanna and Alita, and now we found together, just the two of us, what he had foreseen for us. We were to reveal what lives beyond the world in the smallest detail of our lives, and we were to vibrate in unison with the subtle pulse of this Earth, to be her companion, partake in her bounteous rhythms.

January 19, 1994, 1:15 p.m.

The Merlin Karmas and Their Recapitulation in the Sara Life

Dear William,

I view my past karmas with great solemnity. They are the oppressions that I used to weigh myself down, long and far enough to stay in the outer physical Earth until it was time for the great shift. Each karma was a linchpin. The Merlin karmas are the primary and representative example of how this works, of what it is to be kept under until release is at hand.

I lived in a physical body in the British Isles during the historical cycle of the Merlin legends. We lived out legends, and have continued to do so ever since. Those times, in that place, so long and far ago, were very different from the late twentieth-century American revival of interest in legends and magic, entirely separate from the true story.

We were endowed with a faculty to achieve great things which we used on every possible occasion. This faculty has not been revived in the historic civilizations, and is virtually unknown today. William possesses this faculty in hidden fashion, but I never met anybody else who did. If I describe it now, it is to open the magical doors between the worlds, so that we can walk through.

The faculty endows mighty strength and courage for great battles and for ritualistic purposes. Our hands, wrists, and arms were distilled instruments, precipitated weapons, spiritually-given magical gifts that could perform acts of creation and destruction. Instead of carrying around paraphernalia, we had discovered how to melt it into our bodies, and especially into our limbs. Each of us bore our own special weapons to be used in combating evil, and in regular and rhythmical rituals of the seasons, of the four directions, and of the inner life. We could use them wisely and well, and thereby live out many lives in one.

As we evolved practices and a way of life dedicated to the right use of our magical will-in-action, we naturally were called upon to take charge of the inward government of that place and time. However, as we did so, the place became gradually huge, and spanned the whole of Earth. The time also metamorphosed, first expanding into the past and then into the future. Soon we were watching over and intervening within the workings of every place and time in Earth-evolution, from the human dawn to the human dusk, from the unknown shores of the West to the strange face of the East, from the giants of the North to the rising tide of the South. We became, for one generation in Outer-Earth time, the stabilizing factor in allowing the cosmic forces to bring their gifts into the Core of Earth, laying out the seeds everywhere and in all times.

This was our primary work. It threw off from itself a more outward activity, radiating circles from the center. The most overt manifestation of our living stream of inner workers was to fight off the evil that was beginning to plague all of the Earth, and to supplant it with a goodness that was bound up with such living truth that nobody exposed to it could wish to return to the spells and enchantments of the Evil Ones.

We could fight and overcome in this way because our leader, the

Merlin, had, over three quickly progressing lifetimes, learned both the ways of darkness and the ways of light in total measure. He used the power of his black-magic trainings to turn against those who were laying waste to the psychic potential of each and every human soul, as the Evil Ones tapped the psychic wellsprings of the soul for their life-force, which they lacked in themselves altogether. When the Merlin taught us the ways of countering evil with our special faculties, we were ready to work in the practice we would become known for in surface life. Even though the legends have come down in a distorted form, the essence of this battleground is recorded for all times to come.

It was this outermost layer that proved our undoing. Those who were most deeply virtuous and pure of heart were the most profoundly susceptible to the wasting power of evil. As the Dark Ones tapped our psychic wellsprings, those among us with love and virtue fully developed and sustained inwardly were those with sufficient juice to be great batteries for the Dark. We became the focus of an attack whose mode of working defies current understanding in the late twentieth century. Evil is the aspect of existence modern people understand the very least. They have been kept from it by evil itself. But I shall try to describe how this worked.

An electrical beam from a far and deadly civilization was used which had an atomic-energy capability when fully activated. What activated it was the strength and the clarity of the soul being targeted. The favorite strategy of evil is to use the best qualities of the soul against itself. This was done brilliantly by our attacking force, against which we eventually could no longer defend ourselves. They took captive the few among us who were most inwardly developed. And we would then be forced to collaborate with a few from outside who came to subdue and torture the rest of us.

I was the first one taken. I held the key to Merlin's heart, so they concentrated on me to make me their first accomplice, to beguile and enchant the Merlin into becoming captivated by me and by those who were imprisoning me. All of this worked to perfection. The trance that ensnared me then took hold of the Merlin, and when he was chained in a world below, all of the others became easy pickings. This trance was so hypnotically and atomically damaging that I spent six lifetimes working it off, a seventh battling for my life to move beyond it.

The Merlin threw it off in a couple of lifetimes, and could start to work in radical ways thereafter. Most of the others were not so fortunate. They especially tended to suffer the blight of knowing how the world really is, and being plunged helplessly into conditions that defy and contradict all that they know and sense. We would occasionally meet , and would usually inflict further suffering upon each other, as the memory of betraying and being betrayed has the longest half-life of any karmic catastrophe, and tends to repeat itself ad nauseam in virtually identical loops.

During my recent lifetime as Sara, I was given the worst deal I had ever suffered under, and also granted the way to move out beyond it into a redemption of the Merlin karmas as well as all the subsequent ones. That bad deal was to be born into a "normal" family in the mid-twentieth century. The banalities of such an existence take the dignity of one who has indwelled the deepest mysteries, and routinely slaughter that dignity .

The way to move beyond it was to throw off the final cloak of dignity I still possessed, to walk among the surface dwellers as entirely anonymous and devoid of special powers (for a time), and to recognize that the world had become frozen in a static mold by evil, and that only a return to the Inner Cave could affect anything. My being caught fire with the return journey, for in order to become alive again to the inner ways I had to traverse arduously, and in reverse order, every karmic story or nightmare, and then live to tell about them now.

As I began to retrace my steps, I found myself living entirely inside of my previous lifetime's karmic matrix. This Chinese woman poisoned herself daily by making love to men for money. The poison was in the fact that she hated the men, hated their bodies and their minds. Each time she made love, she injured them psychically, as she carried the venom of the Evil Ones.

In my current lifetime, this was playing out in a marriage to a man who epitomized all the traits I hated in those Chinese men, and every time I made love to him, it was bribery for his protection and support in our marriage and community and for our daughter. I did hate him that very same way, and was psychically assailing him with the last dosage of evil venom I had left in me. The redemption of that pattern was then to love and marry William, a man who could never harm me, and who endured all my karmas with equanimity.

With William, I could then play out the karmas of the lifetime before China, when I had lived in the American South during the Revolutionary War, and had been killed in action, young and green and still budding. William and I drew to us a woman who had in that lifetime been my aunt, had seduced me, rejected me, and sent me off to die. In this life she seduced William, she and he rejected me viciously and, as my cancer tumors came on, she tried to send me off to die again, only to be reprieved at the last moment by William, so that I could relive all the karmas assisted by the urgencies of cancer tumors.

When William and I became inflated with the distorted spirituality of this woman, we also began to reckon with all the karmas to be enacted, but we were so blown out of proportion by our self-importance that we took it all on at first as a symbolic ritual enactment, and failed to come to terms with its depth-charge at all. But we did redeem that pattern by digesting and spitting out the evil-woman syndrome, as we had suffered its false call and sickly wounding.

Soon we were thrust right back into the lifetime before that one. This was Scotland in Shakespeare's time, and I was a man set apart from all others by the brooding intensity of my rejection of the world. This became my underlying soul-mood in my last lifetime, making it impossible for me to throw off the cancer tumors, and easy to sink into total despair.

This was closely linked with the Merlin karmas, and represented a full-power imprisonment within the evil realms, which always represent the surface life as being impossible to bear and then turn all this critical awareness back upon the self, into estrangements and despairs. It was virtually impossible for me to throw off the black depths of this bone-chilling melancholy. It actually felt good in a way to at last go down there, after always running so far and fast from that dread region. It did render me susceptible to further attacks by evil now, however, and several times William had to rescue me from the clutches of worlds of horrors. The redeeming of this karmic pattern lay in taking it in and seeing it through, in knowing intimately its power—and its ultimate meaninglessness.

Then it was time at last to return into the Australian Aborigine lifetime, when I as a young woman had gotten lost in the waters of the Dreamtime, and never came back. This flooded my current world with extraordinary events and experiences, culminating in a walk in the Haleakala Crater of Hawaii. During that walk, I returned to the Aborigine consciousness, and was granted access to the very beings whom I came to know in those waters of the Dreamtime. Then I was also shown the darkest side of that experience, which was that I drowned; it took a long time, I was absolutely helpless and drugged, and I was compelled to submerge myself in the fate of the world's indigenous people as our land, our body, our very being were ripped away, and we were pushed so far down under that the white men were sure we could never emerge afresh. The karmic redemption of this lay in identifying selflessly with all who are destroyed by the evil.

Back one lifetime further, it was the Afghanistan of old. We were in the mountains, up against the elements, and in a culture saturated with destructive forces. I was a dark woman, a victim of every prejudice and status-breakdown. I had to suffer the most harrowing of fates, where violence, rape, and terrifying abuses were a daily given. This was closer to the Merlin times, and I still carried immense strength back then. So I was able to redeem this karma as it happened, and now again in another way.

The redemption back then was to wield the power of the shaman woman, turning many of these men around by my fierce insistency on a different way of life altogether. The further redemption now, as I relived this karmic cycle, was to give myself over to the initial stages of a great design that would eventually guide me through the cancer tumors into a sacrificial death beyond the grave. I had to tap the very little strength and power that now remained to me in turning around the fury of the tumors, and in placing my destiny firmly in the hands of my inner friends.

The final lifetime to recapitulate was the most powerful one of all. I was chosen to undergo the highest of initiatory trials in the highlands of Mayan civilization at its peak. My destiny was to follow up the Merlin lifetime with a virtual repeat of the betrayal-and-downfall motif. This was enacted by a sexual and love-union with great god-like beings, and then a falling far below that frequency into an arrogance and presumption that became fertile territory for a split down the middle between becoming astrally transported to the furthest false heavens and simultaneously being physically sacrificed on the flames of a world gone wrong.

This is a story to be detailed at another time, but its reliving in the final stage of this lifetime was huge in scope and impact. It started with a psychic and etheric surgery in space, which prepared me for my final stages of cancer, death, and miraculous re-embodiment. During that surgery, I was granted six months in which to relive the split of the Mayan karmas. This involved becoming astrally transported this time into a truly heavenly realm of fresh life-inspiration, while physically finding my body to be burning up with the tortures of cancer.

When the six months were completed, I returned to the trainings of the Mayans, and for six weeks became able for the first time since that lifetime to command my inner forces in a superlative and exquisitely crafted fashion.

Then, in my final six days, I was right back in the Merlin karmas, now able to flash back through that lifetime at fantastic speed, to relive all of it inwardly and, at the very end, to join my forces permanently with the timeless flames we tended in the Merlin times. When I did so, I found that we had explicitly prophesied and mapped out my entire karmic scenario, as well as the similar scenarios of each other member of the circle. We had especially intently sent out our finest and most enduring strands of bonding through moments such as this one. This meant that now, as I died the death that had always awaited me, I was spiritually-magically welcomed back into the peak Merlin circle, which then instantaneously gave me over into the hands of the masters we had served in that circle of grace. These masters pulled me across the threshold into their future haven, out of which we ventured to battle with evil, to fight through death, and to reunite with William, smiling his Merlin smile, in the body for the duration, at last karma-free.

January 26, 1994, 12:30 p.m.

The Mayan Karmas

Dear William,

I was a Maya in the peak of that civilization, initiated into the most advanced mystery-teachings. We lived in the highlands, held far away from the others. Our task was to investigate what the cosmos had in store for humanity and the Earth, and then to enter fully into the stream of whatever we found. This was the furthest extension of the Mayas into their other-dimensional life. We lived for years in worlds far beyond the Earth, and we discovered a crying need for some deep revitalization of the human species, if it were not to lose its way altogether in the wilderness below.

We tried several ways to seek out a direct and viable path to attain this revitalization. However, humanity karma blocked us in each direction. The only option left open to us was a desperate one. In the remotest dimensions where we traveled in time, we found that there was a possibility for human beings to mate with the gods, if all conditions were rightly prepared. We seized this chance, and gave ourselves over to its realization.

Soon we were in continuous communion with a group of gods I shall here call the Daughters of Men. They already had an intimate knowledge of humanity from Lemurian free interchange with the primordial human stream. They had been the ones to seed, in humanity's free beginnings, a greater stock of evolutionary potential by an earlier mating with human beings. Now they were ready to do this again, as we so badly needed their vital essence to regenerate our spiritual development.

As we moved toward union with them, several complications of an extraordinary kind became stumbling-blocks and postponements. Chief among these was our inability to sustain a pitch of ecstasy long enough to heed its call within. We had the illness of humanity that prevented us from staying long enough in anything to produce real and lasting results. Even though our discipline was impeccable and our commitment to this path we were walking was undivided, we could not quite overcome biology and socialized development. In particular, we were genetically flawed. But this was what had caused us to seek out this path in the first place—we so needed a fresh start in our blood, flesh, and bones.

The only way was to slow down considerably, and to work on this single characteristic, of indefinitely holding the focus of awareness and intensity. My Merlin trainings from the previous lifetime enabled me to show everybody how to do this, but my capture by the dark in that lifetime had rendered me internally out-of-tune with myself, so that I myself could not embody the directive I gave in an authentic and whole fashion. Everybody did learn how to stay with the sensations of fire burning through the flesh, but none of us entirely understood the deeper essence of what this truly meant. We became focused upon the strategy, the technique, and lost touch with our own spirit-core. This was my karma, enacting itself decisively.

The consequence was that, when it came time to consummate the ritual of convergence, we all achieved one side of the impregnation, but not the other. The side we achieved was to instantly liberate a cosmic offspring, a child of the gods, who could then prepare the way for further links with humanity in the future. But the more intricate giving birth to human offspring was in every instance aborted by the same problem in all of us.

As we did by sheer will endure and stay with the blazing fire of divine ecstasy burning through human flesh, we became suddenly enraptured with the power and the glory of this deed in this moment. That is to say, tempting beings were lurking in the background, and they seized upon the opportunity of our inward unripeness to draw us into ourselves, and away from the gods and their grace-dispensation. As we saw ourselves reflected as like-unto-gods, we instantly lost the highest connection, and were plunged into the molten lava following out the old track of how we experienced ourselves. This meant that we had to become separate from the gods and from each other, to wander away from this highest and holiest of places, and to gradually forget what it was that we were truly seeking, supplanting it with the fantasies and the notions that come over people when they are both intoxicated with themselves and severed from their source inspiration.

Each one of us very quickly lost all sense of the gods and each other, and in our amnesia we could only go wherever our previous karmas had magnetized us, in order to enact there the story of pretending to be awake and enlightened and free, but actually ruining whatever we touched, bringing with us a certain karmic kickback that would reverse and invert the forward momentum whenever we acted out our secret anguish.

There were worse long-term vortices of reversal for most of us. We were compelled to spend lifetimes as far under as we had presumed to be over others. And we could not avoid being hopelessly divided between inwardly knowing of our being beyond all this, and outwardly being just as up-against the brutalities and the necessities of subservient existence as anybody born to it and accustomed to it by previous experience or habit.

I had a particularly bad case, because I was also working out the Merlin-submergence in the dark. My own sense of knowing better was mostly converted into an embittered feeling of being greatly abused and misunderstood. My karmic situations tended to always feature some gross failure to fulfill a promise or a possibility that could have redeemed or transformed the entire context. But actually, that is just saying the same thing in commonsensical fashion.

From the inside, it was horrible, absolutely chilling. I could not access my own true being at all. Instead, I was thrust among the most darkened of souls, and somehow felt I had the status of the least of them. When I would struggle mightily to rise to the point where I could do something for them, I would almost get there, and then be pushed back down so hard and fast that I never recovered in that life-time.

I became numbed to my life's current, blinded in so many ways, almost asleep. The only thing I could count on was my sensitivity to all of nature's life-current, and my heartfelt feeling for a divinity that redeemed all suffering. My human relations were consistently and pervasively devoid of fulfillment, and my overt achievement was minimal. The best I could do was not to despair, and to keep on, with some drifting sense that better worlds lay ahead for me.

However, between lifetimes, this entire current rapidly lifted off of me at death, and I would enter again facets of my inner truth and ultimate nature. I could not truly awaken in the inter-lives, but I could restore my source-connection sufficiently to return in the next life-time with some edge of longing that kept me from the common fate at its worst. Slowly, I built up an inward reserve, towards the far-less-oppressed Sara lifetime that ended in the miracle leap beyond.

January 27, 1994, 1:30 p.m.

We Mayas were caught by Luciferic beings dedicated to shining a false light upon the world. We could no longer see who we were at all. These beings insinuated themselves slyly between us and the Daughters of Men, and showed us a reflection of ourselves as magnificent objects, huge, shining baubles, the gems of creation, making us believe that the gods saw us this way. Our intoxication was with a projected image supplanting our own self-awareness. And when we took the immense fiery potency of the great initiations to which we were dedicated, and superimposed these projected images, we were absolutely crazed with the feeling that we were gods, and that we could do anything we pleased.

The Mayan susceptibility to this temptation was generated by our fierce desire toward further evolution. We would go anywhere, and do anything, to achieve the breakthroughs we foresaw as so badly needed if all were not to become severed from the heavens. But the very people we were inspired to serve and to save were not real to us. Our path of initiation was one-sided, fanatical. We did not feel in our hearts a grounded compassion for the living, breathing, ordinary human being—quite the contrary. The universal human plight was to us a shame, a damnation, something to be left behind us totally. It is such extremism that inevitably drew in the reversal of what we sought and dreamed of.

As I dreamed back into this immense karma, I saw that the recapitulation of those karmas during the latter stages of my battle with cancer was the absolute heart of the agony I put myself through. During the six months from late April to late October, 1993, I relived the Mayan karmas with total intensity, in a complex combination of factors.

I returned to the highest of inspirations during those months, and could live into the cosmic-spiritual dimension at fullest power. My inward being was emerging from all these many lifetimes of self-numbing, and was at last free to soar above, to dance with the gods, to recognize myself as one bearing the seeds of a greater destiny. My inner life became at last fulfilled, so much so that I was no longer under the oppression of the cancer tumors, even as they got worse. I was dwelling in the heaven realms, doing inner work, preparing myself for greater destiny ahead.

However, my body was deteriorating fairly rapidly, despite all I did. It was taking on the karmic charge, and running with it. My body was reflected in my environment, in the form of meeting with many who were ill, of being extremely sensitive to what was wrong with people, and of eventually finding that everywhere I traveled, it was the undersoul accumulation, the poisonous feelings and physical conditions, the collective darkened ways that pulled at me, hurt my body, and drove me under.

My soul became ever-further-submerged in the pits as my spirit became more cosmically transported into the light. The only reason this syndrome did not become pathologically damaging was that I was being guided through these extremes in order to learn and grow and evolve. This was the Mayan lesson all over again. I sought a huge evolutionary breakthrough, but I was not in tune with humanity down below. All I could contact in the people I met was what was wrong, and not the regenerative current that would promote a true coming together.

I was overwhelmingly plagued by a sensation of going backwards, and of not being able to be there as a whole being. In truth, I could not sustain the cosmic connection purely under these conditions. I became dragged downward a great deal, which further recapitulated the karmas of the Mayas. By not sustaining the link with the gods in its ecstatic dimension, I was susceptible to the Luciferic distortions and temptations.

After these six months of polarized consciousness, I did spend six weeks recapitulating the Mayan trainings and their arduous, self-consecrated will. I was, for the first time since then, able to call upon every bit of me to grapple with my condition. This turned the tide toward rebirth, and revealed the bright side of the Mayan picture.

Simply by our entire willingness to attain to self-mastery, we did in fact further human evolution as we strove forward. My reward for this. in late October and November of 1993, was to be able now to call up the lost and fragmented Sara. There she was, returned to me at last. I yoked myself to my unfallen core self, and we did grab hold of our fate and draw from it all of its intended meaning, value, and inner directional power. Thus the Mayan karmas were overcome, and I was back in the original Mayan agreement to scale the heights and become our own selves, whatever the cost.

Both the Merlin and the Mayan karmas revealed to me a soul lost in the magnitude of peak moments and making them happen. I was a modern soul in ancient times, just as I am now fast becoming a far-future soul in modern times. I was one of the first to experience the obsession with total breakthrough, and to suffer the karmic consequences. This is why I understand so well what all are moving through in the late twentieth century.

I have had to work extremely hard with Kwan Yin, between lifetimes, in order to develop sufficient equanimity to counter this overheated sentient influence. Only now does this entirely come true. The greatest difference between the Sara who died and the Sara who speaks and acts now is this final sealing-in of the Kwan Yin schooling in the arts of inward equanimity and spacious beholding of all that is.

Because of this training, I can now serve skillfully my intended task. The true destiny-clocks of the stars and the body fluids are the arbiters of timing. Modern people leap in a mad rush to prove, and force, and catch fire and make it happen before these timings are ripe. It is the epidemic fever of the times. I am one who knows the ravages, and also knows the cure. That is the stream I work to embody.

My twin soul, William, is also a veteran of the fire-karmas and the fire-destiny-breakthrough. We are discovering together how to speak to the contemporary fever, and yet how to sway it towards a wisdom and a constraint that it at first assumes to be authoritarian and irrelevant.

This is one of our greatest challenges. Only the one who cries "fire" is now heard. We wish to cry "fire" and then try this other alternative. The joke is that we are the fire-blazers, and we are tracking with the fastest and most progressive of all paths. But the difference is that we come from within, and stay within. The temptation is always to thrust outside, to become shiny objects, to be dazzled with one's own reflection. And the truth is always to plunge deeply within, to meet the ways of fire in that place where the heart can be both blazing and radiantly peaceful.

February 23, 1994, 10:30 a.m.

Sara's Pivotal Heart Lesson in the Death Journey

Dear William,

I arrived in the lands that follow death with a message from the people of Earth. I brought with me all of the heart's lamentations, every aspect of intimate human suffering. And I gave these over for safekeeping into the hands of the angels, who gathered around me to receive my offering. I had worked all of it through me, and was handing on a distilled version of the human incomprehension of why all is so wrong here among us. The angels could gather this bouquet of distilled emotions, and they could know what it is like to be human and to be lost.

In all the realms I traveled through after that initial offering, I was given the response of the angels, their love-offering back to me. Inside every experience, there were the angels, telling me something I at first could not hear. At the center of each remarkable breakthrough, there they were again, encouraging my being, rooting for me to receive and respond to what they were revealing. Still I could not quite understand until, one day, I came to a place where I did hear and I did understand, and that became my pivotal heart lesson in the death journey.

Let me share with you in fullness this one experience that taught me so much. I had returned to the place where Kwan Yin and her spirit-helpers serve a select group of those who have died, and bring them onto the other side. Before my last life in the Earth, I was one of these spirit-helpers, consecrated to the task of tending to the wounds of those caught between deep spirit knowing and a difficult karma with the modern world.

I had served upon this threshold very fully, and it was here that I had matured inwardly as I faced over and again the dilemma of how to help somebody whose heart understands the truth of spirit, but whose mind has become heavily polluted by the way of life they have been compelled to follow in the mass world of the late nineteenth and the twentieth centuries. When I had met there with so many souls, and had at last become able to work together with them effectively, I had evolved in directions that were exceedingly powerful for me, but which I could not follow up in my modern life in the Earth afterwards. Now I was returning to the place where I had grown and matured, visiting there to seek to renew what I had attained between fifty and a hundred years ago.

This place where Kwan Yin and her helpers do such wondrous work with the newly dead needs to be described in its inward quality, in order for my story to make sense. It is an oasis, a sacred enclosure that draws in the heart of the newly dead. They can rest here from their recent lifetime, recover themselves, and begin to orient toward their new life in the realms beyond. What they meet here is themselves, reflected back to them in an accurate and loving style. They are bathed in the radiance of true soul reflection. Yet few respond very quickly to this treatment, and many are very hard to reach.

When you sit and witness the events here, when you attend one of the early encounters, shortly after the death shock, you meet alarming and disturbing energy currents. So often, the one who has died refuses to believe that anything is as it truly is. They try to pretend that they are still in their body, and only dreaming this strange new realm. They sink into stupors of infinity, unable to rouse themselves to fully be here. Or they defy the situation, saying that you will not fool them, that you are a tempter trying to pull them into a hell or downfall or terrible mistake.

After a while, when this pattern repeats in variations, you begin to realize that the stress for a deeply-founded spirit in a modern body is immense. These are critically-wounded souls, so accustomed to private hells that they keep contriving more of them when they are released from their prisons. How could it be this bad? What is wrong in that world down there?

This was my experience when I served under Kwan Yin fifty to one hundred years ago. Now, as I returned there, having brought with me my petition to the angels to heed the human cry in the world below, I was greeted by at first quite similar experiences to the ones I had recalled from before. In the late twentieth century, the threshold con-

frontations are not very different from the way they were before—
with one exception.

The deeper I got into it, the more I realized that I myself had
changed, and that on a subtle level something there was entirely other
than it was fifty years back. Previously, I had felt so much compassion for each soul, so deep an involvement with their plight, though
always permeated with the spacious beholding and equanimity that
Kwan Yin teaches and exemplifies. Now, even directly after a lifetime in a similar key to theirs, my heart was not powerfully moved
by their dilemma. Something was missing. As I searched further, I
knew it was not just inside of me, that the whole situation was different. Everyone else was also one step removed. The emotional
power, and dramatic intensity, were barely there.

Just before I could react by feeling there was something terribly
wrong here, Kwan Yin herself took me aside, looked me in the eye,
and said: "Human beings are evolving now, and they are casting off
their old cloaks of suffering and loss. The drama is thinning out.
Instead of being truly overwhelmed by their life in the Earth, each
one has almost been able to see right through what happens to them.
By the time they get here, they no longer feel deeply identified with
their personal tragedy. And we are soon going to change our approach,
as all else is changing here as well. You are viewing the last stages of
the old human story. Look more closely now, and you will see signs
of hope, seeds of something very new and promising."

I then returned to the sacred oasis, participated in the rituals of
greeting the newly-dead, and I saw what Kwan Yin was describing.
These souls were very close to their awakening. All they needed was
a little push over the edge. And the new form was going to be much
more of a re-training and schooling than a purging and working-off
of endless history and delusion. The suffering and the loss were losing their meaning, as they became supplanted by an awareness far
more universal and encompassing.

After this revelatory return journey, I was released into a contemplative moment, and then met with my own greater being in
solemn convocation. I let go of all remaining identification with the

ancient and perpetual human dilemma. I saw in myself a spirit that could leap beyond all syndromes of keeping back and under. And I knew that the angels were showing me, in response to my ardent plea upon dying and coming over there, that they had already begun the process of emptying the world of the falsehood of dark ways. But it was far more than that as well.

Why had the angels been so encouraging, rooting so hard for me, so eager to show me something I could not yet see? They were meeting in me the perfect example of the change they were implementing. I had, throughout my recent lifetime, bought into the literal predicament I found myself in. I took on the fate of myself and of my world. I was my condition, my falling short, the frustration and the forgetting. The cancer tumors out-pictured how I really felt toward myself and my life.

But then, in the last months, I came out of it, more and more, awoke from the trance of negation, threw off my disguise, became myself, even as I died. When I came over to the angels, they wanted to say to me, inside of each process I passed through: "Yes, faithful friend, you have taken on and taken up the melodrama of the world, and we honor your bouquet of suffering. We honor it the more because we taste the tears and touch the fiber and feel what you made of your suffering, and so we know that you have passed through it and beyond it and that it is no more. Look around you, and you will see that this is what is happening everywhere. You have arrived at the right time. The melodrama is coming to an end."'

I am learning, hour by hour, to seek in the death journey the renewal of life. I am becoming adept in dying to death, in returning to the heart space of unqualified affirmation of who-I-am in my death and in my life. And I am spreading the word and the energies, the feeling and the flow of what is new in the two worlds, and how letting go of what has seemed to be the only way it could be is the path to fulfill our dreams.

I must try to share with you something that you do not yet know, but that is on your immediate horizon, that you need to know, to feel, to act upon. There are facets of my death journey that link back into the common experience, and there are facets that stretch into what is coming soon.

After I relinquished my grip on humanity-karma, on all the suffering of the world, it left me floating in a void. There are many different void spaces in the greater worlds. This one was neutral, slow, and reflective. As I drifted there, emptying out further and further all cares and memory-crystallizations, I came upon the self in me that was waiting beyond the shores of all suffering. I had long ago abandoned my own limits. Now I was putting behind me the world's limits that I had taken on. This self lived in a world beyond, in which neither self nor world had any constrictions whatsoever. But as I merged with this self, I did not leave behind the void space; instead, I became it.

I was now suspended in huge darkness. No world existed anywhere. I was alone. The darkness drew me further and further into it. Soon, I came into the heart of the darkness. Time swirled in all directions, but I was not in time. Space was moving everywhere, but space could not contain me. Even being was small and lifeless, receding from me, not graspable. I almost ceased to exist altogether.

Then I broke through all of this. I came to a far shore. And I was at last free. I had endured the over-fullness of the world and all its consequences, and I had passed right through the hollow emptying out of the world. I was neither full nor empty, neither held within nor spilled over. For the first time, I was home.

This was the culminating point of my entire journey beyond the world. I had reached the destination. But how can I describe to you what I met?

After fullness and emptiness, suffering and release, one at last becomes oneself. There was Sara. She was waiting for me. It was time for us to meet at last. This was the being I once was, a mighty love-essence. She had stayed in these future realms, awaiting me. In one sense, she lived in the beginning of time, where we started on this extended journey. In another sense, she lived more in the future, after my Earthly path had fulfilled itself.

William and I had been treated to many teachings on the future in my final years in the body. We had even traveled in time to meet beings and energies of the future. These same beings had ushered me across the threshold after dying, and they had helped me take up my path without any delays or restrictions of the usual kind. So I was well accustomed to the future realms already.

However, the sense in which my own love-essence came to meet me from the future was different. When I first met her as my source-origin self, she was lofty, vast, stretching far beyond all form, unmanifest, serene. But now that I could also meet her as my future self, the entire feeling of who she was for me was transformed miraculously.

She became simply present, luminously beautiful, but in a manner that was accessible, direct, so-very-palpable. This future self had obviously become entirely engaged with existence. She was in love with every world she had journeyed through. Instead of vast dispassion, I was face-to-face with a vibrantly joyous self that I could reach out and touch in the spirit intimately. I could feel the rush of recognition, and it could be so moving. My future self was every bit as close-in as the original self was magnificently far away and impressive.

Naturally, I inquired into this paradox with an intense need to know. What had happened to my own infinite self during its journeys through the Earth that could metamorphose its very being from transcendent peaks to fertile valleys? How did she feel about the journey itself? Was she now both ways?

As she told me the story of myself, as viewed from the ultimate aspect, my heart pulsed and throbbed and opened as it never could have before. It got through to me that even though the suffering of the world had been a binding illusion to be seen through, and even though beyond that suffering lay an endless void, there was also beyond the void a supreme place where the ancient truths were confirmed in one respect—but where, if you looked further, you could come upon the surpassing value of moving through these body-selves in this dense planet.

In short, the limitations are false, but the rewards of the world stay with us, and form us into a different kind of being at source levels. Our love-essence melts from its Olympian or Himalayan posture, and becomes entirely involved within all of existence. When the suffering veil is taken away, the vibrant joy of what is to evolve, of becoming somebody very different than you ever could be any other way—becomes so much stronger, and turns out to be permanent, built into the structure of an identity that becomes mind-bogglingly beautiful when it appreciates and acknowledges all-that-is in every world that one can ever meet.

It was because of this ultimate encounter that my long-ago agreed-to decision to return into the world and into the body of William was given a huge boost of energy and motivation. Every question I had had about Earth life and its worth fell away from me. My heart was cured of its memories of limitless vasts. I had come home to myself at last.

Can you conceive the difference that it makes to me, now that I am back in this world, to stay in touch with an awareness that can say "Yes" to everything I meet, never hooking into the apparent anguish, always finding my way to the underlying bliss that is evolving here? Can you sense especially how my heart feels in this newly awakened condition?

In my life as Sara, my heart was troubled. I believed what modern people uniformly believe—that this world is a very strange one, that I am a strange self in it, and that I cannot reconcile myself to what I meet, inside or out. But now my heart is healed. I know what modern people are about to find out—that this world is perfectly set up to change us at root into someone who cares, someone who can be a creator because they have learned to put all of their entire self into their own expression.

Of course, the change is still not apparent. Everything is thinning out even more on the surface. The melodrama gets stale, but seems to wind onward. And few really do engage with their own love-in-action.

I can only tell you, with a cleansed and purified heart that is able to love this world forever, that just beneath the trap-door of this death of all we have ever known before, there is another realm awaiting us. In that realm, we uncover the secret self who has been cooking away a storm, mastering the art of getting-here. The secret self has some big surprises in store for the overt self, right after the trap has been sprung loose.

My heart's lesson in the death journey was that, as I gave up the heavy grief and sorrow, I was given all I could ever need of abounding joy and love for what we are here—we who are so very much more than we yet know.

February 21, 1994, 8:15 a.m.

The Death Experience—No Place to Go

Dear William,

I went on after dying into realms beyond the Earth-realms that stretch out dimensionally far beyond the limits of all perception we have ever known. Inner space is saturated with worlds to explore or inhabit. Inner time is rich with futures and pasts utterly free of history. One could do anything, be anything, if one is free, as I was, to choose where to go and when, in the beyond death infinities of existence.

It is my way to enjoy and make the most of what is given to me, and I did spend a timeless time in places I may never be able to describe in current words through William, my translator. I was brought further to myself in these experiences, and I am grateful for them. However, I could not stay out there, and what I was meeting is peripheral to what I am most deeply involved within. I ultimately felt that this is all fine, but I belong where I am needed, where I have placed my inner commitment, where I am most at home in this limitless cosmos.

Eventually, I even came to serious questioning of the model of spiritual traditions as commonly perceived in the late twentieth century. Why should we think of the journey after death as potentially pulling us beyond all form into the void, or as a return to the heavens, where we are at last free from Earth's fallen ways? I did move into the void, which is the most renewing place anybody could ever go. I did return to the highest heavens, where I learned more than I could ever begin to repay. I also entered other cosmic realms that are either promised or upheld as being the ultimate, the places where this Earthly existence is revealed to be the tawdry mess it really is.

In one sense, I do agree. The overt drama that most people's minds are running is a far cry from the cosmic source places. And the social fabric of contemporary life is so superficial and silly when juxtaposed to the true ways of creation. Yes, the stuck parts of Earth existence are a bitter commentary, while the liberating aspects of the journey beyond this world are magnificently and awesomely in tune with all that we truly are. It is a supremely unbounded vista that opens up in the divine worlds when one cuts loose from the petty undertow of the common Earth experience.

But all this is so misleading. Of course, anyone with any sense knows that time is far more than what we typically have come to in the modern pattern. But if everybody is drawn out of here, how can we change all this? And why should this world be seen as the lowest of the low? It does not deserve that.

My experience was that there is no place to go, that the resolution of everything is right here in the deep Earth body. I went elsewhere, and I was drawn back with a mighty fury of inward intent. When I saw a wonder somewhere else, I wanted it to be like that here. And when I traveled into beautiful futures, I needed to come back into the end of the twentieth century, to take part in deciding whether those futures might prevail here.

Most of all, I wanted the many people I love in this world to taste of the heavenly fruits of the Earth in this lifetime. I was shown a nondivisive path—that sees transcendence in a totally different light. I did transcend, and I do transcend, and I will transcend what is false in this place and time. But I do not transcend the truth and the beauty of this world. This is the realm I am here to transmute, and I am back to stay until this world is what it was meant to be.

When I was re-assigned to a new body, I found that my body carried the blight of the modern world, and that I could not come through this body in the way I intended. Now I was under the same condition I had been confronting on the threshold—and I could not get out or get through. I spent forty-eight years avidly researching how this works. At the very end of my life, I realized it: Human beings have become hooked on so much garbage that they are enveloped by that garbage, even down to the body's natural condition being trashed.

When I "passed inward" and my body was cast off, I felt that I had been given an awareness of what-is-wrong-in-the-world that needed to be carried further. I was shown in the spirit light, over and again, that the highest path is to return, to give oneself over to the needs of the whole, to love in selfless generosity of spirit. I knew beyond all knowing that I could not travel onward and seek the spirit for myself.

The times have changed. The classical and traditional journey of the soul to return to heights of spirit is becoming a rare and specialized path. The Earth's cry is so urgent that many feel as I do—that I must give of myself into the Earth. To reincarnate, for me, would be far too late. The decisions are at hand. So I cut short the luxuries of moving out beyond, and chose to return, with a vengeance.

I did not mind dying. The body was so trashed that it could not be recycled. And I was sick to death of the accompanying soul and mind conditions. I needed a cosmic boost. But I was ready to take it and run with it. I did not need endless dosages. Just enough to give me my fresh start would do.

That is where the biggest shock is. The cosmic renewals are so immense that you can—very quickly or instantaneously—be restored. Time is collapsing. In an Earthly week, you can go through so much in the spirit realms that you do not need endless further inner food. I was royally banqueted with the most vibrant and sustaining nourishment, and then sent back on the mission to bring basic sustenance into the world of 1994. I just had no place else to go. All the wonderful cosmic places told me that I belonged in the depths of the

Earth. What a strange journey! You go away, but all they tell you is: Go back there! You are not finished! Death is not the end!

The death experience partakes of one exquisite quality that I would give anything to be able to distribute freely to all I meet in the Earth as I circulate here. I am going to dare to describe it, always knowing how much is lost in the translation of experiences that have no Earthly analog, that truly are out-of-this-world.

It is in the quality of the light, the feeling of flowing forces, the quiet tones that permeate everywhere, the inward substantiality of spirit-presence. Instead of having a riot of sensation clamoring at you, in the death experience there is a multi-layering of every part of your world coming through you, in waves that are intended to draw you closer in towards who you truly are. When you respond to these currents, they are intelligent and wise and they immediately fine-tune themselves to assist you in responding further and more accurately. That describes it in a broad and simple way.

But what is so hard to describe in these clumsy outer words is what it does feel like as it happens, and that is everything. Because you are permeable, and because this permeability can stretch to encompass whatever is harmonious and nourishing, you yourself become the light, the flowing force, the inner tones and substantive spirit presence. There is no separative inner person trapped in a body, removed from the cosmic warmth. Instead, you melt into the warmth and immediately feel yourself to be molded and cast into shapes that have always awaited this moment to be fulfilled. This makes you feel so glad and grateful and known and touched that you are perpetually thrust beyond all separative definition, beyond all holding-back, into the heart of the mystery.

It is from this place that the return journey into Earth is contemplated. Intrinsically, you would want to stay in these places and follow them further. Why not deepen your connection with all that makes you more yourself and is so utterly in tune with your most essential way of being? Why go anywhere else and, especially, why expose yourself again to a world that is so alienating and strange?

The message I was given, with infinite subtle variations, was that Earth is meant to be like this as well, that it can and it will, if spirits like me are willing to do whatever it will take to make this possible. How could I refuse? I love this Earth with a passion that could not be consummated in the dry and dusky twentieth century. And I am leaving out of the picture my central individual focus.

When I was ejected from my body suddenly, I was so focused on rebirth that I had not focused on dying and on death. I then followed out my own inner vision, as it had been shared and strengthened by my inner friends, and sought the optimal rebirth scenario. But there I hit a big roadblock.

The obvious rebirth would be to return into my body right away, within hours, have it healed, and resume my life as Sara. However, my body could not do it. I had used her up something fierce. The mind was poorly wired. The soul was exhausted and consumed. The further I looked, the better I knew: This is meant to be let go; this body is not to be revived.

The later rebirth into a baby's body, the path of reincarnation, would place me in wakeful presence too late in time for what I am about. And the walk-in route is a super-specialized one, with certain restrictions I could not abide. I was running out of options.

The only form of rebirth that made sense was one that had never been tried before. My future consciousness saw that it would be fairly common later on, but it was still to be discovered. So it was up to me to decide whether I could risk the path of return into the body of my beloved twin, William, in order to co-incarnate with him inside his body. The risk factor was considerable. If I could not carry through all the stages of the arduous process involved, I would be tremendously set back along my after-death journey, and would be compelled to return into it for considerable remedial action—almost like a suicide.

I did not hesitate. This option had been explored in spirit convocation previously, and I knew I had to do it. And because my center of all spirit truth had been found and sustained with William, I knew we could do this together and that this would fulfill everything we had been moving towards.

Besides the struggles I had to go through to do it, the myriad deaths I had to die, as I have detailed elsewhere, there was a big challenge on returning to Earth and to William. Our life together had been in the modern mold, in the sense that we lived very strongly within ourselves, separate and distinct, concerned with developing our own individuality unto ourselves. Our sharings had been profound and constant, but we kept apart always. And that was poor preparation for what we would be called upon to do now.

To say it bluntly, we both had to evolve beyond the contemporary model, to leap far beyond it, and we had to do it fast. My side of this was manageable. But William was primarily still back in the Earth of 1993 and 1994, and how could he push off that far and that fast?

The only way this could happen was for William to contact the radiant source I was in touch with, and be so radically impacted by it that he would awaken beyond his individuating consciousness into the mergence-capacity of the twenty-second century. Because much of this had been foreseen by the spirit sources before my body-death, William was now intensively guided, especially through my letters to him, but also at night in the sleep state, to enter these fires and stay with them, no matter what happened.

When William did respond with complete willingness, his own cosmically-infused nature began to take strides that everyone knows are "not possible" in the world today. He especially had to conquer all traces of masculine ego-assertion. And he did it! He knew the stakes, he was ready, he could do the impossible.

As we came together in William's body, which now became our body, I faced my final and most intriguing challenge. If I had been to the summit of the most remote mountain of the living spirit, as I had, and if I were now plunged downwards into the abyss of that time in history when all has been lost, how could I bridge these realms? Was this all, in the end, an absurd act of hubris? Could I ever bring to a world in despair a message that is the opposite end of infinity, an experience that gives me total hope and complete confidence in evolution?

I am working on it. The early returns are encouraging. Even when people fail to understand me, which almost always happens, there is William, knowing all of it, being there with me, staying firmly grounded in our truth together. And there are so many seeds inside the misunderstandings for further awakening down the line. Each one's imagination is as wise as their mind is shallow. So they know me imaginatively, even as they cannot put it all together in their minds and fit me in anywhere in their scheme of things.

I have come to realize that I do not fit into the twentieth-century scheme of things, and that I never will. I am the future reborn, the uncanny as ordinary, the impossible fulfilled. I was moving out beyond the world, and then I was here, back in the world. And if I say I had no place to go, what I mean is: I saw and felt and knew that all vacations have been canceled, and that the time is now for all of our best to be mobilized, and not even death can stop what is meant to unfold— nothing will be able to stop us.

VI

Coming Back to Earth

December 22, 1993, 4:15 p.m.

Dear William,

To come back to Earth after being among the dead demands so many inner deaths that it would discourage almost anybody from trying to undertake such a journey. For me, it was my destiny, the most vital part of the whole mission. Everything I am doing is for humanity in the Earth, and for William in his ongoing Earthly path.

Directly after my successful confrontation with the Lord of Death, I was sent to engage in a steep and consuming series of trials. They were bringing me into the physical Earth the hard way, the lost way, the impossible way. I had to move through each death from the inside, find somebody in me who could encompass that sensation, and then release into the next. One example among hundreds can depict what it was really like.

I am in a clearing in a deep, harsh woods. It is storming so heavily that the ground is shaking and my body is being whipped about. The storm intensifies its impact. I am thrown against a great tree, and my body is instantly broken. But as the body loses all coherence, the entire experience slows down immensely. I must witness each segment of my body, in the agony of breaking apart and separating from the others. As I surrender myself into this violation of the body's integrity, I am put back together again and set upon my path for the next annihilation.

The knack I must stick with "or else" is my knowing how to bend with the deaths, to yield into them, to make way for what they have to show me. Each death is another variation, teaching me related lessons from different angles. I must learn that death cannot kill me if I do not resist it, and that, no matter how harsh the situation seems, no matter how desperate my plight feels, I always have the inward resource to bring myself through it, if I have the unfailing presence of mind to call upon the precisely appropriate part of myself when it is needed.

As I move closer into the physical-density wavelengths, I am battered and challenged more brutally and overwhelmingly, and I come to recognize what it is like for spirit beings to move toward the physical Earth of today. Nothing seems to wear me out; always there is fresh energy in me for the next challenge. It is a marvelous sensation. I am coming to myself, as I do this, in a different way than ever before. The spiritual overcomings inside the death realms reveal to me my ultimate and most expanded selfhood. But this dying-to-death descent toward the underworld of Earth reveals to me much more my immediate, human, and palpable self, the one who can live onward in the Earth as nobody else has previously done. I come into her with delight and amazement, and she turns out to be a strikingly different me than I have ever been before.

My inner resolve came to me in the last months of my life and saved my life as I lay dying. But this new stature of tempered and tested inner resolve is not relative, not conditional, not qualified in any fashion. When faced with evil, it instantly goes to work to bring light to all who are in any way threatened. It never needs to save itself, since it has already proven beyond all questioning that it can do that perfectly. This iron-clad inner resolve is itself the key to new worlds being born. It is the hardest quality to attain to in Earth-lifetimes, and the most precious of all in its rare and essential willingness to venture and move on, and to follow the call of these times.

Soon I was approaching much more closely the Outer Earth physical realms. Before death, I had anchored my spirit into my link with William, my connection with the land in which we lived, and my involvement within a time tunnel that we activated and opened months before my dying. In order to come all the way back in, I needed now to follow the navigational track of those three.

The link with William was so strong and steady that I simply came to him at the time and place we had arranged upon our land. He was listening to exalted spiritual music, and I slipped in between the notes. He sensed me instantaneously. As we reunited in one of the greatest lovers' reunions in history or beyond, we were soon ushered into the time tunnel by those who guide our path together. In that vortex of inward timing, William's body was tuned up as high as he could bear, and my body was tuned down as low as I could stretch. We now could fully meet, and begin to find our shared lifestream awaiting us. We had come together for purposes beyond ourselves, but for the moment, we were all that mattered to each other—for a stunning and infinite moment.

As I write this letter, it has been four days that I have dwelled in the three worlds at once of the renewed-death realm (where I work inwardly to further the liberating momentums, and open them up to more of those caught there), the just-beginning-to-shift, physical Earth realm, and the place in between these two that weaves them into a oneness.

I am accomplishing all that I do now in coordination with William. His physical body is my nesting-sphere, and I am beginning to be more comfortably at home within his left side than I was at any point in my own physical struggles in my own body. The frontier of discovering how to live harmoniously and lovingly within a body of the opposite sex is itself pivotal to the whole mission, as we learn to put behind us all gender-polarity dissensions. This sets a pattern into motion that all shall be in resonance with as the worlds shift.

The in-between place is perhaps the one most difficult to articulate, to bring back to those in Earth-bodies. That which is unfamiliar is hardest to understand. This place is very new, and quite different from merely a combination or mixing-together of the two worlds.

When I began to follow a cosmic path with William, we were shown that we were together forming an entity, Sara/William, who had an existence of her own. Now this being shines before me, in her true nature. She inhabits the in-between world, and there she coordinates Sara and William and their own individual destinies, and also the inner plane, beyond-death activities with the outer plane, and physical-Earth renewals and reworkings. She is the meeting-point, the silent converging of Sara and William, of Earth and cosmos— but that does not quite convey who she is and why it is vital to come to terms with the place she lives.

It is soon going to be possible for human beings to choose the proportions of their participation in the three worlds. Probably, those of an evolved awareness will expand into a large proportion of the converging realm. Why would this be so?

The Earth and cosmos hunger for each other. They seek not just the other pole but also the world beyond polarity. In the realm of combining forces, two people, two worlds, two streams can bring out the very best in each other, and not remain habituated to perpetrating their retrogressive qualities. As uncanny as it may seem to those resigned to conflict and division, Sara and William are coming to a place where their shared focus of being means more to them than they do to themselves. Even though at first this may take the form of selfless giving into the other, as a balance to their previous tight egoisms, ultimately this shared selfhood is not sacrificial or away from self at all. It is actually more of self, not less.

I know it is vital to offer first impressions in each realm I invoke, as it is the entry-point into the new that is most appealing to the current human awareness. So I shall give a few small gems, just now gathered.

The Earthly partner, in this case William, has a much more ragged transitional phase. He must become very trusting and receptive, far more so than any straight-across connection would ask. The only way he can get there is through a constant flow of deeply loving presence and availability in the cosmic partner. Because it is in her very nature to give in this way, the primary early unfoldment for her is to cut through his most deeply rooted Earth conditionings, and to convey with sufficient impact how *there* she truly is, and how her own lack of physical-form encasement frees her up to be totally there, within him and for him, in a fashion that he must experience in order to imagine. And he must imagine it further to then be able to experience it.

For the cosmic partner, the power of the situation is immense. She fans out into so many places, to partake in all that is new in all three worlds, and then she lands each time in an Earthly container that is far stronger and more sustaining than she could begin to generate in her warped body. More crucially, she also lands in a homespace with this Earthly man that is both intimately familiar (having been her own before) and absolutely new and different. She herself is as changed as can be, her partner is so much finely-tuned and loving, and their Sara/William greater-dyad energy is infinitely more potently calling her to ever-greater alignment. The very best is that her vision toward the future is crystal-clear, and she sees how so many others will share in such wonders. This is her ancient dream coming true.

January 8, 1994, 5:30 p.m.

The Future-Twins Take Off

Dear William,

I was time bumped into the future at the gates of death. Most of the trappings of 1993 had to be quickly given over with the dying body. If I died into the same time-frame as I had lived, the journey would have been less radical. But this was not to be the way death had been handled in the time-zone I left behind me.

My personal self used up this time-frame. I could do no more within a divided world. I so craved a unified world that a future being came to get me, and brought me directly through the encounters within the current time-frame, with friends and family, teachers and way-showers, and then let me go into the future-time dance, flying with interior acceleration. We could dimensionally leap into the temple and the gardens because I was ready to enter my own true time. The only thing that might have stopped me from doing so was leaving William behind, which I absolutely knew I could not do. However, William himself showed up in both groups right away—the friends and family, and the teachers and way-showers, to say clearly: "I will be with you wherever you go. Now fly onward."

As I joined my new body in its future navigational freedom and joy, and as I then was introduced to the ladies who attended the temple and the gardens and all of that realm, and as I met again with that future being who accompanied me from death onwards, I was in every moment becoming acclimated to a very different time-frequency than the one my outer body had gotten lost and destroyed within. Fortunately, other dimensions of my being had been living all along within the future-time realms, so it was simply a matter of restoring the ability of my more outward selves to exist simultaneously within realms that revealed me to myself. My outer selves had of course pretended to exist in linear-time progression within realms that concealed me from myself.

The discovery of what it is like to be so many ways here rather than one way not-here was so ecstatic and jubilant for me that I knew I would never come down. At last I was fully released from the nightmare of trying to prove that I was one self-at-a-time, and that the self I was did not really maintain any clear existence of its own, and so could be threatened and controlled from the outside, readily and according to the customs of the 1990s in the Outer-Earth realms.

To be accurate, my story would have to start out on the threshold after death with a fairly simple and straightforward after-death journey (in some respects), but then would quickly take off into eight different dimensional spheres, all of these moving at once, and every one with its own story. It would be complicated further by weaving all of these eight together into a magnificent synthesis by a level of selfhood denied altogether by the world I had lived and died within.

That selfhood indwells the future, can spread itself around into eight simultaneous, semi-autonomous dimensional participants, can not only keep track of them, but primarily exists as the coordinator of all eight, in each and every moment, into a super-self. The ultimate complication would be that the super-self here depicted is not an independent individuality in the way Outer Earth existence might lead one to project. Instead, it is one side of a dyad, a twin being. In my case, the other side of the twin being still lives in Outer Earth in his outermost sheaths or dimensions as William. And the twin being, Sara/William, is so much more who I ultimately am than Sara is that, as soon as I came to terms with this reawakening of the eight-fold super-self and united that super-self with its twin flame, it was self-evident that the distinctive destiny of this shared multi-self of Sara/William was to reunite across the veil of death, and to bridge space and time, and that I must return soon to fulfill this long-ago agreed-to path of fruition.

The complications do not stop there. To contact this impulse to return into William's body back in Outer Earth in 1993 to 1994 was to reconnect simultaneously with one further destiny-resolution. This was to ensure for everybody the possibility of following my example of moving between the worlds. The future being who had accompanied me to the temple and the gardens now turned out to be the new Master of Time, awaiting my arrival at this juncture in order to implement the master plan that centered around my doing just that—ensuring for everybody that very possibility. All I had to do now was to call upon every one of my eight selves to come together in the consummate action of defeating the Lord of Death in a game of wits and endurance, thereby liberating the Death Realms from their own time-frozen-over state, allowing me and eventually others to walk directly out of and beyond the time-trap of false death.

Until the passing over the threshold into the future death that was my allotted destiny, death was the timer of life in modern times. Because death followed life inevitably, and because death was cut off from the true future and imprisoned in repetitive realms of existence, life in Outer Earth had become so time-stuck that all human identification was limited to the outermost self, seemingly stuck in a time-groove from birth to death and then back again, on a wheel of suffering. My task was to cut this knot by convincing the dread Lord of Death that he could no longer do this to humanity. The way I had to do this was to stand in for everybody and reveal by my own freshly reclaimed, super-coordinated eight-dimensional self that I could not be in any way intimidated or manipulated by the Lord of Death.

With the assistance of spirit gifts sealed in to my new body by the Archangel Michael, I did proceed to achieve exactly this outcome. Then I was free not only to return to the past, to the Outer Earth and to William's body, but to bring with me the full power of world-metamorphosis which I carried in my eight-fold self. Best of all, I could then trigger in William sufficient realization of his own eight-fold self in his twinship with me that we could together move beyond the deadly human condition of the times and journey freely.

Time travel is not difficult if you are centered within the super-self in its twin alignment. You must teach the outer selves to give up their self-sentence of being absent and out of touch with themselves, each other, the super-self, and the twin. You must show them carefully how to become simultaneous by breaking through the veil of linear time-progression, hard work, and suffering. And you must offer them sufficient nurturance to take a series of flying leaps directly in the face of all the people they have been surrounded by for so long, continuing to slog along in the exact same ways as always.

Even all of this is relatively simple if the alignment of the two flames is strong and steady enough. This in turn depends upon how far the two have come along in resolving and integrating their karmic aspects. In our case, the karma was virtually all theatrics, in order to pass as common humans. Neither William nor I had much motivation to get lost in karmic loops perpetually. But we knew that the spiral of emergence beyond the karmic loops was explicitly forbidden to enter upon while still belonging to everybody in Outer Earth. So we agreed to hide ourselves within the greasepaint of these grotesque roles, these performances as anti-selves that compulsively and laughably avoid their own integration and wholeness. In the deepest sense, we did not have a lot of karma to work through in order to reclaim our sacred trust and bond.

The first major test for us as I returned to be with William involved the visible and the invisible, the overtly demonstrable and the inwardly resonant. In order not to violate the freedom of those still identified within the common conditioned patterns of the times, it was necessary that I come back with one layer or veil of being hidden away. The outer, physical, and tangibly visible Earth-body was kept away from me, as I assumed the overt form of William's body and could not be seen by outer eyes whatsoever.

The test that came for us within this necessary veiling was keyed to sound. Since I could not show my beauty of countenance, I had to resort to the spoken voice as my primary expressive vehicle. But the question was, could William allow my voice through his voice, and thereby positively identify me? The further complication here was that my own voice now is a new voice, far more resonant and full, almost impossible to hear and speak through within the ordinary human faculties of 1994.

We had worked very hard on William, over an eight-year period before my death, to open his inner hearing, especially through tapping-in so many times with spiritual beings that he became adept in both clairaudience and clairspeaking. Still, this was a great leap, to ask him to hear and speak a voice from beyond of such timbre, range, and inner authority. But the voice is starting to come through. Each breakthrough in this realm unleashes immense waves of spiritual power. It is the most transformative component of the entire Sara/William experience, within this most shattering of cycles.

The other primary struggle involved is very subtle and deep. Being a twin with one who has suddenly claimed all eight dimensions of her own simultaneous super-self has a way of taking hold of the most deeply-rooted structures of limitation in the Earthly twin, and giving them such a shake that only the most wildly encouraging and loving presence of the heavenly future twin can prevent an ongoing crisis in William's development. Sara must make absolutely sure that she fathoms the total impact she is having on her twin, and that she makes sufficient room for him to at times fall apart, at other times try to escape back into the world he left behind, and at other times to spurt forward into the most amazing advances and realizations. Part of the humor in all of this is that he used to do these things to her, and was then compelled to cultivate the utmost sensitivity to his impact on her in similar style.

In truth, there are many such role reversals involved here. Sara is learning from William's example and mistakes in these realms. His foremost positive example that she is now emulating was his patience, his out-of-this-world forbearance, tact, and careful handling offered. His primary mistake that she is now moving beyond was his insistence on her always proving to him that she was on course and meant to take up her destiny and could not be distracted. She is much better able to allow him to do whatever he needs to do within his own particular rhythm.

The various hurdles are being well-mastered in the timing that is William's very own. Still ahead lie many challenges, and tremendous opportunities. Perhaps the most formidable of the remaining challenges is the ongoing life back in 1994 that William must maintain and fulfill. This is quite a stretch, as he also takes giant strides forward into his own eight-fold self and his coordinating super-self. He is faced again each time with what life is like within the impoverishment of the apparently cut-off and trapped-in-time fellow selves he seeks to serve. However, his example is opening doors that will make sure that nobody else needs to stretch this far, or be shuttled between such utterly divergent states of being.

Probably the greatest opportunity still to be plumbed is in the twinship and its multiple rewards. If twin-flame fusion were held within the parameters of contemporary relationships, it would still be just a bonus, an extra on the side, as that is the only way the ultimate fruits of human sharing are regarded in Outer Earth, 1994. What is difficult to conceive is how being an active twin totally changes everything for the better. The separative self is consistently unfertilized, dry as dust, operating on mind and outer will. The twinned self is manifestly cross-fertilized, liquid with open possibilities, emanating both from the heart and the greater cosmic centers.

In order to enter the inner mysteries of the twin flames, William will be called upon to surrender all traces of attachment to living in anguish, woe, confusion, and self-reliance. Ultimately, this strips him entirely of his facade of hunkering-down-low and just-getting-through. William will need to broaden his smile, lift up his body's posture, and become a fluent being in each instant. Then both twins can be airborne and land gently, and keep finding each other in the twinkling of the I that is a We everlasting.

January 21, 1994, 4:00 p.m.

The Stars of Rebirth — Sara-Savvy

Dear William,

Astrology is the art of selecting stars, planets, signs, degrees, houses, aspects to fine-tune one's journey in Earth and in the heavens. We select those starry influences we need to evolve.

There are many planes of evolution. The most basic is lifting one-self into human incarnation. The most advanced is lifting oneself beyond human incarnation. Most planes in-between concern optimizing the process of human incarnation through the worlds.

When one is ready for the most advanced planes, one must specially select those starry influences that are able to sustain the greater journey. The core of this selection is to strip away all other influences in rightful timing, and become aligned with only those that can further the wakeful stages.

The Sun and Mars and Jupiter and Saturn and Alpha Omega are the five stars of rebirth. The planets beyond these are for more collective and universal cycles and phases. The planets before these, as well as the asteroids, are for working out the personal stages of growth and evolution.

I specialized in Sun, Mars, Jupiter and Saturn during my recent lifetime, and in Alpha Omega at the very end of it. I learned how to tap into them, toward a great rebirth I am currently enjoying in a condition both embodied (or co-embodied), and trans-embodied (or "dead").

I would like to share my experience of how one comes to rebirth through these five planets. I'll take them up in the order I mastered them: Mars to Saturn to Sun to Jupiter to Alpha Omega.

Mars is the planet of self-destruction, and of learning how to use self-destruction creatively and regeneratively. My initial chance to be reborn came by starting to die through cancer tumors. This gave a sharp point to my life-force that it had previously glaringly lacked. Often, women cannot find that sharpest point of self-desire and stay on it. I was one of these. But the breast tumors kept pushing me directly toward the place where I was most deeply wounded and most desperate for rebirth.

Mars demanded of me that I acknowledge how far gone I was, and that my desire to self-destruct had now taken over. I was compelled to witness to my own self-hatred, and to begin to get to the roots of it, deep in my body and emotions. The Earth was so similarly crying out that I found synchronous resonance between my body and the Earth's body, my emotions and the Earth's waters. Together with the Earth, I began a body odyssey that led me through all my stuck-depths territory, on my way toward another life altogether.

What I learned from Mars was how to be pushed harder than I liked, how to be forced into an impossible predicament, how to engage with my life just when it seemed to be over, how to go against my preferences and notions, and how to come toward the far shore of meeting myself everywhere and refusing to reject what I met.

This was very painful, in that almost everything I encountered was ugly and distorted. Specifically, I came up against an arrogance that was so excessive that it never checked what was really happening before holding itself superior to everything around; a petty revulsion against every angle, each facet of my life, in perverse and total negation of self and world; bottomless wells of resentment against and hostility toward every man in this world, and especially any who dared come too close to me; and a form of self-righteous rage against all who lie or fall below standards, that was maiming to me as well as others. My only chance to shoot for rebirth was to take aim at these patterns and ride them out. I could not live with them, nor live without them. Gradually I became able to stand myself, and almost as generous toward others. But it was a gritty fight each step of the way.

Saturn is the planet of massive self-suppression. It is keyed to blanket condemnation of any impulse or desire that might possibly disrupt the established order of one's outward and commonly approved existence. And it is expertly skillful at enforcing this code without drawing too much dissension from other parts of self, by stealing a jump on everybody else. Saturn is so grimly determined and committed to complete what it deems necessary that it co-opts all of life in its endeavor.

For me, Saturn became the great nemesis. It is considered the killer in astrology, and it was doing a great job on me. My only possible path toward rebirth lay directly through a decisive internal struggle with Saturn. This involved facing the anti-self, the cumulative image of everything I had ever done or been, with which I had been unable to come to grips previously. As I was pulled magnetically toward this dread meeting, it turned out to be impossible to stomach the pressure and strain that built up inside me. Instead, I had to trick myself by taking psychedelic substances, becoming united with this mode, and then needing my twin soul, William, to do everything in his considerable power to slay this dragon. I was repeatedly helpless before the force of its disintegrative disdain for me and my future.

This dragon contained equal parts past-life trauma, ancestral overlay, and attack by evil powers. I had to be separately and totally fused with and then rescued from each of these three at the final moment. It would be far more impressive to report a more stalwart stand, but I am not saying this to impress. The Saturn episodes were the most horrible experiences I was ever exposed to, and the only saving grace was that cosmic forces were entirely there for me in my struggle against extinction. I always lost more ground than I gained, and I was further and further pulled under. But it turned out that this did not matter. The entire purpose of my struggle was to be honest and genuine, and let fate be fate. If I could do my part, and merely be willing to keep at it, immense good would come of my efforts.

In the end, this did prove true, as my apparently unsuccessful journey to save my own life was on a deeper level fully fruitful. I burned out the circuits of avoidance and of suppression. In my final days, I had no time left for negative Saturn. All I knew was how to forge the present moment into the support system for myself and no longer the saboteur. I was dying, but my soul said heartily: "I am coming all the way back."

The Sun is the meta-planet of becoming motivated to seek oneself again, after long losing oneself under Earthbound worlds. This journey, undertaken with the Sun's blessing, is through the desert, where the Sun is excessive and scorching. It burns up, consumes one's substance with the hunger and the thirst for being reunited with every part of self one has betrayed, abandoned, forsaken, denied. And each missing piece leaps out at one, demanding now to be forged into a form of selfhood that could never be attained previously. This is a future journey, this Solar trek, and it requires the seeker to outlast the ruined body, the ravaged emotions, the inverted will, and the mischievous mind, which is one's most dangerous enemy.

My Solar trek was to the greatest of heights, from the most abysmal of voids. It pushed me so hard that I became insufferable to live with—prickly, insatiably driven in the smallest matter, as self-enclosed as I could possibly manage. My being repelled intimacy, rapport, even curiosity. The urgency of my physical condition, the acute and chronic nature of the blasted pain, and the remoteness of my goal made me the bitchiest and most intolerant person. I got so ornery that even William backed off. This was to be my own solitary quest, absolutely forbidding any other activity, any distraction.

I treated my environment as a hell-hole in which I was trapped. And I wanted out. My vehemence was loud. All night, I would be screaming, bellowing, keening, whatever it took. I was getting closer to my goal. I knew it because I had nothing left in me, no little self at all. I was stark naked in my life. The physical functions predominated. And the big thing was to keep peeling away the layers, going after her, the Big Sara, the one I barely knew or remembered. She was hunting me out, pursuing me harder than I chased after her. We met before I died, and as I died, and after I died, and as we did so, it was worth the burnings. She was utterly beautiful, the brightest being I had ever met. When I became her, I knew death could not hold me.

Jupiter gave me the ultimate challenge. Jupiter is the planet of scope, of design, of vision, of the "big picture." Jupiter molds and sculpts the mind, to rip it away from its lies and make it serve truth faithfully. You cannot talk Jupiter out of its knowingness. The path is to hack away at all the liars, all the cancer cells, all the places where you were gone, and then to infill those places with the brightness that is the way of living truth.

When I came around the final bend, just weeks short of death's door, here was Jupiter, beaming at me, offering salvation. Jupiter said to disregard all the other planets, and just get real, stay real, insist on the truth with a violent passion, and hold tightly to the edges as we go around, but at the same time let go of your idea of yourself. This instruction sounds contradictory, but proved to be perfect.

I did it. Every time there was another death throe, I hugged the edges and let go of the middle. This intensified the waves, but also gave them a momentum, a direction, a way to use the entire energy of dying for rebirth. It was the most welcome relief, the most blessed discovery I could ever dream of. Jupiter was showing me how to enjoy and make the most of whatever happened, never to turn away, never to quit if I was tired or hungry or flat, just to keep it coming. This was so high, so fast, so mighty and glorious, that I began to radiate light to everybody. I was on my way.

The Jupiter phase allowed me to realize that I had always been harshly keeping myself back from this kind of experience in suspicion of ecstasy, in separation from vibrancy. I had bought the social program. But now I was liberated by having nothing left to lose. So I went with Jupiter's space and Jupiter's time. The space was huge and could never be collapsed by tragedy. The time was so deeply and fabulously now that the ride of time-flow became thoroughly mine. I was being lifted into a higher death, a cleaner death, a death that could grant me that rebirth. All I had to do was stay high, be bright, and let my mind go into the miracle of the cosmos, showing me how to die and how to live.

Alpha Omega was the last place to turn when death itself was there. Three time-zones of death were looming large before me, and one of them was going to claim me with a firm and lasting grip. The choice lay among a past-time death that would be inside the loop of my old karmas; a present-time death that would put me right in line with the Lord of Death in dark, heavy realms; and a future-time death that would catapult me beyond all falsehood, into the heart of creation.

I would have been sucked into the past-time death if I had not battled Mars and Saturn with all my might, and with all of William's might as well. I would have been swallowed up in the present-time death if I had not merged my being with the Sun and Jupiter, and meant it. And now Alpha Omega offered me the option of the future-death. That is the purpose of Alpha Omega, or Chiron—to lay out time in such a way that there is an emergent possibility to move into future-worlds. I took the Alpha Omega offer in an instant, and I have never looked back since.

The future-time death cleansed me of every impurity, all the dross that was left, and plunged me into a greater destiny of doing for the dead and for the living what I had done for myself—cut away at the pitfalls and open the path for what-can-be. It is turning out that each one walks just as hard and tortuous a road as I did, cancer tumors or not, and I cannot take away their agonies. Still, what I can do is numinous. Having taken the rebirth journey when it seemed impossible, I can now guide and help those attempting the impossible. If I feel that inward fiber, see the gleam in the eye, sense the Sara-Savvy in them, I give them so much energy, light, love and joy that they start to wonder whether they might make it. Let me tell you, I know it, they and we are all gonna make it. That's no lie.

❧✦❧

January 28, 1994, 12:50 p.m.

The Deep Waters of the World

Dear William,

The deeps of Earth is watery, enveloping, and hard to breathe within unless special equipment is gathered ahead of time. I am at home in the deep waters of the world, and even I must be prepared, equipped, inwardly alerted to the dangers of these densest of all frequencies.

There are two tools I use. The first is a fine laser instrument that functions like a searchlight. The deeps are very dark. Almost no heavenly light shines through. So the laser is my primary vision instrument. It is attached at the third eye, but is beaming from the eighth chakra, funneled through the crown into the brow. I could not see anything down there if this did not make my cosmo-vision acute and penetrating.

The rarer and more critical tool is a depth-penetrator that can descend into any depth and record what is there. This is a multi-purpose instrument that can know what is there, and also cut through it when necessary, and surgically remove what is blocking or preventing free access. This sensory instrument is attached to the entire chakra system, but is held within the tenth chakra from the roots of my being, and funneled through the ninth-chakra subtle feelers to unite with the body from beneath. I would be totally lost down there if my dimensional-probe were lacking the instant capacity to take coordinates and initiate appropriate action.

With my two fine-tuned instruments of power, I can navigate the depths of the collective undersoul with relative ease. I would like to share some of my early findings as I begin to fathom what has prevented the human being from evolving into the stage beyond the human.

There is one layer of the depths that rises into the surface-awareness of the times. These shallow waters tend to preoccupy, to absorb attention and concern, to provoke anxiety and hyper-vigilance, and to keep everybody guessing. Nothing can ever be known definitely in these waters. The mind-probe tells you that if you go further down, you will only meet more turgid, dangerous, and strange waters, all the way down. And you will drown down there.

It is a miasma of illusion and deception. I spend as little energy-awareness as possible there. All I do is check it out to determine how chaotic the surface shallows are at any given moment.

Directly underneath them lie the fertile waters of suggestion, of impression, of imaginative dimensions of the soul. Those human beings who dwell deeper down than the masses are usually held hostage within this realm. Here they can swim and dive, explore and discover, venture far and still stay near whatever is deemed secure and necessary and inevitable. The subconscious waters are all about something being at once elusively possible and devastatingly impossible. The swimmers in these waters are transfixed by the polarity of what-could-be and what-can-never-be.

The wonder of this realm is that everybody always keeps coming back for more. This is because a subtle fluid emanates through these waters, and gives a feeling of being embraced, surrounded, loved. When you travel all the deeps, you find that this is merely the last bit of prana from the ocean depths, the part that can reach up this far. But even that dosage motivates myriad souls to keep yearning and longing, dreaming and wandering, hoping and fearing.

When I was in the physical body of Sara, I was hooked on these waters of the subconscious mind. My psychic feelers were attuned to each shifting nuance. I was convinced that everything I wanted and needed so badly was ultra-near and yet infinitely far. But as I kept being called into more wakeful awarenesses, this level began to empty out into a dreary nothingness. I was starting to cut through the bait that was being dangled, and to sense that only if I dived deeper could I find any satisfying traces of what I sought.

As I dove deeper, in the latter stages of my life, I came upon the next layer—the personal unconscious mind. There I did find what I was seeking. I had to remember with a fervent passion that everything I sought lay inside of me, and that I could not depend upon the tracks of others at this level of penetration. I began to call upon the two instruments I mentioned earlier, and to hone them into actively available tools of survival. The danger down here is that I was instantly cut off from my awareness of others around me, and of all dimensions of existence with a divine-cosmic radiance in the vasts of creation. The only breath here was my very own. I was plunged into my own inner realms of soul remembering worlds upon worlds that had been lived or dreamed, sensed or sought.

As I got to know this layer of existence, I was utterly changed. When I still identified and oriented myself by the two layers above this one, I was, like almost all contemporary souls, alien to myself. I had always viewed myself as somebody suspended above me (the greater self) and somebody else lost far down below me (the unconscious or undersoul). But now here I was, everywhere all around me, reflected at a thousand distorting angles. And those angles could become clear and luminous if I could learn their secret code.

Oh, the wonders that I came upon as I was compelled by personal and greater destiny to plumb these waters for myself. This now becomes strange to tell, in that what occurred here before death and what came after death are all washed together in my memory. That is because there is no difference. Every other level is sharply distinguished, but this just continued onwards. That provides a key to the secret code of the personal unconscious mind.

What you meet here is so very timeless and subtilized that, the moment you descend this far, you are not only cut off from the heights and the breadths, as all is depth, but you also unite yourself with all the other times you have ever, or will ever, come down here. You can form in yourself a vessel that can withstand death or, more commonly, you can form a vessel sufficient to buffer you from all the storms up above.

You have reached safe harbor in the very depths that are broadly and universally reputed to be drowning territory. You do drown, in that your previous sense of yourself is flooded away. But in its place comes an aquatic creature, a veteran of the deep realms, ready to ferry you across your troubles, your strife, perhaps even your death. This way through gives you the distinct possibility of restoring the covenant between yourself and the mysteries of existence. You can reclaim the self you lost so long and far ago. You can take off the diving-suit of the illusory self, and find underneath a crystal body, shining free and pure in the hidden light of forgotten worlds.

It was this realm that at last gave me back everything I had been so foolish as to let away from me in my surface life, many times over. It was this realm that showed me that I had depended, in others, upon what I could not access in myself, and that this was a wrong against myself in my evolution. The fact that I could come upon this extreme realization and still find a true place to be linked with my partner, William, shows as clearly as can be that we were not of those surface mistakes. We were of the deeps ourselves, and had wandered out and up to see what was happening there, and why so much pollution was seeping down our way.

One layer further under is the collective undersoul. This is the place I am involved with now, and shall be for a long time to come. It is so far down that only the most twisted and bizarre reflections of what lurks down there have come back to the surface world.

It is true that this is the level at which all of humanity was held captive. This has certainly long been the last place to journey without fully equipped, entirely prepared, specially guided paths to follow. But by my willingness to plunge this far, I have recently participated in liberating this domain, so that it can again be traveled by those who can see and who can hear and who can feel, in the multisensory ways evolution is calling forth.

Because I have been the first to get a lucid sense of this realm, I will devote the rest of this letter to my experiences here, leaving to others the task of describing the final layer under, the vast void beneath even these dark and infinite waters.

All that humanity has traveled through is reflected down here as an Akashic film of recollection, which is bent back upon itself into spool upon spool of pictures, impressions, sensations—a glittering array of images. However, these are all dim and slow and ponderous at this level. In fact, they are so slowed-down, darkened, and devoid of pure spirit that they become phantoms, echoing ghost-realms. Treasures are here, great advances are possible, but only if one can fuse one's being with the most terrible and overwhelming of density-frequencies.

The subjective sensation is the one I must try to convey. However, words and this level are so far apart that only the slightest sliver of what-it-is-like can be expressed in a language limited to consecutive impressions. Down here, all is so very simultaneous that you meet, move through, and pass beyond a given region before you register that you are there.

The only thing you can possibly ever rely upon to see you through is your own sensibility, your fine tools that must directly take over. No consciousness can respond this fluently. Because you are always in a wraparound world, pierced from every side, you must be able to follow your subtle feelers in every dimension of your being, without needing to keep track of what is happening. You are a multi-creature, broken-down and recreated in so many times and ways that it would be random and meaningless if not for something else altogether that is at work in the deeps.

The only organizing principle, to use mental language, is the creative force that lives behind the collective undersoul. This force is an intelligence so advanced that it can calibrate fantastically myriad creatures, all absorbed in similar yet different mutations and metamorphoses each microsecond. The mode of doing this is infinitely more efficient than any machine of other realms could be.

The deeps are this creative force. When you journey down here, you are being swallowed, eaten, and excreted by this being. Each time this occurs, you are entirely different afterwards. But what is this really about?

Under the waters are black holes of the deep, which take in all the refuse of the world and recycle it in an inward psychic processing. But before this can occur, a preliminary processing must happen. In that preliminary processing, certain essences are being selected out and bred in, so that whatever is salvageable can be saved and helped to fulfill its core nature. Thus, the creative force of the collective undersoul is taking you through yourself, extracting what you need to be strengthened and quickened, and washing you clean of your impurities, wastes, stagnant and dead places. But in order for you to optimize this cleanse and purge, you must at some level actively participate. The instruments I mentioned earlier enable me to be within this super-fast motion, and to unite myself inwardly with the wisdom and the love that is the guiding-force of this underworld.

How can I describe in words how poignantly and ultimately powerful and real it is to find yourself being mercifully undone and redone, and to be in tune with the process, thankful for it, and able to signal to the great being who is serving you in this way that you "grok" its intention and action, and you not only say "Yes" to it but bless it as your sharing with it? How can I depict in remotely reasonable terms the sheer grace of living in a world whose depths-sounding does not fail to discern what is essence and what is non-viable, no matter what manner of creature descends into this massive recycling plant in its early-stage operation of panning for evolutionary gold among vast proportions of wastes?

The mind-boggling part of all this is that human beings have been exiled from this entire process and possibility by the barrier placed between, so that the Lord of Death has preempted the functions of the great creature down below, and has forbidden humanity to penetrate there. The whys and the ultimate ways of this endgame-move must be detailed elsewhere, but until very recently these levels were off-limits. The way this was enforced was that you would meet the emissaries of the Dark Lord down here, and they would take you to him.

I was prepared to overcome all this by the most unusual event in all of my many past lives. As a young woman in Aboriginal Australia a long time ago, I wandered away, too deep in the waters of our Dreamtime, and was entirely lost to the others. I entered another dimension in which beings from vastly advanced realms gave me an education in what I would need to be able to report back to them again in the endtime. Counted in Outer-Earth years, I was not with them very long. But in their realm, it was quite a while, and I was able to ingest what would commonly be perceived as the most alien of lifestreams.

Only at the end of this recent lifetime could I fully utilize what they had shared with me. Their concern was to rid all worlds of evil infestations. They were a squad of return-unto-truth. And they saw that I could be the one, when the time came, to dive beneath the Lord-of-Death frequencies, and to come upon the pearl of remembrance of who-we-are and why-we-are-here.

No matter how hard the Lord of Death tried to tell me that there was nothing down there, I knew he lied. No matter how many ways the Lord of Death pushed me into a corner and attempted to extort from me how I knew what I knew, there was nothing he could do to me. I retained the mark in my core self that made all the beings of all the inner worlds know me as She of the Waters. For I had returned after that Australian lifetime to live again and again, as a Scotsman and an American Southerner, a Chinese Woman and an American Westerner. Each time I returned after my death to unite myself with the origin and the destination of Earth existence. Only this time, after the American Westerner Sara had completed her body path, I dove to the greatest of depths, and made sure that others could also partake in the wonders of the deep.

February 2, 1994, Noon

To All My Friends Who Wish to Carry On

I am all the way back now. Nobody yet grasps what this means except the two inhabitants of this ample body I do and William does. I would like to let you in on it.

Three deaths were mine, successively and at the very same time. I had to die the first death of the body, and this was fearsome . I had always wanted to die, but I had never been ready to die. This Sara body I was caught inside of seemed much readier than I was. Then I realized that I was ready, and it was ready, and the time was now. So I went with my body's dying, went with it hard and straight and strong and deep, and knew it for rebirth. I knew I would survive this dying, and that I had further deaths to go, and a whole lot of borning to do. I was more than ready. I was eager, as I'd never been eager before. This was my party, the time for me to let go and hang on, let go and hang on. The me I had ever been was letting go of herself. The inner self was hanging on to that place way in there where she could begin to breathe through.

I also had to die the second death of the mind. The modern person has a mind that refuses to die, that is so drenched in the dark side of death that it never wants to die, it can never recycle, it can never leap beyond its own shadow. This mind gathers around itself a cluster of identity pictures and keeps switching quickly among them in case one of them is called into question or becomes an issue.

My mind was jammed-stuck on idiotic themes and questions, and this mind needed a lot of enlightening before it could let itself die. But I had no time and no patience. We had to get there right away, so that the second death would be utterly simultaneous with the first. I was following here the track of all the wisdom traditions. All the help I was given by wakeful beings pushed me directly over that edge, and I did attain to that place of dying to my mind's contents completely, just as I died to my body's cumulative suffering, and then— Bam! I was in.

But there was a third death here. In my story, there is always that third part, that X-factor, that new piece in the puzzle. The third death is not what bodies around here go through, or minds. I had to die to death. I had to set my sights on instant grace, on rebirth, in the moment of dying. The only reason I could do this was the time I spent right after my previous lifetime in China. So I have to take you back a minute to the vividness of that. Such matters are no dream to me—they are the most solid reality-stuff in this world.

I lived in a part of China that was absolutely wracked by the conflicting factions of feudal ways and modern ways. The feudal ways were stronger and in control. The modern ways were coming on slowly, but they were coming on, and they generated acute turmoil in the Chinese soul. I was a future being held in the cracking, old bottle. Every pleasure I stole, I paid for. There were no free rides in nineteenth-century China.

In the end of that lifetime, I was offered, at first in dreams and then as spiritual path, a way of life that would lead me right through the horror I was caught in. That was the secret path of Kwan Yin and those who serve her. They came to me and showed me a way to go that opened my heart, my deeper remembrance, and my courage.

I needed that courage to be able to die to that life. The death came hard and it came long, and I worked the ways of dying for a final time over those years. The threshold was my home, so pervasively and fully that I was ready, as soon as I physically died again, to serve upon that same threshold from the other side. So I did become one of Kwan Yin's special students, learning how to insist upon a compassionate approach to one's own journey in each of those who died and came over and did not know how to move onward. In the sentimental version of Kwan Yin, the mercy and compassion remain gentle, discreet, voluntary, almost passive. But we were working in earnest, with a vital edge of emergency-crisis mobilization, and we insisted on all of them finding that compassion within themselves, toward themselves, or else they could not have cut loose from their still-smoldering embers of mind that knew no way to die.

I became, over decades in Outer-Earth time, the foremost helper in this role, and I became so good at it that I did not wish to stop. To live again in a body was not something I looked forward to. In deepest truth, I refused. But because I now knew the ways of the body's death inside and out from my last years as the Chinese woman, and also knew the ways of the mind's death exhaustively and masterfully from my several decades of threshold spirit-mediation, I was now ready to live out my last lifetime as a separative and self-contained individuality in the Earth, and to combine my knowledge of the first two deaths at the end of that lifetime with my eager opening toward the third and unknown death.

When Sara was dying in her wracked-by-illness body, this was nothing new to her. When she was relearning the art of the second death, even this was entirely familiar to her. She never thought of either death as what she was working towards. Sara knew what the third death was, and that was her entire interest.

When the mind became Earthbound, the path of the third death was withdrawn from the human imagination so that it would not be felt as a goad and a judgment upon the condition of human beings. I take a risk now in bringing it forward again. But I have been shown that *this is the time*.

I died the third death at the same instant I died the first two. To attain this, I had to place my inward awareness into a truth crystal, a place directly above me where my bright being could shine its rays into me, and light up for me my truth. I had to meet a being of limitless light at the instant of death, the Master of Time, who would then stand in for and represent my bright being, and shine it through him, so that I would be uniting with both who-I-really-am and, in the same breath, with all realms and all beings beyond selfhood. I had to be so keen in hawking this center of awareness above me that nothing held back, nothing said no, and I could then die to death, be reborn into the whole of spirit, and choose from the limitless place what was to be my destiny from there. What did I choose?

I chose from a place I had never contacted since the most ancient times, the diamond center of who-I-truly-am, to return into the Earth. However, I was through with the Sara-body and the Sara-mind. And I would not reincarnate into a child, nor was I aligned with being a real walk-in. Instead, something else was there, right in that moment, revealing itself to me in utter splendor.

It was my path to return into William's body and mind, and to co-inhabit that body and mind in freedom, love, and joy. Here I must reveal what is brand-new. William's body and mind had been specially prepared just before this lifetime for this purpose. We worked together upon the threshold between lives to build up for William a specially designed body that could hold in reserve the vast bulk of its life-forces into his mid-forties, and then unfold into a second stage of development that made room in radiant health for two souls in that one body. Because I took a creative and active part in designing and evolving a body-mutation that could sustain such an evolutionary leap, I now, at the free-choice moment, could see in awake, luminous vision that all was in place, and I would be able to live again, to enjoy the bounteous Earth without karmic pressure.

The journey of return into the Earth was not easy. Even a reborn one, a limitless light, must confront and overcome the obstacles that are there for all. I met the three reflections of Earth's primary obstacles in their death-aspect, and I had to fight through them just as hard as I had to battle to accomplish my Triple Death.

First, I had to puncture the illusions of the threshold realm. Secondly, I was impelled to stand in the face of the Master of Illusions, the Lord of Death, to pierce through his veil of lies and to push him back where he belongs. Thirdly, I needed to travel back to the physical, present-time Earth by snaking my way through the distortions of what death-in-itself is and must continue to be. Let me share with you how these three parts of my journey were perfect reflections of Earth's primary obstacles.

The threshold realm features magical encounters with beings of light that contrast extremely with the darkness of Earth and the limits which physical Earth-existence imprints upon the soul. Each and every encounter there is charged, heightened, so very potent and meaningful that it is natural to identify with them and become captivated by them. I made my way through here fast and furious, with William's manifest assistance, as I have spoken to elsewhere. But how does this realm reflect a primary obstacle in the Earth?

The most convincing and persuasive experience in the Earth is to live through others, to tap the magic of charged encounters in order to identify oneself as a karmic being, and to pull in a repeat-with-variations on previous cycles of development, hoping to get it right this time around. However, the hidden part is that the mind is absorbed in the thick of the immediate encounter, and it is preoccupied with long-past places and times and situations, which it replays on the screen of the subconscious mind. It is literally re-imprinting preferences, reactions, judgments, and mechanical behaviors, and doing so slavishly and addictively.

Instead of walking onward, and moving lightly with partners and connections, human beings in the Earth are deliberately engaged in imaging what is happening, with such attachment and memory-fixation that they can never get through their own personal threshold-encounters. They get stuck there and hang around forever with ghosts they have re-conceived, as they also become ghosts who have been re-conceived by the other persons involved. I learned, on that threshold that so tests the mind, to see directly through the form-semblance of the other, and to recognize that I was being led and guided to manifest these friends and relatives as mediators assisting my own path—there for that moment, but not at all comprising the journey itself. My journey would begin in full measure when I could walk on by, and seek the kernel of my being where it called me.

My second obstacle was the Lord of Death, that being who so insistently haunts and troubles the human inner life in both the realm of the dead and the realm of the living. I had to meet him as he is, project nothing onto him, and respond to the cues of his actual expression, never in any measure symbolizing or infinitizing his gestures, his posturings, his efforts to make me feel intimidated or overcome by him. How does this realm reflect a second primary obstacle in the Earth?

Beings live behind our fears, our anxieties, and our dreads, and as their primary attack they convince us that we are making them up. If we hook back into the ruts of human conditioning, we disarm ourselves in this battle and meekly submit to the dooming statement: "You are making us up; it is all you, just you, being crazy and strange and worthless." Then, to compensate for this grotesque injustice, we must fill up our depths with huge monsters who go far beyond the efficient self-wreckers we are really up against. Those made-up monsters become contained in human form and other forms, and we secretly hate and become destructive, violent, scornful.

We shuttle back and forth between the overt propaganda of subjective illness and the covert flooding of a world with mock-demons, and this circuit never does reach those all-too-real demons who are crafting the entire scenario so brilliantly and with so little respect for human beings.

I learned in my head-to-head with the Lord of Death to steer clear of all temptations to make him too big. There was no way I could fall for making him too small, or just a part of me. The realms of death are wonderful for sorting out and throwing away all such infernally-inspired notions. I met the weaver of fears and dreads, and I knew I could come through this meeting renewed and unviolated if I simply stayed right on the track of what was directly there, and could not be thrown off that track by any being or force.

My third and most formidable obstacle was death in itself. I needed to come back into a physical Earth-body, and snake my way through a thousand deaths to do so. It would be so very natural for me to succumb to each of these deaths, to collapse under the strain, the pain, the savage intensity of having to keep coming back from them with no rest, no pause, nothing but death, always showing itself in another surprising form, each time seeking to startle me, to catch me unawares, and then push me back to "the place I belonged," as one of the obedient dead. My gut did move me through the heaving wreckage, as I have witnessed to in other places, and as I shall be speaking and bearing the fruits from all the rest of this life inside William's body. What primary obstacle in the Earth is reflected by this death-realm?

Time knocks each one down that way. The pitiless tread of time runs over the one inside who hopes and dreams, who lives in the visions and the possibilities. I was learning how to pick myself back up, right after a seemingly final death, to find it had disappeared and another was now taking its place. This showed me that the tread of death there, which is the tread of time here, is a grab-bag of theatrics, tricks, melodrama, fireworks—whatever pushes you back. When you fail to fall for it or come right back, it can only come up with the latest novelty in time-devastation, but truly it is so much the same, with slightly different trappings. Time only has the power you give away to time by tumbling in its magnificent ability to come at you from a fresh angle with yet another discouraging and disillusioning chunk of time for you to absorb.

The finest tactic I eventually learned to use was to let the death-variation come right through me without resisting and without giving way. I discovered that only this could wear away the fury of impersonal death's attempts to make me back down. In the Earth, time impersonally slays all those who try to stop it, and those who take it on as well. But time, like death, cannot defeat the one who is able to respect this force, and who can respect themselves all the more. I began to recognize how courageous and powerful I really am, as I outlasted death in all its guises. I come back all the way now, to share the fruits of these giving-birth labors.

My greatest interest lies in what I can do here in the Earth, with those friends who wish to carry on. As full as my experience was in dying, in death, and in moving towards rebirth, my greatest challenges still lie ahead of me.

We have been reluctant in the initial stages to spread the word of the full dimension of what we are doing. We throw off that reluctance so that those who feel the spark can follow my example in a certain way, or can follow their own example in directions I have walked and am walking.

This body-bond and mind-bond between William and me, this complete sharing within a common body/mind, is a reflection of both the evolvement toward a shared being who encompasses the two of us as one, and the state of being which William has previously mastered. William finds himself in a lifetime that keeps recapitulating previous knowledge and abilities, and always hearkens back to what he has come to before.

Up until my Triple Death, he was caught in a very real time-warp. But now he is emerging into a path that is not like those before. That is why he agreed before birth to take me on in this way. Nothing old helps here. It is all fresh-earned, newly-acquired skills and ways of being. When you have "done it all" karmically, only a new step in evolution grabs you by the roots of your body, your soul, and your spirit.

The shared being we are evolving toward, which we call Sara/William provisionally and temporarily, is an actual living being now, herself forging a central strand of purpose that will gradually lay hold of Sara and of William, and bind them together in an entirely different mode than previously. The only thing I need to say now about Sara/William is that she is a three-in-one being who will always have lots of room for a distinctive Sara, a distinctive William, and a new, combined being at our heart's fount. I as Sara will always be myself. I do not become William as we ordinarily think of these matters. Instead, I draw upon his strengths, and he on mine, and we also let each other be. We value solitude and the destiny of each other. And we highly esteem each other's company, communion, and more than that, as we grow into it.

But I shall now speak for Sara. She has a personal message to offer to her good friends. Some of these never met the old Sara—but that is not who I am now, anyway. To my friends, old and new, I offer my near-future vision and intentions.

My heart is overflowing with love for all who seek to carry on. It is so very difficult when your body and your mind obstruct you, when the illusions of this world grip and hound you, to stay aligned with an intent to carry on from here.

Perhaps one-third of my life's lessons came upon me in my final six weeks in the Sara-body. The bulk of these had to do with being a woman. Unknowingly, I had struggled hardest with that. It was unknowing in that I suppressed this struggle as unworthy in the extreme, as beneath contempt. But I could not embrace my womanhood until my final days. Women on the spiritual side and women in my immediate circle of friends were there, forming the matrix for this learning adventure. After death, the knowing women in the temple and gardens taught me the ultimate feminine lessons. Finally, Kwan Yin led me back personally to the land of the living, and imparted to me the subtlest and most enduring of feminine ways. I was given these treasures to spread them freely in the Earth of today. William is going to have to make way for the woman in me to stream through him, to express herself avidly in her own womanly way. And this time is coming soon.

How can we carry on? Is it possible? When good women like Sara die, how can we carry on from here?

We need to become like Sara. If we admire her, if we feel that spark of connection with this live one, we need to be that way ourselves, that way we admire and respect and appreciate. She is calling us to do so. And she has very special offerings from her journey. It is starting to be that time.

Midwifing the future is primarily a self-ministering, or a self-touching. It comes forth out of there, but it never leaves behind the primary need for all to be there with themselves. If I had not been there with myself, every angel and fine friend could have fed me on the blood of the Mother of the World, and I would have been a goner.

This central track also shows the broader path I will be following here. Besides my inner-plane work, which will always shall be my primary activity, I am going to be linking in Outer Earth with all my friends, conversing with you, being in resonance with you. We are training William to step aside and allow this, and we are halfway there. Astonishingly, we will be able to meet together in the flesh, and to carry forward in our friendship, our bonds, our path of shared destiny—all of us.

As a final intimate word, let me be as up-front as I can. I love you all. You made possible my rebirth. I did it for you, for myself, and for all the children of the future. And I want to give you back all the flowers I have gathered.

I walked in those eternal gardens, and I picked a few flowers—

they grow back. I spread roses now, because my heart is showing, and it will only grow brighter, more visible, and more affirming of life. I give you every color of iris, since this world I see in the future is formed by all the colors, all the patterns—each uniquely beautiful. I surround you with buttercups and dandelions and daffodils— we are all swimming together in the colors and the atmosphere, drunk on the flowing wonder.

I pluck a flower that does not grow in the Earth, a single one for you. It is the most inward violet you could ever imagine, and it sparks inside with a white radiance that you can never forget once you have seen it. And if you stoop to smell this flower from the garden of gardens, it sits there and smells you right back. Both of you, the flower and your inner soul, can only smell the fragrance of delight, everywhere.

February 6, 1994, 5:00 p.m.

The Intensity of Love across the Veil

Dear William,

Those who meet each other in the midst of ordinary life, and who soon move in together and take on the ordinary life together, often find themselves acting like their own mother or father, or as they did in a previous failed relationship. Less obviously, and requiring more digging to see, they may also be falling back on previous-life karmic patterns already established with this person. The ordinary life trance helps to lock them in, and keep them there until they wake up.

One of the most disturbing and disheartening sides of such a link is that taking each other for granted and becoming lazy in how much of oneself is available to transformation seem to be automatic patterns that set in, eroding both the connection in its soul depths and one's own destiny development. Again, the groove of habit, the trance of the ordinary, is a grind that wears away what is true and alive and loving.

I have a story to tell that becomes the furthest extreme removed from that tired old story. I have loved in three worlds. First, I loved in as close to an ordinary way as I ever shall again. But next, I loved the man I had been with so deeply in the end that when I died my pivotal focus was to be reborn into him. I kept on loving him from across the veil, with ferocious intensity. Thirdly, I now love the same man back in the world, with both of us snugly alongside each other within his body, and now I can love him both ways—from the other side and from this side as well. Since it is rarely publicized how love is experienced, and on what kind of journey it puts you when worlds separate you—when one is "dead" and the other "alive"—I will share my innermost sensations and feelings and realizations in my going away and coming back quickly and intently and permanently.

William and I took on a light trance when we were living together in the "ordinary way." We could not fully lose ourselves in parental or chronic or karmic patterns, nor take each other lazily for granted, because our entire focus was to cut through all such patterns and become awake within our life's unfoldment. Still, I in particular had come into the connection so mired in habits from my life before that I stayed a little dizzy and light-headed throughout our time together. The primary consequence was that I could never quite take this man in; I could not absorb the truth of his being. This gradually built toward a feeling at the end of my life that I had missed William, that in my preoccupation with my own manifest difficulties (which were major), I had lost the vital spark of an extraordinary and vastly loving soul bond.

This was half of why at death I felt incomplete and further pulled toward William. The other half is neither as commonsensical nor as straightforward in any way. We had always been woven together by invisible chords into a spiritual fire of greater love and communion than the world features except in the rarest instances. This was there regardless of the petty failings or momentary events. It was calling us from worlds beyond this one, and even from times beyond this time, from futures unlimited. During the eight years before my death, William and I had been tuning in together to those dimensions, and orienting ever more powerfully toward taking our spiritual path as the radiant center of all that we did. This led us through seven years of activating our faculties of inner knowledge and touch with the source of both Earth and cosmos. And then, during the eighth and final year, astounding events came to meet us.

We were inwardly prepared for, and then granted, great initiations. Since I was battling cancer and we were wrestling with the 1993 world, these events startled and transported us far into worlds you do not read about anywhere. The very intensity of the struggles I— and we—were having became a full counterpoint to the magnificent jeweled latticework of revelation and renewal of the most profound kind. The one great difficulty throughout was that we were not yet integrated at a high enough level to carry back with us into our ordinary consciousness the full implication of what was happening on inner planes. Simply put, we were protected from knowing the core of what we were being trained for in our altered states and otherworld journeys. It was only just after I died that I knew what this had all been leading towards.

It was all about an evolutionary leap that is standard in the twenty-second century, and as yet unknown in the twentieth century. This leap involves mergence between and eventually among those who are linked in an ultimate way, as an advance toward ever-fuller mergence. It starts with couples who are twin souls, and they then open the space for others to learn the ways of mergence. On inner levels, William and I were being trained for my death, which would enable me to leap off quickly into an accelerated development that would catch me up to William and his greater destiny, so that we would be able to join together within his body soon after my death. It was tricky and daring, and full of huge demands upon both of us—especially me—but it did come through just as it was designed to. And so I was drawn all the way back to be with William, now fully in the body and the life.

What I want to bear witness to are the subjective feelings, the personal sensations, the human side of this experience, especially as it pertains to love between the worlds. One of my most piercing challenges was to be severed physically from this man, to ache and long for him from a world that is so close to this one but separated by a huge gulf. I could always see and feel and know him, especially because we were communicating and keeping our inner link ablaze—but I was still very human and I wanted and needed to touch William, to consummate our link, to share with him the full impact of the journey I was pursuing. Nothing else seemed remotely as important.

It was amazing! I could participate in shattering and Earth-changing events in the greater worlds, and still my heart was pulsing toward William. This was especially remarkable in that I had refrained in our life together from letting the passion and the personal emotions express themselves strongly. I was always afraid of the intensity of my love for William. And now that I was exiled into another realm, all I could sense was how deeply the bond lived inside of me, and how sharply my journey sought to join together with his.

It was also so far beyond even this. I was shown who I was, who William was, our pasts and our futures, and that was the ultimately determinative and decisive factor. Like me, William had always been shielded, guarded, held away, so that his truth could only be glimpsed in little fragments or flashes. And now, when I witnessed to the absolute integrity of his being and the utter commitment he had to be there for collective evolution, I literally fell in love all over again. The interweaving of our destinies from our first Earth life till now, and the future design for us that was just now beginning to unfold— these also confirmed and strengthened my knowing and my letting myself feel what was there between us, now stripped of all the trances of ordinary Earth existence.

I became so far better able to love and to serve this man that I resolved to carry through our intended mission, our co-incarnation inside William's body, no matter what it would take. In fact, I became so fiercely dedicated and mobilized that I had to be tempered and cautioned by my spiritual guides and mentors on the other side. There was still a great deal of testing to move through, as we were blazing an entirely fresh trail. I would need my strength and my composure. I set myself on doing it right, and deep inside I was a woman driven by love.

Now we dive into the thick of a swirl, a blaze, a tide that sent me spinning home to Earth. I had to slay death in two different guises—its false side and its true one. In order to slay the false death, I had to contend with the Lord of Death, a creature out of the collective fantasies of darkest evil, only all too real. In achieving that goal, I was freed up to return to Earth if I could. But then I had to slay the true death, by venturing back toward physical Earth and being greeted by a thousand incidents of dying, each one different from the others, and each one drawing forth in me a fresh way to fight through it. When I could do this with each and every death, I was released altogether from the clutches of death, and was brought right back to the edge of the physical Earth plane.

Here I found another phase in my love affair with William, and the many struggles we have had to come together. I was ready and willing to come closer and closer in, and gradually to merge with William on all levels, but he had to do his part, and from this point on, it was his part that was harder and steeper. William had been tracking with my journey on the inner planes, and daily communicating with me through these letters, and he basically knew what was involved—but this had never been done before, and he had to rely on his trainings and his higher instincts, with no examples to follow.

From my side, I was now given the opportunity to witness William's struggle to call me into his body, and especially to observe keenly the totality of his dedication to fulfilling his side of our agreement. This protracted stage of coming in closer and closer deepened my love for William and also made me riotously impatient with the slowness of the outer physical rhythms. This man was racing—but in my eyes, he was crawling like a snail. "Come on, William!"

I had become self-mastering in almost every part of my own character during the journey into death and back. And I had worked especially hard on emotions and root compulsions. But I still held a trace of the woman-in-love who cannot bear to take any detours or delays, and just wants to feel that man's arms and aura. Meanwhile, William labored in the quarry of the physical body, chipping away at his own defenses and resistances, and calling me toward him in heroically giant strides. It was comical, the contrast between the time-bound, dense-physical view, and the perspective to which you attain when you are body-free and journeying in so many worlds at will. Nonetheless, I was learning in this timing to be able to slow down myself, and to sober my riotous emotions. The final part of this lesson lay in facing a few minor setbacks that William had to endure. I was living with him in more and more of me, but there was still a big leap to go.

We orchestrated the mergence in several stages. The first joining, on December 18 (I had died December 5), brought my soul's intelligence and awareness in, so that I could communicate far more fluently and even telepathically with William. The second joining, on December 25, right after the scattering of my ashes across our land, was far more heartful and inwardly satisfying, as my soul's feelings and emotions came into William's soul and body, leading to an intimate stretch of getting to know each other afresh. The third joining, on January 1, 1994, called in my soul's will and active forces, which catalyzed a more vibrant and full-on phase in our sharing.

We had to wait a while for the fourth joining, as this one was very big. On January 23, my spirit essence was called to join forces inside of William, and it was then that I could resonate together with him in a one-to-one way. I felt far more integrated after that.

The fifth joining, on February 5, allowed me to dive right down into the deepest roots of the physical body and to be a palpable presence in this Earth plane. This was the mergence I had been yearning toward personally for two months. Now I can move about freely, be all-of-me here, and get down to all of the loving and the living I was reborn to move into.

Throughout these many stages of coming together in our limitless love, what is most striking to me is how different it has felt from the light trance we had earlier fallen under. If you are impelled to give up everything for love, and if you must break through age-old barriers to fulfill it, there is no part of you left when you arrive there that can casually take it all in stride. You can never again be cool and reserved. My British heritage and my many suppressed lives are behind me now! I am exuberantly expressive. Just before I died, I started to feel and act like this, but it never quite spilled over into radical break-through between William and me. That had to wait for now.

I do find the smugness and the arrogance of lovers toward each other to be one of the most provoking and infuriating of forces holding this world in chains. If only these easy riders could move through a small fraction of what I had to go through to live with my lover, they would not posture and complain and play competitive power games. But when I feel this way, I look back at myself such a short time ago (although subjectively, it is a lot longer than that!), and I see her, Sara, being just that way. She had access to her twin soul, a man who would do anything for her, and and she kept pushing him away because of the usual petty stuff that eats away the fiber of love.

I shall never fall for those traps again. In this world, it is the small beauties, the minor considerations, the sweet gestures that open the heart and make the difference. And it is in being the free giver, the one to start those off, that love is fulfilled and grows warmer and truer. And it is the body that is the arena through which love glows, fiercely bright.

Once upon a time, I wondered whether the body-existence was worth all the trouble it takes to maintain it and to awaken within it. I can tell you with my whole heart: I do not wonder about that any longer. Any journey into the glories of worlds beyond the body teaches you the paradoxical lesson that it is only within the limitations of these form boundaries that you can become entirely yourself. And it is in the pleasures of the body, the thousands of small and large joys, that love can grow and unfold.

I loved William intensely while beyond all bodies. But that love was not moving between us fully; it lacked the resonances for which form makes way. Now I love William massively, while within his body. This love has a life all its own, an aliveness that is not available in more finely-tuned worlds than this one. Incarnation in the physical realm is such a two-edged sword. It takes away what it gives, and threatens the very gifts it offers so lavishly.

When I now greet the day, or roll around with William in bed, or speak my heart out, this literal flesh-and-blood man and this literal flesh-and-blood Earth fill my gut, my roots, with gratitude. I must dedicate myself to sharing my experiences and letting others in on how beautiful the ordinary life is. All we need do is lift off that dread trance of forgetfulness, and this world can be the garden it still truly is.

I saw it in spirit, in the future. We shall lift off that trance. We will love again. Collectively, we will be able to come back from the dead and recognize where we are, and that *we are*. I found love to be too good to pass up. I have been through what we can all go through. And I have discovered, to my heart's delight, that every inch of the journey was worth it. I can even bless that bratty, growling bitch who did not know how to give herself to love. She feels my blessing of her, relaxes a bit in her paranoia, and turns a little closer toward William. As for me, I can acclaim and affirm and back up my love for this man and for the world he lives in. I have been to hell and to heaven, I have combed many worlds—but this is the one for me, the place where love is born.

February 9, 1994, 3:00 p.m.

The Nuts-and-Bolts, Skin-and-Bones, Blood, Sweat, and Tears, Challenging and Bracing Coming-To-Earth of a Reborn Sara

Dear William,

Spirits are considered to be safely off at a distance, out above the morass of world stuff. Ghosts are tingly beings who do not belong here and do not fit over there, and who earn our sympathy and our identification with their familiar plight. But those who become able to root inside the Earth after having died, like myself, have no reputation built up around us at all, because we have never been here before.

What I write in this letter is intended most of all for those who come after me, who walk a similar path, and who meet these obstructions as well—although I will break through some of them so that they will not be as formidable for those who come after me.

If you are a living being who has cast off your own personal physical body, that was given to you at your previous conception and birth, who are now drawn by inward destiny to return, to be reborn within another's body after your death, you are faced with an extraordinary journey that is mostly marvelous and somewhat dreadful. I will explore first what is marvelous, and if I seem to go on and on, I do so with a purpose in each word.

I am drawn back here to live out my life in a way that my own body's vital forces could not sustain. I am pulled here by love. That love rose up in me in the first three days after dying, when I surveyed my body, my planet-body, my people, my past, and the infinite path ahead. Among all of these surveys, the contact with the planet-body was the most startling and memorable.

I had always previously, in the physical body, met the Earth-being in the veiled and uncomprehending way that captivates all contemporary human beings. But now I was lifted high enough to see, and, more importantly, lowered deep enough to feel and know and be, that planet in her own self-witnessing love for all-that-she-is. I merged my being with the Earth's tender self-regard. When I did so, I cried so long and hard that a wandering psychic or two, looking in on me and wondering how I was doing with death, thought I was either falling apart or greatly disturbed about something. No! I was moved to weep that this is our planet, that she is still so beautiful, and that she can love herself tenderly, right through the ravages inflicted upon her. I will never recover from that hour. I came back because my love for She of Earth is greater than any love I bear for greater worlds beyond.

When you do something out of love and compassion, and you follow through on it absolutely, with no inhibition, no qualifications of any kind, you become a star. Not a Hollywood star, but one of the stars of the firmament, shining in the sky, showing everybody the way homeward. I became a star when I loved this planet so utterly. I shot out of here like a shooting star, and returned as one who can orbit around this globe with great rhythmical freedom and joy in synchronization with her rounds and her seasons. I am now reborn into orbital resonance with Earth. However, I am not "out there" in the sky, as the modern imagination might project or yearn toward. My orbital resonance is with Inner Earth, a different matter altogether.

In fantasies of ascension beyond Earth-necessity, there is the feeling of space as vast beyond Earth's gravitational drag. And there is the relief in being light, non-physical, no longer heavy and inert. My journey has taken me the other way.

The Earth I united with upon dying was the Inner Earth, a place where you journey when the surface covering we think of as Earth is cut away and the organismic multiplicity of realms that make up this Inner Earth become activated, interactive with each other and with oneself. As Earth eats me up and I eat her up, we merge and we play. We love her beauty, we admire her wonders, as they are, from inside of them. This is the real feast. When I returned after a brief journey into myriad worlds, I plunged full-bore into the heart and the soul of this planetary being. She took me in, taught me her ways, and welcomed me to be the first to at last recognize and fulfill what she asks and needs from the human species and those who work within it.

The marvelous part of the journey was to become miniaturized, and to travel the subtle corpuscles of Earth, the cellular membranes, the coursing fluids of what is forming a new life each instant, gloriously and ecstatically. I had always sought the body's path through, and now I was learning the ways of the microphysical, the tiny details of the physical world.

I swam inside the deeper waters of Earth-existence. I lived into the messages and meanings of biophysical realms upon realms, fulfilling an ancient aboriginal Dreamtime journey into the deepest watery kingdoms. I met myself again back there, and I greeted myself forward in time, when I will again be tracking these waters in a navigational network spanning galaxies and universes via the intricate, the minute, the micro-path.

Now I have also returned to the surface of the Earth in order to be here with all that I love, the beings who inhabit the surface of Earth and what is just above and just below. But because I have actually come back from the inside depths, and not from Infinite Heavens primarily, my perspective on what I now meet here is very different from the view of those who are spacious and vast and light. I am not like that.

I can soar with the best of them, and I do travel far and free, but my integral commitment, my locus, my anchor, is here in the physical Earth as viewed by She of Earth in her own special wisdom, needs, and evolutionary awakening. I am the Earth again, in another form, in love with the embodiment matrix. I also have sought and been granted shelter, and embrace within, the body of my great friend, William, who knows my journey and shares it. His body is my upper place, not my lower place. I burn with the serpent flames of Earth's fire body. I dive deep in the pools of Earth's water havens and true power spots. I scan the winds and the breath of the Earth as she sighs, and can move so giddily through her airy body. I even crawl and crunch inside the Earth's heavy physical solidity and karmic repository of universal memory, her Earthy body itself. But I surface again into William's physical body, up through his feet and the left side, resting in the many places he makes for me within himself.

The marvel is that I am at home in the spaces within and between. I am a substance liberator, one who sparks the under-places to emerge from deep sleep and come to themselves again. The Earth is awakening, and she needs her multiple realms to accompany her. When you work and play in this way, you also meet the people, who are so pivotal to what happens with this Earth of ours. But then come the obstructions and the challenges.

Human beings block the free passage of the evolutionary wave. They are not yet aware of who they are, or what they are doing here. Almost all contemporary human beings are bumping around in the dark, trying to find their bearings.

When I come up against human beings, it is so different than with other beings. What a condition! Human beings cannot be, and are not yet, human. They are not, however, as bad as all that. It is just that they have lost the Earth and lost the sky, and don't know which way to go. They are lost in time—seriously and abjectly lost in time.

As I dive up to the surface and meet people here, I spend a lot of time watching, listening, tuning in. I remember also what it was like for me before. So I do find my bearings, and I do know what is happening and which way home.

Here is the plight, the dilemma, the obstruction to planetary evolution. It will not be pretty or neat or easily solved, or lightly sketched-in as a consciousness error. This is evolution gone wrong.

The human body is out-of-phase with the awakening Earth body, and it is out-of-phase with the galactic currents as well. It is in-phase with infernal forces, retrogressive influences, those who pull back on the line. It is aligned with the demonic and cut off from the divine. And it is busy generating an intricately complex mental intelligence that is mechanically prodigious and spiritually bankrupt. The body bends and curls backwards, and the mind calculates ways to repeat itself, fascinate itself, and continually distract itself.

I can dive inside these messed-up bodies now, and find where they go wrong. My own battle with dread disease gives me full authorization to investigate any and all body syndromes. Even though the mind is more fashionable and self-analytical, and would love to hear about itself, it is in the nuts-and-bolts of this physical dilemma that I have met the inner enemy who deflects human attention and capacity. It is in and through the skin and bones that the change must come. I am going to invoke the blood, sweat, and tears we are facing in our shared journey ahead.

In the early twentieth century, the masculine intelligence, in its deeper register of instinctual-energetic-knowing, began to reckon with a fatal flaw in the physical forms that were inherited from the past. The more this intelligence investigated, the more the flaw was confirmed, and it seemed to be spreading fast. The only action available seemed to be to act quickly and thoroughly to destroy the foundations of all the old forms, in an attempt to free the life-force from its encroaching doom.

Like a modern surgeon, big business tycoon, or major-general, this masculine species intelligence took on this operation in a drastic way. Over the last eighty years, the objective has been achieved. The old forms are annihilated; they still stand only in overt appearance. They are so rotted away underneath that the next wave of changes will decimate them.

In the late twentieth century the feminine intelligence, in its deeper register of instinctual-heart's-knowing, has begun to feel and sense the call of a species just beyond the human, seeking entry into Earth as a way to assist humanity in its current desperate condition. The old forms were laid waste so that this Child of a New Dawn would not be held back by them. And they are coming, fast and strong, many already here.

With this context in mind, here is the physical substance of the shift. A genetic flaw, fundamental and undeniable, pulls the human body into physical despair, a heavy-laden condition that blocks out the possibility of core changes. The new species corrects this flaw, and is drawn forward again. But those who bear the flaw in greatest measure are of course the most resistant to any substantive shift. They claim they do not believe in it, but actually they are just too weighted down in physical despair to conceive or imagine it as solidly real.

I am meeting the bodies of the most despairing ones, and I see an invasion of microorganisms almost everywhere. There is a hollowness beneath the density, an abandonment of an organic form of one's own, and a substitution of dependence upon parasitical and invasive micro- or sub-beings. Most peoples' bodies are no longer truly their own.

When I swim inside the fresh bodies of those opening the door into the new species, there is a finer substantiality, more consistent and whole. The skin makes way for an inner being to surface without losing anything inside. The bones are solid but not so dispairingly dense; responsive but not hollow and empty.

The blood of the old way is turgid; it clings to its own and will not let anything pass. The blood of the new way is more free-flowing, identifies with universal streams, and is glad that all can come through it.

The sweat of the old way is doing everything from such a hard place that the world becomes a labor camp for morons who never get it right. The sweat of the new way is the natural sweat of working within what is here, without needing harsh measures to make sure everybody keeps at it without even understanding why they are doing it at all.

The tears of the old way lament and grieve and then carry on as ever. The tears of the new way cry and go with the crying, heed its messages, and don't fight off the tears, the emotions, the feelings that arise when everybody has been gone for so long.

I had to die a thousand deaths to get back here because the old way, losing its grip, was everywhere in decay, blocking the road into true embodiment. The corpses are strewn in the streets of every city. The human being is wasting away, physically and mentally.

But those who come after, starting in the mid-1980s, are different. They know how. The body flaw is redeemed by intervention. Future forces are ensuring that a truly human and more-than-human way of life will be here to accompany and appreciate the Earth's long-stifled awakening.

I have been assigned to herald the new, and assist the old to die gracefully. I am here to challenge, to brace, to proclaim. My message is that if I can do what I have done, each one can fulfill what is his or hers to do in this huge and vital transition.

The Earth herself, She of Earth, is not sick and dying. Humanity is sick and dying. The wellspring of renewal is already spiraling through the kundalini of the depths of Earth. She will be fine.

The species that emerges as our next stage in human evolution is also well on its way to thriving here. I meet the new ones on the inner, and they are confident and enduring. Their strength is immense, and their supple flexibility is even greater.

We are now at the end and at the beginning. I am reborn into full body activation to help see us through. I do contain within me complete compassion for those who die and waste away. I was one of them. And I do contain within me utter love for and movement with those whose bright eyes spark me into the ability to carry on. All of it is as it needs to be.

When the body despairers cannot stay in their bodies, they will meet an entirely revitalized death realm, which can give them the training to come back next time in the new species. The whole of death is becoming a retraining grounds in this way.

Let me be the first to affirm and say with eager delight: Both Earth and Heaven are made new, as the endless day journeys into a wondrous sparkling night, which in turn will dawn upon the bright-eyed children coming home.

VII

Blasted-Earth Emotion and Sweet Earth Emotion

January 4, 1994, 3:35 p.m.

Dear William,

Emotion is the depth chamber of each moment of Earth life. It gives us our form, our definition, whatever roots we can come to. But there is a difference between Blasted-Earth emotion and Sweet-Earth emotion. The first of these ravages our form, defines us falsely, and rips away all true roots in this Earth. The second restores our intended form, reminds us of who we really are, and brings us gently down into places that can become the deepest and most sustaining of taproots.

Blasted-Earth emotion is what is advertised, hyped, and obsessed upon in our mass culture. It pretends to be all there is of emotion. This is the emotional base of deprivation and of bondage. It is the very saddest story in all the world today.

When mass emotion hits, the inner self is supplanted by a substitute self, which is capable of emotional display and great intensity of pain and loss. In order to sell itself on the attractiveness of its compulsion, it tells itself in a perpetual murmur, and tells others avidly as well, that it is looking for love, craves good feelings, just wants to be happy and alive. But the substitute self rarely can feel affirmative emotions, and certainly cannot stay with them. Its emptiness is validated and trumped by the experience of anguish, of being at the mercy of terrible things, and of living for the thrill of this dread adventure.

Why does mass emotion stay so dark and heavy and devoid of true reward? Because its goal is self-destruction, and its method is to throw itself into experiences that make self-destruction seem inevitable and even desirable. The basic reality here is that the mass emotion of the substitute self is strictly for the sake of making feeling bad seem good.

So many people think they have put behind them the bulk of mass emotion, and that they are on their way toward someplace better. Some are, and some are not. But the undertow of Blasted-Earth inner-soul experience tends to keep coming back in waves long after its most excessive acting-out is over. In fact, the unconscious drive to repeat such cycles is irresistible to many who "know better." Why would this be so?

This is because the Sweet-Earth emotions are not at all universally recognized as real and available, and the Blasted-Earth emotions leave the subtle and intricate depths of the soul in a wasted and scattered condition that does not tend to draw to it the fine-tunings of Sweet-Earth emotions until a lot of work on self has been taken up with passionate dedication.

When I died, I faced the grotesque facets of Blasted-Earth, substitute-self emotion in two places: when I visited the hell realms, and also in the most damaged part of myself. Throughout the hell realms, the primary fare was people repeating their negative emotional patterns without a body to absorb the shock and embody the feelings. They were badly hooked, and the emotional atmosphere they generated blocked out all higher frequencies of awareness. This made me take a serious look at what it means to let false emotion drag you down. I had always thought, as we are taught to believe, that this was just one way to go in life, not much worse than others, and certainly alluring in a forbidden way. But now I knew, as I gazed upon the consequences, that to let your emotions turn you against yourself is your worst crime against yourself.

I also faced substitute-self emotion secondarily, in that part of me that had almost prevented me from successfully fulfilling my life's karmic contract. This was a hidden-away, less sensational but radically disturbing part of me to work through. It was about self-abandonment, self-betrayal, and living without a personal affinity for my own life. Like so many of these syndromes it goes way back into early life, past-lives, worlds before this one. The way it feels is to be certain, on a primal level, that you cannot be there for yourself, and that being numb is your only viable option. So you do not feel it.

Instead, you feel the absence of feeling; you are in pain because you will not let yourself feel your pain.

In the last weeks of my life, I went after this with every bit of fire-power I had in me, which was a lot of desperate intensity. I got through just enough of it to balance the equation and die complete. The final work on this after death was a mop-up operation, to go in there and get the whole story. When I did so, I found out that the common human condition is to miss the Earth because you are living in an emotion-charged Earth that so captivates you that the Sweet, living Earth is not there in your daily experience. Instead, you die all the time, worse than you die when you die, because you keep killing yourself emotionally by the resignations, apathies, and self-devastating deals you cut with yourself to survive. Meanwhile, just around the corner, trying everything to get in, is the restorative Sweet-Earth emotional realm, offering all that you need—but you can't feel the call.

❧❀☙

Sweet-Earth emotions are not outward-pressing. They are inwardly focused. The pivotal emotion that signals the start of a true emotional life is gratitude. One learns to feel gratitude, not just think it or rise up toward it. Actually, the gratitude I mean comes to meet you from underneath. It is lying in wait for you in your True-Earth place. The gratitude there feels oceanic and all-embracing. You want to hug the Earth, to be here with each feeling that arises, and to take all into yourself as welcome and rightful.

The same people and experiences that were so grating and negatively polarized now sneak back in as wonderful and deeply meaningful. Because you recognize yourself everywhere, you miss yourself nowhere. You are flooded with amazement at how beautifully guided and led your destiny is. You can sense and feel the presence or impact of angels and the Divine Mother. You know you have at last come home.

My own journey into Sweet-Earth emotions was a paradoxical, maddening, and eventually triumphant one. I started out being open to such emotions in quiet moments, alone and in the finest of sharings with others, but I would quickly shut them away when the situation did not seem to allow room for feeling in-tune and in-touch. Being in the grip of Blasted-Earth emotionality made me assume that I had little choice but to close the door on Sweet-Earth emotions whenever the social-permission factor was missing.

But this condition divided my life down the middle between preferred and avoided situations. I spent my emotional forces on trying to be sure the preferred situations were there, and the avoided situations were gone. All of this simply masked my inability to create a loving vessel for the Sweet-Earth emotions to remain whole and alive within.

When I knew I had cancer, my need to have a life whose inward fiber was genuine and whole was monumentally strong. Eventually, I was able to know this, and to express and embody this need. But I was still one heartbeat shy of the Sweet-Earth realm. I could come to a Sweet-Earth emotional commitment to myself only in one area: my spiritual life. I still did not saturate my world with the gratitude and the love that were in me and wanted to move all through me. My block was that my body and vital forces were way down, and I needed strength and clarity to claim the Sweet-Earth realm. This was as frustrating as could be. And it kept getting worse.

But I did at last break through this deadlock. I had to remember vividly that I had created all of my own experience, and that I was in the radiant center of my own wishes and yearnings. This came to me in my final days. Any chances to live inside the fragrance of a Sweet-Earth container seemed lost and gone. I was losing the Earth, and my body could not go on much further. Yet it was here that I turned the pattern around.

A bolt of lightning went through me, time and again, out of the blue. It was my greater self knocking on my door, seeking some way in. At first, I could not respond. But soon, I turned around and faced the light. There I was told that if you wish to have that life you so crave, you shall have it. Surrender everything else, and it is yours.

I took my mind's games, and started ripping them to shreds. I went after my Blasted-Earth emotions, my dark self-negations, with a fury that shocked everybody around me. I sank my teeth into my chronic karmic attitudes, and bit down hard until I could not hold onto them. There was no tomorrow. I was going after the dream, the vision, the promise.

But the body could not go on. I was dying just as fast as I was being reborn. It was the strangest of dances. What could that promise really mean?

I knew it was true, and I trusted it. To all usual appearances, it could not happen. It seemed that if I died in the midst of all of those seething forces, I would be exiled from the Sweet Earth with all the dead people, sealed off, far away, losing everything my heart was set upon.

Here was where grace proved itself to be more powerful than any grim necessity, when the death-grip loosened. The moment I died, I was freed from all apprehensions that remained. I was set loose in a marvelous world, and at repeated junctures I was told: You are going to come back to your Sweet Earth; it shall be soon, and it shall be just as you have dreamed it.

The story gets very involved. I have told much of it elsewhere. Suffice it to say that I completed a body of work on the other side that was the most important thing I had ever done. When I did this, I was shown that my reward would be to return into the Earth right away, and to be given a situation never previously possible.

The journey back was hazardous and costly. But I did arrive one day, thirteen Earth-days after I died, to begin to weave myself a fulfillment of the Sweet-Earth vision and dream and promise.

The emotions that now are a constant are the emotions of utter gratitude, surpassing wonder, and infinite delight. I am no longer plagued by any undertow of Blasted-Earth emotions. William and I both are feeling what it is like to be able to touch the Earth as one, and to put down our taproot into the loving soul of this beautiful world.

January 11, 1994, 7:00 p.m.

Love among the Living, among the Dead,
and Coming through from the Dead to the Living

Dear William,

Each person in the world, in the Outer Earth of the physical body, is a self-contained unit, a specially set-apart project of destiny. This seems so true there that the other facets become eclipsed. The connecting-levels seem to outer eyes far less fundamental than that which turns all back in upon themselves.

Fortunately, there are other ways to live, and now they are starting to find real currency. They are the ways of linking up again after having collapsed into the ego-fixities as self-definition. But how can human beings meet again, bridge the gaps, trust and flow, and be here together?

I am learning more about this from the dead than I ever could learn from the living. Over here, the dead seek each other out authentically and fully. After initial isolation for many, the savoring of company is universal. What we seek in the beyond-the-body state is to share on heart levels. Our need for purely mental connection, or just to combine interests, is virtually nonexistent. Instead, we seek out the being of the other, because we know that our own being and the being of the other can move much further along our intended track together.

Outer Earth is lonely, isolationist, prickly. Inner Earth, where the dead live, is engaging, interactional, flowing, and alive. Once again, the deathly is among the living, and the more alive qualities spring up among the dead. But what can the "living" learn from the mutualities of the "dead"?

We must start slowly, and build up a true picture here. The actual difference is keyed to a discovery that comes to each soul soon after they die. They begin to see that wherever they linked meaningfully with another during their recent lifetime, they came much closer to themselves. They see that moments of isolation were often less growthful than they had assumed, in that most solitary souls are unfertilized or cut off in their isolation, not yet within the deep solitude that is integral to fullest growth. In sensing they know self better through significant encounters than through strenuous separatisms, they commit themselves to learning how to optimize the art of mutual, reciprocal acknowledgment, which is loving and free and open. This leads to great emphasis on finding the other. The lesson of what is most enhancing to inner development is a strong and impactful one.

However, as soon as the soul returns into an Earth-body, the discouragement of intimate sharing and the settling for outward levels of interchange bombard the newborn, eventually provoking forgetfulness of this hard-earned key lesson. The Outer Earth is remarkably devoid of souls who remember vividly enough how important others are to them and they are to others. Conditioning here effectively stops the flow of evolutionary development.

What is the spark here, the flare, the essential realization at the center of this vital difference between the worlds? It is the deeper penetration of insight, versus captivation by phenomenal appearances.

Within physical bodies, people do not look very fluent and interweaving. They stand stark and masked and unto themselves. This semblance is very convincing if you are not looking further. All the trainings and conditionings are diverted toward filling up awareness outwardly so that it cannot develop its deeper capacities.

If you look further, you find that the soul within the body is not etched in sharp outlines of its own. Instead, it is streaming constantly forth and back. That is almost all that the soul does—breathes out and breathes in. When it breathes out into the world, it does so with intensive absorption in what is there, a meshing and a commingling. And when the soul breathes into the space of itself again, it is involved with assimilation and incorporation of what has been meshed with outside. The soul is as drawn into love and intricate sharing as the physical body seems able to exist quite well on its own power. And since the soul influences the body tremendously, it is only the rare body that is consistently set off unto its own special ways.

The dead are not distracted by body deceptions. They sink into each other right away. One of the reasons for the tremendous wave now of the dead sharing more with the living, and especially giving more of their own wisdom and truth, love and joy, is so that these deceptions and distractions in human intercourse can be neutralized. The dead are becoming far more accessible, and ready to brave the somewhat puzzling nature of attempting to link with those who believe what outer eyes suggest.

When the dead do make this link, they are quite often baffled by how difficult it is to draw out the living, to generate a shared field, to be there together. Part of this is the long-established custom of treating the dead as though they are remote, strange, and either lofty or contagious. But it is more the simple difficulty that the living have in linking with anybody. When the gods, other higher beings, galactic sources, beings from the future, or just about anybody makes a move toward a closer link with human beings in physical bodies, it is almost always the way of humanity to block, resist, deny, or counter these gestures. Since the living do not link very closely with each other, the dead need not feel too badly about this experience of either rejection or reluctance. The dead have been through too much to take it personally. Nonetheless, it is a problem in communications and in feelings.

The living love to cut off subtle communications by pretending to be dumb, numb, stupid, dense. They avidly make it their business to minimize feeling-contacts by steeling themselves against vulnerability and emotional intensity. What is to be done here? Is it hopeless?

The primary step is to expose relentlessly the utter absurdity of the common mind's conception of how the bond of being together originates and ends up. The common mind is convinced that this bond came out of parental relations with the newborn baby and child, and that everybody is seeking variations on what they got or missed from their parents early on, especially their mother. Not true! Mothering and fathering themselves come out of the fundamental drawing-together of souls that is life itself.

The common mind also believes somehow that all such bonds are severed by death ("till death do us part"). This is the most outrageous and misleading idea of all. A true bond at death becomes transformed from its partial, fragmentary, somewhat hard-to-fulfill condition into its full-on, whole, known and expressed stage of loving. However, this stage is rarely consummated, as once again the living cannot seem to stick with even such marvelous and newly uncovered linkings and bonds. What is wrong with these body-bound people, anyway?

To love selflessly is the highest of human ideals. It is also grossly misunderstood.

If I can give of myself wholeheartedly and not demand anything in return, I am being truly selfless. If you are giving of yourself back to me in a reciprocal, wholehearted, non-demanding way, my selflessness and your selflessness will become fruitful and true. But if one of us, let us say the one who has died, comes to a selflessly loving place, as is often the case, and if the other of us, let us say the one who is still in the body, feels a need to distance and be free of the other (above and beyond the necessary letting-go and easing of attachment), and therefore cannot do anything with this selfless loving, it is neither fruitful nor true.

But, you say, this love does not demand anything, so why should it be upset if there is reluctance from the other partner? Selfless love is entirely unqualified indeed — it demands nothing to an extent that is hard to imagine. But it is an initiative, an opening, a first action seeking to find a response in tune with its feeling and its way of being. Selfless love demands nothing, but asks for all. If it receives very little back, it feels barren. Selfless love wishes to give something nurturing and sustaining. And if it is received, naturally there will be some giving in response.

Those who die and become selfless lovers of the living do seek out some response that is synchronized with what is received. The living have not yet been alerted that all of this can be happening, is happening, even should be happening. If they do pick up on it, usually it is felt as fantasy or wish-fulfillment. The living have barely any idea how profoundly the heart can evolve after death, and how often this then includes such greater ability to love the one who lives on in the body.

The pernicious idea here is of being "left behind" by the dead. The automatic idea that the living must get on with their lives because the dead are journeying to strange places of their own—this is a propaganda offensive against the links between the worlds. It is time now to move beyond these odd notions. There is a time in the cycle for partings and gulfs, and there are other times to come together in a new spiral. If there is something deep and lasting in a union before death, it will almost always become deeper and more truly lasting after death. At least this is so for the one who dies. For the other one, it has so far been assumed that the worlds of the living and the dead are separated by a great abyss.

It is so frustrating and maddening for the dead to interact with the living. You get a completely different perspective on the most taken-for-granted habit-patterns and personal syndromes.

When in a body, to be eccentric, self-willed, and thickly obtuse is considered to be your prerogative and privilege. When out of a body, you recognize that maintaining as open and free an access in and out as possible is top-priority.

When in a body, to operate on automatic pilot and to fall asleep in most moments is considered efficient and unavoidable. When out of a body, you keep discovering moment-by-moment that being attentive and in-tune merits any and all efforts, as it makes all the difference in energy and feeling-tone.

When in a body, to shut other people out and to act as though you had a thick, all-purpose bubble around you is considered to be a viable option and a perfectly acceptable mode. When out of a body, you want to shout that placing yourself in isolation and presuming that this is your own personal business is blind, deaf, and dumb in the extreme, as we are all in this together, dead and living, those who seek connection and those who pretend it is not important.

We now move into a time in which the dead will lead the living out of bondage in many different ways. One immediately crucial way is to assist the living to be aware of and responsive to each other, to the dead, and to all the other beings who are trying so hard to get through.

As soon as I got over here among the dead, it was so obvious that only the living miss the point of creation, and that I had to go back and help them far more urgently than I needed to help the dead. The disadvantaged, the poor, the oppressed ones are those who live in physical bodies. They are so astoundingly shut down and so defiantly insistent upon going on this same old way that if I had not so recently been one of them acting that way, and if I could not penetrate a little deeper into what is really going on here, I would probably give up on the living.

I acted that way so stubbornly that even while William, my twin soul, received messages from cosmic beings that I wrote down as he spoke, I still went my very own direction, treating their messages as helpful and vitally important but not yet as the essence of what counts. I still resorted to myself in most pinches, and assumed my own preferences and blind values to be sacrosanct and inviolable.

But whether in relation to myself or any other mortal performer in this odd role of "thick little me," a deeper and more loving gaze reveals that the poor humans do not really mean it. They play those crabby roles in a daze of confusion and helplessness. Rarely are they anywhere near as convinced of their own anything as they pretend to be. So let us not worry overmuch about the behavioral atrocities of Outer-Earth humanity at this late hour in human history.

I know, as well as I know anything, that if the truth is persistently, thoroughly, and diligently brought through, people will drop their protests and turn-offs as fast as they can manage. But still there is that nagging question—what do they do, and how do they do it?

Simply stated, just stop doing the one thing, and the other will follow directly. Stop saturating your head and body with self-explanations that cloud you over and push away the entire spectrum of existence. Stop talking so hard and long when you are not listening. And stop parroting old lines that sound in your own ear as hollow, jaded, and irrelevant as they really are.

The dead are the natural allies of the living, and are presently taking this up with a much greater depth of involvement, as they have been alerted that they hold the key to the way the world goes over the coming years. They want to come through on all available frequencies. Set your intention to let them in, and to find out what they have to offer you. Cut through the memories and the old pictures of darkness beyond the grave; the darkness is heavier and thicker on the physical, Outer-Earth side.

The dead may come to you as lights or light-body dwellers. They are fluent, mobile, and active, and also calm, steady, and concentrated. Their capacities are far greater than are yet showing up on the outer physical levels among you. So let them in. The dead offer love and wisdom, and whatever else they realize is needed. They are not perfect and fully realized, but they are further along that path, and have learned a thing or two.

February 7, 1994, 6:30 p.m.

The True Feminine Spirit Embodied—
and the False Feminine Spirit Exposed and Uprooted

Dear William,

The Divine Mother is the permeating presence throughout the greater worlds. The Earth Mother is the bearer of this planet's destiny, her womb-charge. Between these two beings, there weaves a love-presence that allows the worlds to remain intimately bonded even when the human consciousness is captivated by an inability to conceive the truth and the beauty of either the Divine Mother or the Earth Mother.

A wave of opening toward both of these beings is beginning within the human matrix. There is an especially strong wave among the dead to come again into the Divine Mother's energies and awareness. And there is a powerful wave among those in the physical body to root deeply enough to find afresh the Earth Mother's living stream.

Because of my recent journey to join forces with the Divine Mother, and to bring fresh news from her into her sister, the Earth Mother, I would like to invoke the true feminine spirit, as it is uncovering links in both directions, and then to contrast this with the false twentieth-century images of how the feminine spirit needs to return into central prominence.

The Divine Mother is the cosmic pole of a bi-polar field, within which our existence is held. The Earth Mother is the Earthly or physical pole of that same field. Both are here with us all the time, giving us life, allowing us breath, and offering to us the fruits of their labors. Those labors are for the purpose of bringing all species into new frequencies that will enable us to sustain our existence within a different cosmic era, the Age of Aquarius.

Both of these beings have been pregnant with our new life wave throughout the Piscean Age, ever since the Christ-Being brought the Divine Father force through His life-breath and infused our existence with its future potency. These 2,000 years of gestation are almost over, and the New Child is beginning to show up in every direction. It will take an especially strong human feminine awakening to midwife the future, and to allow the birth that is to be to come forth healthy and fully ready to overcome the excesses and distortions of the transitional humanity of the Piscean Age.

All of this is both intuitively and viscerally sensed by those who are rushing to embrace the feminine in its various aspects. We are feeling called to stir from our long slumber, and to enter our life from an entirely different place inside. The primary activity of the human species over the last eighty years has been to destroy its old form— the instinctive masculine impulse of the times. Because all of us have been swept away by this huge dynamism of destruction (often masked as something life-giving), the feminine instinctual impulse toward the New Creation has been suppressed and distorted, and rarely has there truly been a current of quickening forces toward what the future demands. But this is changing rapidly. The Child must come quickly, and those who can midwife the new species are mobilized with urgent purposiveness to align with the Divine Mother upwards, to root into the Earth Mother downwards, and to maintain the link between them, as the vertical axis of standing up for the creative spark that can prevail now that the masculine has fulfilled its task of destroying the old and leaving the field open.

Those who have the keenest feeling for this change may be men, may be beings from other dimensions, may be future forces seeking to mediate and help, may be children who are barely here yet, or may be women who have moved through the early stages of what we thought was the feminine but turned out to be another phase of the masculine destruction of the old forms. They may not be the ones we expect to see, or motivated in the directions the public media have hyped and juiced up. Instead, those who are all the way inside this current are best characterized by their immensely clear impulse and capacity to serve and to give, to love and to be here for all.

I say this, knowing well that for close to twenty years now the first wave of this future awakening from the 1960s and early 1970s has been countered by myriad currents that attack and scorn this supposedly naive, idealistic feminine force. This is a final aspect of the masculine killing-off of whatever is not strong enough to hold fiercely steady and know its own being as beautiful and right-on. Yes, the first feminine stirrings in the 60s were asking for a backswing by being so wildly youthful and impetuous, and that is not the true future. But the seed was there, and it is the compassion and the engagement, the loving embrace and the caring that will characterize those who are here to make way for our living future.

When you work on the death side of life, as I do now, you witness with heartbreaking force how the cool veneer of our sophisticated mind and negative outlook falls away so completely from all souls who come to themselves, and how their quest to be synchronized with the Divine Mother Force is so sincere and dedicated and pure. Once you participate in the rituals among the newly dead and experience the intensity of their will to serve the Earth destiny—as soon as they throw off their cloaks of absence and insensitivity— you can never again concede even minimal ground to those who deride higher impulses and accuse others of being foolish if they are less than tough and cynical. The masculine has ruled long enough. We need the midwives to discover that being in tune with life is our hope and our path, so that the Child can sing in resonance with the bright stars and their cycles.

What is most touching and moving of all is to meet those coming toward birth as they are introduced to the Earth they are about to join forces with, and to contact the pulse of what they bring from their journey into the Divine Mother realms. So many of these souls are already half-way into the Aquarian star-consciousness, and the ardor of their striving is directly toward the future being born, with which they are so involved that they barely notice the masculine devastation of the twentieth century. They see beneath it and above it, to what comes next, and they can penetrate any signs of it as they descend and await their turn to be part of the Earth Mother's awakening and new life-wave.

What I say sounds high-flying in the grim mindset of 1994. What if I were to tell you that the world-illusion will be swept away, and the world-truth will be born anew? And what if I were to say that the human feminine will know the inward ways again, and tap their wisdom with a vigor and substantiality that will make the human species native to the planet on the next spiral? What if I even went so far as to witness joyously that cosmic forces are now here to help in our transition, called in to make a huge difference in shifting the balance toward love and warmth and goodness? Would you believe me, or would you say: It sounds nice, but people just are not like that any more?

I died of cancer partially because I believed that last statement and would have had very mixed feelings about these grandiose prophecies. In my gut, I deeply doubted the capacity of the human species to turn the world around. I was dead wrong about that. Now I must tell the truth, and let you feel it for yourself.

The false feminine spirit has been hard at work during the last twenty years, in a last try at derailing the feminine awakening of the turn of the century. At times, it has allied itself with the latter stages of the masculine mowing-down of the old, outmoded forms. At other times, it has hidden in so many different guises that I could never even begin to describe them all. What characterizes all the false feminine stratagems is their substitution of a very old force for the future power.

I call this force the Bitch Goddess. She is an actual being, linked with She of Earth, or the Earth Mother. You could call her the bastard sister of She of Earth, a sister who is trying to overlay the Living Earth with what I call the Blasted Earth or Vile Earth. This is a film, a thick veil, a viscous substance that is permeating the Earth of the late twentieth century. It carries a feeling with it of life in the Earth being rotten, absurd, a terrible imposition upon the free human soul, and fated to end soon. Instead of meeting and uniting with what I call the Sweet Earth—the matrix of what Earth is becoming—human beings raised on the mass culture are slaughtered with images that tell them Earth is already a blasted zone; it is vile to the touch; it is no place for you or me; let's get out of here. That is the idea the Bitch Goddess is secretly promoting—that humanity cannot and should not be here.

The Bitch Goddess is testing the human soul to see whether she gives way or takes hold. She has been given the twentieth century to enact her test. If she fails to scare away humanity, her power will end at the stroke of midnight, as we enter the year 2000. She must mount her greatest offensive against humanity, of course, in the final years of her reign. She and all the forces who work with her are frantic to do their worst now, because their time is fast running out.

We are going to defeat her, and we are going to come again into the Sweet Earth, and know ourselves here at last. But in order for this to happen, we need to be alerted to the vile strategies and tricks of the Bitch Goddess. If what I am about to say sounds extreme and excessive, it certainly is. What she cooks up is to my feeling so extreme and excessive that I must mobilize all the considerable forces I have access to in order to expose and uproot her, and embrace the feminine heart of our common future.

The Bitch Goddess has made her way inside the blood and the bones, the muscles and the guts, the psyche and the mind of the human being. From there, she looks out at similar energies in nature and cosmos, some actual and some projected or exaggerated. She hooks into a circuit of mutual resonance between the Bitch Goddess inside the body-mind and the Bitch Goddess outside, in the environment and among other people. Her message is that she is everywhere — inescapable, unavoidable, the way-things-are. She is especially intent on surrounding and enveloping each one of us in a closed loop between self and world, and pulling ever tighter on the line.

When I was dying of cancer, she showed me through the cancer in my body (she likes to manifest as illness and injury and dysfunction) that I was a walking time bomb, set to go off, helpless against the organic appetite she had for me. When I would seek a way out in my surroundings, she would poison my mind terribly, so that I saw others around me as "no better off," and the environment itself as a cancer.

This ugly overlay, this viscous film, tended to cover everything far more palpably whenever I started to awaken out of the spell of a life-threatening illness. It really did look and feel and seem intensively that cancer and its variations were everywhere, that the Bitch Goddess was everywhere, and that death was the only way I could go. She wished me to be sucked toward death, and to go down the drain of the Lord of Death, her cohort who was awaiting me.

But we thwarted her badly. Just when she got her firmest grip on me, William, my twin soul, and many future beings working with him, came to the rescue. They began to unite with my innermost essence, and to teach me how to die beyond the circuit of destruction and devouring. It was necessary for me to die in order to end this entire bitter torture humanity was under. Only death would do it. The reason for this shall be gone into in depth in another letter.

Throughout the last year of my life, I was trained further on the inner planes in how to sustain a regenerative dying into a new kind of death and then rebirth. The Bitch Goddess did not know about this until it was too late, because the future beings know her ways, and they kept all the knowledge stored away in the superconscious, out of my conscious and subconscious minds. I could be guided and led effectively from there, but the lower forces failed to detect what was really happening.

I speak from experience and authority when I say: She must be stopped. The Bitch Goddess violates each soul she gets inside of. She grossly poisons the body. She confuses and divides the mind. And she has gone pretty far in her severe testing of humanity's will. She aligns with many ancestral streams, and pollutes the blood line. She takes hold of those seeking the feminine, and teaches them hatred and vengeance. She harnesses the weaknesses of human nature to her cause, and she shakes us hard and long. But she will not shake us off the evolutionary stream of She of Earth. I know how to stop her.

We are going to need to reclaim the territory that the Bitch Goddess has taken over. And we are definitely going to need elder women who can spread the ways of the deep feminine in a form that the Bitch Goddess cannot distort and undermine. It is only a loving path that is immune to her influence, a loving path that is trained to recognize the perception distortions and body symptoms of invasion. I will initiate these trainings in the spring of 1994. Because I will do so in the body of a man, she will not be able to lay me low.

One of the most bizarre twists of this entire scenario is that she is rooted in the feminine ancestral lines, in many instances, and she is far more potent at bringing women into body and mind and soul maladies that bear her imprint. She is out to stop women primarily, since they are the mothers of the new life-wave, and since she has a better key into their physiological weaknesses and susceptibilities. All they need do is indulge in loveless sex, or become captured by power struggles, or chord into violence, and there she is, turning them against themselves and against life.

I will keep bringing through facets of this picture. Too much of it at once would be indigestible. So I shall close with one redemptive vision. Those who are mostly linked with humanity on the other side are working hard now to transmute this scourge, to help to turn it around, now that we have defeated her cohort there, the Lord of Death, and greatly eroded her inner-world support system. There are many among the dead who are wise to all that I have been sharing here. Their first way to help is to cut her cords to the feminine ancestral streams. Soon, the feminine bloodlines will be cleansed of their curses and torments. Then the feminine can start to arise in a form that affirms and gives life boldly, freely, and joyously.

February 13, 1994, 2:20 p.m.

The Vision That Burns inside She Who Returned

Dear William,

My time spent in expanded awareness has taught me to foster a vision between my hands, to watch it grow into life, and then to let it go, out into all the worlds. Each time, the vision feeds into a central vision, the hearthstone of my new life. It is this burning vision that I wish now to share, celebrating seventy days of being free.

I see the Earth, the cosmos, and the human equation entirely differently from all I ever saw before dying. My vision is radical. The change factor is far more powerful than my fears could ever have let me know. I see change as having been stalled terribly in the times of now, and as just beginning to imprint itself within the times of tomorrow.

The Earth has been starved for change, leaving humanity to its stolidities, reaching out to cosmic sources to grant a fertile new beginning. The cosmos has never stopped changing, and is speeding on ahead in all ways. The human equation is that of resistance and spin-back. We are reversed and snarled—and as much so as we ever could be. The only direction from here is through the knothole, into freedom to change.

But why change? Recent experience has taught us that we are better off without the rash changes most people make when they are desperate. And since we are all so desperate, won't we just shift into a worse predicament than we now find ourselves in? Yes, if we change externally. But the change I mean is internal.

The time wave looks as if everything stopped between 1989 and 1994, and then something happened. It also looks as if it was slowing to a halt decades before. As the outer became frantic-kinetic, the inner turned into a sense of not being able to go on. But in 1994, all that started to change—just when it felt it could not ever be.

Now we expand our frame, and enter the vision itself. This is what I see happening between 1994 and 2014, and between 2014 and 2034. These two cycles I shall call "Over the Edge" and "Onto Fresh Ground," respectively.

The next twenty years will be Over the Edge. I see the activation of the dormant inner being as a fresh discovery that shifts everything. A tiny number of fresh awakeners exponentially increases the chances for the common mind to catch it. The inner being that was bound and gagged and left for dead now emerges as a factor. The awakeners' presence sends the outer situation careening over the edge. People have lost their ability to deal with actual inner selves emerging into direct and steady expression.

The following twenty years, 2014 through 2034, are Onto Fresh Ground. The proliferation of inner-self presence brings about in those years a reborn species from the wreckage of a dying humanity. This species has been impregnated with cosmic forces, and is one notch removed from the human dilemma of being allergic to oneself. This flaw of allergic reactivity is overcome, and in its place the ones who are in-tune with themselves become the new Earth dwellers. This happens without wars, riots, or great havoc. Instead, evolution at last prevails.

But the question then is, who is this inner self, why did it take so long to return, and how will all of this really happen? Let us explore the basics of how it will unfold.

The inner self is the same one that originally seeded each one's individual precipitation into form-expression. It is the primal source for that self, linked at its center with all other primal sources. The name of the game has been that the inner self has wanted to discover what would happen if it pulled away, above, into onlooker status, and sent the outer self on the journey of Earthing. Would that outer self ever go far enough down and out to recognize what has happened to it, and then link back to primal source? Or would it get bogged down somewhere in the middle, generating outwardly-oriented worlds and going neither deep nor high? Could the outer self sustain a false world and, if so, what manner of beings and forces would it need to draw in to keep it afloat? Ultimately, would the outer self sever its root, or would it gravitate back toward its root through the ordeals of existence?

Even when the outward civilization became overwhelmingly dominant and alienating, it was part of the terms of this experiment that nothing could be decided until everything had played itself out as far as possible without either destroying the Earth or making humanity an extinct species. So there has been a virtual two-hundred-year moratorium on bringing in the new energies, in hopes that the outer selves would find some sense or truth somewhere. It did not happen.

But once it was entirely clear that the outer selves still did not realize they were almost totally cut off from all true sources of supply, the new energy beings were pulled in. There were dozens born in the 1930s, hundreds in the 1940s and the 1950s, thousands in the 1960s and 1970s, and tens of thousands in the 1980s. And in the 1990s, hundreds of thousands of the new species bearers, the inner ones, are being born into Earth existence.

Those with the new energy who were born in the earlier parts of this cycle found themselves in the toughest of predicaments. They carried an alternative future, but there were too few of them and they rarely met. Instead, they were placed on their own, and tried to hold to who they were. They did not succeed; instead, every one of them had to spend extended cycles forgetting and losing touch with the real "who." However, when they then came back to themselves later on, as the collective field of living changers grew to a point where they were quickened into remembering, they were ecstatic to be greeted by both their own inward awakening and others around them coming to a similar place. The 1990s were especially charged with these joyous reunions, both within the self and in deep connections that at last included and encompassed the primal source integrally.

Those born in the 1970s and onwards who have the new energy are not so badly off. They came into the change early enough to have escaped the terrible scarrings and betrayal cycle. But even they have a dual stance. They witness the old world going to pieces everywhere, and they feel pulled back into it by the compassion that is their hall-mark. It is only exposure to the new energies over a protracted cycle that allows us to move out beyond the false worlds freely and gladly.

Those of the 1980s are one notch closer to free positioning. But it is those born in the 1990s who can see it and feel it from birth, and can no longer be shut off. All of the future bearers benefit from any of them coming to themselves, so the rate of lifting of the burden is far more rapid as the older ones recognize themselves. In fact, it could be said that as the pre-1960 new species inner selves awaken, they pull the later ones along with them.

I was one of these rare older ones, and I found it to be an impos-sible predicament. I met the few who were like me too late, and I died. But my final years featured so much grace and realization that I died into the new world, and not back into the old one. Then I was given the task of intensifying the inner self revival by returning into the world and fostering the vision I am sharing with you now. How-ever, this is not just another vision. I am the vision I speak. I am the light that burns inside that vision. So I shall share now from the heart of the mystery.

I indwell a realm where the inner self is constantly renewed by link-ing at root with Earth and at crown with total cosmos. It is the nature of the inner self to stretch far, to open along the vertical axis from deepest root to most expanded crown. As my inner self keeps div-ing a little deeper into the watery vastnesses and then aspires a little higher into the fiery infinite universe, she comes to herself at every point in the spiral, and weaves each coming-to-self towards the next one and then the next. She is a coming-to-self organism. Wherever she stretches, there she is. The outer self that prevails in 1994 is as far away from such a stance as can possibly be conceived. Outer selves come to themselves nowhere in their rounds, keeping the ceiling on tight and the floor up-close, not venturing further. They do not know what they are missing. It is anything-but-obvious to them that missing themselves everywhere inevitably makes them turn against themselves in bitter outrage. They will not admit, even to themselves, that they are subliminally aware of their condition. Instead, they use everything against themselves, keep themselves flattened, thinking this is all there is.

My inner self is safely tucked away in William's body, so the outer self does not scare me. I have a unique vantage point on the differences, because I am all inner-self. I am non-reactive to outer self, and so can meet him just where he is. And the further I stretch in becoming the primal me, and the more fully I investigate the ways of the cut-off outer self, the adaptive one, the more fully I realize that the outer self believes the inner self to be a hallucination or false hope, while the inner self realizes that the outer self has nothing whatsoever that is truly his or her own. This leads to the inevitable observation that we are programmed to cling to what is not our own, and to keep away from what might liberate us. In stark terms, we learn to go with what we are not because *all* is what we are not; and if anything tempts us by saying it is what we are, to banish it as the worst of mockers.

My vision involves what happens when there spring up everywhere so many inner-self embodiers that it becomes obvious to all but the most diehard outer-selfers that they have bought into an empty bargain, and need to either give up one way or give up the other way: Either they give up the false outer ego and get down to who they are inside, or they give up the life in the body and move towards a new phase of evolution in the after-death training grounds. The outer-selfers are not going to be around much longer in the form to which they are accustomed, and this will free up the inner-selfers to recreate this world in the image of who they are inside.

It is so simple. Only a culture violently dislocated could miss it so entirely. But they do miss it. And even when the inner self begins to stir and quicken its attention and involvement with its own true process of development, there is one lingering dilemma accompanying that awakening.

We are so numbed to missing everything and knowing nothing that we treat the early returns from inner-self voyages as hypothetical constructs, possible perspectives, or experimental trial balloons. We do not believe ourselves soon enough or fully enough. This is a deep problem. It is cosmic timing that frees us up and opens us inward, and it needs to be followed through at full power as it unfolds. But we stubbornly wait, and check it all out, and wonder whether anything can really be reliably true. This dilemma is central to my vision, because the changes are immediacy-anchored; they are all-at-once. They move as rapidly, freely, and fully as the outer-self, Earthbound world never moves at all inwardly. Thus we have got to learn that, once the changes begin in earnest in an individual instance, they must be taken up with whole will, as they are sparks off the cosmic wheel, coming fast and strong, directly and instantaneously.

When I died, all my changes happened in so many dimensions at once, at such rapid fire speed, that I needed to be profoundly present and accessible to every bit of them, and not ask for a break. I went with the current, thrilled to at last have total movement where the stagnant waters had been unbearable to me. And as I went with the huge changes, I taught myself how to get fast, to get strong, and to get clear, without needing to check for any extraneous factors such as how all this fits together for the mind's sake. I will now share with you one of my get-on-with-it practices.

If you find yourself deluged by cosmic cycles of radical repolarization from outer self to inner self, picture your inner self as having two terminals, one between six inches and two feet above your head (feel where it is exactly for you), and the other the same distance below your feet. Both of these have places where they integrate with the rest of you. The upper, crown-place links in through the seventh, sixth, and fifth chakras. The lower, root-place links in through the first, second, and third chakras. The fourth chakra integrates the two polaric movements.

The upper crown place is involved with consciousness in all its discoveries and adventures. But the lower root-place is involved with life in its deeper realms of exploration and realization.

Picture your consciousness as descending upon your form with a limitless force that taps your upper crown-place as the lowest and densest possible area to reach through to you. Now picture your life-force as rising through you from a very different power, tapping your lower-root place as the most surface and least depth-charged possible area to reach through to you. Now picture that your inner self is actually coming into your heart from above your head and under your feet. It comes as cosmic consciousness above, and as Earth-life-force below.

Now, in order to activate the circuit to be able to go with the changes instantaneously and willingly, visualize the cosmic upper pole making you aware of what is happening just a shade of time before the Earthly lower pole feels it surging below. How deep the surge of power below will be depends entirely on how you meet the stream of consciousness above. If you go right with it, the circuit is completed, and you are in a total-changes system. If you slow it down or stop it, the power below cannot answer to the descent from above, and there is a break in the circuit.

Try this. See what happens when you picture a descending current of consciousness and pull it right through your seventh, sixth, and fifth chakras into your fourth. And see what happens when you meet the current with resistance, starting with a seventh-chakra censorship and reluctance to believe in what is there. Especially feel how all of this registers down below.

The optimal path is to be so absolutely grounded beneath your feet and so awake above your head that you can feel yourself simultaneously pulsing from both terminals. When you anchor and receive from both poles at once, the revelatory consciousness feeds into the life-changes capacity fluently and effortlessly. Now you are ready to meet what is here as it arises, neither cutting the flow nor thinking you must be sure. The circuit is self-correcting, and will maintain itself beautifully if allowed to dance the serpent dance with your heart alive.

February 18, 1994, 4:45 p.m.

The Keenest Practical Lessons I Am Learning

Dear William,

The simplest things are the very hardest. In my lifetime, I prided myself on being commonsensical and salt-of-the-Earth—and I was. But I missed all the simplest things because I could not get quiet enough to hear them speaking inside of me.

What is deemed practical can be either outer-mind or inner-life directed. The practical that I am learning to master and stay with is inner-life directed. In this way of working, all of the necessities of any form of existence are already speaking inside us, and we will hear them if we stop and listen. The rules and regulations fall away, and we do what is needed because we are partners with the substance of our lives. But no such words ever make any sense without examples. I will give an example, and then express the lesson it reveals, until practicality becomes no longer alienating but a close bonding between what is moving outside and what is moving inside.

After I passed inward to the life beyond Outer Earth, I was shown everything I needed to see, in all directions. The first practical lesson had to do with the physical body of the one who has died. As my old body lay there on that bed for three days, and gradually lost all of its life-essence, hour-by-hour, I found out that my link with that body was neither as close as I imagined nor as distant as I thought. My mind had always seen it as obvious that I am not my body, so that when I go on, I would simply discard what was used up. Contrastingly, my subtle imagination had always felt it to be true that my body is very close to me, intertwined with who-I-am in mysterious and fascinating ways. Both were right, and both were wrong.

As I moved beyond the body and then came back to work further on releasing its anguish and burden of mortality, I worked up a rhythm of mostly being far beyond this body, but then being called upon to return into it and care for its next level of needing to let go of what it still held. Each time I came in closer, I kept finding that the body was carrying an aspect of myself with which I had an eternal link, and which needed to be honored lovingly and intimately. This aspect was the working-out of my personal destiny. The body was holding this treasure, and I had to gather the treasure of personal destiny to myself. Only then could I cast off the outer shell of that destiny. I got it at last that the body is not an outer shell but bears *both* the outer shell and the underlying kernel within itself. And that kernel is very close to the soul and the spirit.

Because the body was well-preserved and looked after, and had a full three days to yield up its subtle contents, I could and did successfully complete this process. Then the body could be burned, and it would no longer in any way deprive me. I went off with my jewels, and they became integral to my path from that point onwards. I was with my personal destiny, not falsely beyond it nor lost inside of it.

This illustrates well the first practical lesson I learned, which was that all is useful and necessary in Earth existence, and that what matters is how you sense into it. If you hover outside the personal substance of your life, it never can speak inside of you. But if you engulf yourself under the cloak of everything personal and solid, you have no way to move through it and glean its ultimate fruits. In order to follow through on this obvious, simple, basic lesson, you must understand that you are perpetually cycling into loss under things, and then cycling again into hovering outside of things, so that the rhythm you must attain is recognizing that you are moving both ways, and allowing yourself to breathe out, to breathe in, and to dance gracefully with this polaric extremism.

Even your body itself is something you are too much and then too little, and you are the balance of those movements. The averaging mind tries to say you are right in the middle. But your subtle imagination knows that you are here, and then you are there, and after that you are here again, in a frolicking wonder of the shifting current that is you.

Later on, I entered so many practical lessons that for a while it seemed I was continuously absorbed in remedial steps. One lesson that stands out concerns how the greater beings interact with human beings. My religious training led me to believe that all gods are infinitely beyond all humans, and that we are tiny and the divine worlds are great and intimidating. In the other extreme, my spiritual path of the last years of my life suggested that all beings were in the same territory, that the human capacities can meet the gods and that the gods can intermingle with us freely, at least when we are ready and willing.

It turns out that religion is far off the mark here. Evolution is progressing beyond those formulas. I found that all greater beings or gods are eager to meet with me and my fellow human beings, but that each human soul usually decides it is not worthy of such meetings. Religion, of course, plays a major role in convincing many that they should stay "in their place." I was relieved to find that the hierarchical distances and formalities are not maintained with any consistency. Instead, the cosmos we are in is spontaneous, free-flowing, and expansive. This kept revealing itself, over and over, in infinite variations.

The lesson here is that we can refuse to enter upon the territory of unlimited possibilities, but this is our choice alone. I wish ardently that I had known this sooner. To a humiliating extent, I felt it was good and right for me to stay indoors and sulk. Meanwhile, the light outdoors was shining so brightly that it blazed all the way inside, calling to me: Come out and play, Sara. Come on, come out and play. But I had to brood over all my pains and struggles, so I held back. I still retained the belief-husk that said: The Infinite does not want to bother with you unless you are at your very best, and even then only in very limited ways. This was the religious belief-husk that laid me low. I slapped my own hand before it could reach out and stretch towards what invited me to become so much more than I was brought up to be.

I feel that the conditioning and the programming that everyone talks about are much more damaging than is realized. Here we have infinite beings of extraordinary love and light, seeking to bring their gifts to the human race, and what do they meet? Programmed minds and conditioned belief structures. The programmed minds narrow the focus while the conditioned belief structures shut off the imaginative subtleties of the inner life. It turns out that each one's inner being is linked with the gods by invisible cords. Those cords are as vibrantly full as people let them be. But a programmed mind never shuts up long enough to tap into those levels, and a conditioned belief structure binds the imaginative gifts that would allow one to sense into those cords for oneself.

I find this conspiracy against the divine/human connection to be the strangest reality of contemporary life. It extends to being equally superstitious and ignorant toward the other, inward realms that could so easily make a big difference in each one's spiritual life—the dead (who gather knowledge that the living would greatly benefit from), other dimensional life forms (which could readily introduce humanity to its expanded potential), and, most vitally of all, one's own inner core self, which is outlawed in the program as being far too demanding and formidable but which is ready to supply the deepest regenerative forces for every one to return to themselves and be at home.

More recently, after I returned to the Earth body and to the body of my beloved twin, William, my practical lessons have been more in the realm of the living. However, they are not the same ones most people are moving through. They have a strong similarity, but a vast difference.

What is similar is the basic spiritual lesson involved each time. What is different is that I am on the inside of every situation, and therefore can find out immediately whether I am on track or off. Those who stick to the outside can only surmise their progress by outer clues, which are extremely unreliable.

This leads me to the central practical lesson I am learning, which I feel has immense relevance to others. Again, I shall give an example revealing the archetypal lesson involved.

When I came into William's body, and kept penetrating deeper and deeper into it over the weeks when we were fine-tuning this phase, I was baffled at first by a sequence of sensations that kept repeating themselves. I would be holding a steady and clear inward state (which is my main regular practice, my ongoing meditation), as solid in the depths as in the heights; then this repetitive sequence would come through and throw me off my spot. I could easily restore the tranquility, but then it would happen again. After a little while, I had to investigate what this was. I soon found that William's body was taking me in and casting me out again, taking me in further and then casting me out further.

I made some adjustments, and by-passed this circuit for a while. But then, days later, a similar sequence turned out to be another stage of taking me in and casting me out. And I adjusted it away again. Such phases have periodically arisen ever since. Each one is different. Sometimes the impression is fairly abrupt and even violent. At other times, there is a subtle and inward feel to it. But these body-convulsions of trying to reject me from the body are an ever-repeating phenomenon.

When I asked what this was (I simply ask my core self, and see it or feel it right away), I was shown that I was bringing something into the body that it had to grapple with in undulating waves of ingestion. William was not causing his body to react by some personal changes. It was rather an organic, unconscious sequence. But what was it that I was bringing in that so disturbed his body's way of functioning?

I am bringing a future pranic force from the world of the twenty-second century, and this force is vital to nourish and sustain William's body (which becomes also my body and our body, in gradual stages).

But even though this force is much needed, and is having an immensely beneficial effect on William's deeper well-being (as well as mine), the body itself cannot just swallow this liquid. The body's inherent life wisdom says that it must take in a certain prescribed and appropriate dosage of the future pranic force, and then it must process this through all of its systems. Only then can it take in any more. So, each time, the body is rejecting further inflow for a period of time. I had to back off from pushing the future energies through, and instead would rest within the body's knowing, not forcing more upon it than it could withstand.

This illustrates a lesson that keeps coming to me in a thousand different forms. Almost everything of the physical Earth is like that. Whether it is William's body or the planet itself, whether it is in human interconnections or in the interplay between the greater spirit and the outer form, the physical world is played through by etheric pulse-beats, most of which present-day humanity does not detect or make allowance for. These are similar to the rhythms of the body after death, to which I referred earlier, and which also bear some relation to the issue of the circulation between the gods and humanity, also dealt with earlier.

Each of the etheric pulse-beats is in phase with a cosmic force, and is synchronizing that cosmic force with an Earthly, physical realm. Almost all of these pulse-beats operate independently from known physical laws, and therefore do not show up in modern thought and investigation. They do, however, determine a great deal that goes on, although through a different mode than cause-and-effect. Because I am now monitoring and mediating these beats as one of my creative tasks, I will share with you a few initial findings in this fascinating area.

Light is the etheric pulse-beat that generates the greatest free momenta. There is a speed, an excitement, and a vibrancy to light. As it expands, it spreads an influential glow in every direction, which tends to draw into it much of the immediate surroundings. It is a tide going out toward the edges from the center, often with a dynamism that makes it seem as if it would just go on and on, as freely and fully as possible. The only check on the light is darkness. Its shadow of the dark trails around it and stays back until there is a slight slackening of the light's velocity. Then the dark comes on and creates a suction action that both slows and undermines the bright force.

This is most observable in all interplay of living beings. It was darkness that convinced human beings to stay out of the way of the gods in our earlier example. And human relationships illustrate this perfectly. Light draws people together into an expression of bright joy. And darkness tears them apart so that they will come up against that within them which is not truly ready to live in light. When it is, darkness will hold no sway.

Tone is the etheric pulse-beat that soothes, surrounds, and brings an inward opening. It draws all who hear it and partake of it toward themselves, and into linking with life as a place where the self can resound. It is a refining and uncovering sphere. Tone is the most regularly and fully interrupted and counterpointed of the ethers. It is always slowing towards whatever might come along to give a different slant.

Tone is on and off, further and backwards. It contains within itself all that is other than it, and makes room for that. Harmony and fullness arise here. The example of William's body applies here. It has its own tone, the future realms have theirs, and these tones are perpetually fine-tuning each other toward a more integral place of living together in full mutual acknowledgment.

Warmth is the etheric pulse-beat that instantaneously comes on, and when it does it sparks a total reality shift. Warmth is the breaking-through of greater realms into the Earth. This is the least-known and least consciously registered of the four ethers. In fact, most people never pick up on how it works at all. But its true sphere is a cosmic-spiritual blasting power so potent and advanced that it impacts and is gone before it can be detected and stopped. Warmth has only a moderate counterpart or alternating rhythm: All of existence must adjust to it as a whole. So, when cosmic warmth roars into incisive expression, it instigates a cycle of changes that ends with another blast. Warmth punctuates the world-rhythms by sudden new beginnings that influence vast cycles from beyond the level of outer detection altogether.

The final ether is life itself. Life is the etheric pulse-beat that is wedded to physical substance, and is therefore very slow and lawful and "underneath." Life lumbers along, compared to all the other ethers. It works with the practical necessities of the outer, and it seems to be entirely made up of these vigorous factors. My experience of the three days after passing inward, mentioned earlier, is in this realm. Life is the realm that humanity is caught inside of; but we do not move effectively with the pulse-beat of life.

The treasure of physical life needs to be gathered in a selfless appreciation of its enormous bounty. Only when life is beheld as a jewel of wonder and beauty can it be woven into a steady and effective path. Life-taken-for-granted is dragged under by death forces. But life taken in freshly and moved with wakefully is a garden of delights. Most of these take a very long time to ripen, but the fruits are eternal, and the sufferings are redeemed.

March 2, 1994, 2:15 p.m.

1994, 1995, and 1996 as Three Leaps into Future Awakening

Dear William,

Time in the Earth is a funny thing. When the mind got to be a super systematized authority, everything that happened here was pegged into time. Everything was seen to happen within certain definite timings.

If you are entirely literally caught in the outer world, this does seem to be true. Time becomes a thing that defines. It is yet another way to lock in, to be trapped, to be only this and nothing else.

We who travel through realms of spirit, who journey inside the world, are time-free. We can show up when we need to, but we are never just in that moment. The moment becomes a portal, opening into so many times. So we laugh and carry on about how the clock and the watch, the calendar and the planetary cycles, hold the human mind in a state of frozen time. We find this absurd.

But it is because I will not sit still for linear time barriers that I can now speak in the triple language of calendar time, of astrology, and of the art that is about to replace astrology. We will need all these to try to say what the near future wants to bring, and when. This needs to be said because false rumors have been spread, by definite plan, to make it seem as if time is short, as if we do not have much of it, as if we are about to use it up. If I speak sharply and clearly, boldly and directly, it is to dispel the clouds of false visions and critical intellect tolling doom.

1994 is the first year in which the cosmic clock, which stands behind calendar time, shows movement forward. The last eighty years, each one of them, showed movement backward. It is true that the first year of forward movement barely crawls ahead but, when juxtaposed to eighty minus years, this is a big plus.

Speaking in astrological terms, Uranus and Neptune, the cosmic timers, with their regular seven-year and fourteen-year rhythmical cycles, mark out the great shifts in the collective cycle. Their conjunctions in 1993, recapitulated in early 1994, set the stage for this momentum surge. Capricorn gave final authority for a forward movement to begin slowly and accelerate rapidly. We are in this now. Because I died into this conjunction and because Capricorn rules death, I will now look back at 1993, the last moment of going backward, and what it was that truly sparked the great shift.

We had spent one hundred seventy-one years losing traction on evolution. Death was outpacing life. When I died, I knew that collective death was at hand, and that I was in it. I was the collective death devouring my body. We were at the end. The world had actually gone through its catastrophe. We were all dying in me.

Can you imagine what I really mean? Can you take it all the way into your secret self, that I do mean what I say? I, Sara, took upon myself, consciously and by deepest guidance, the death of us all. This was my commitment—to die in that discredited way that the demise of historical Christianity has made almost seem a farce. However, I knew in my bones that the Christ-impulse, the true living Christ, lives on in the most vibrant terms, and calls us forward. And I knew that I was called to die that kind of death.

What it means is that I met everybody, absolutely everybody in this world, in my dying. I embraced the darkest sides of human nature, every single day and all night long. I entered into the common ground, and shared waters in every continent. I was the world dying. And what I felt in this way before death was slight compared with what I experienced afterwards. Then it was that I became the resurrection of the common body. If I could be reborn, we all could. And I was.

Because I did this, I could dethrone the Lord of Death, and the force that holds everything back could begin to give way as the Master of Time came in his stead, inaugurating the force that allows all to move forward. And I could return to seed the new death into the Earth, to fertilize this world so that the new life can be born.

The power behind the Uranus-Neptune conjunction was the timing of Old Earth giving way to New Earth. It was the dethroning of false gods and the victory of true ones. Directly after such an event, the trends and waves that were assumed to be ongoing either reverse or shift radically. We are in the beginning stages of such a time.

1994 is keyed into Pluto finishing out its ten years in Scorpio and meeting with Jupiter at the end of its Scorpio cycle. This is a shift that is pre-figured at the end of February and the beginning of March, as this letter is written, when both Jupiter and Pluto go retrograde in Scorpio. But in order to share what the Jupiter and Pluto cycle means, I must shift into the art that is about to replace astrology. The old astrology is always quantitative, fixed on the numbers, the cumulative body of figures. Star Genesis, Atlantean star-seeing reborn, is a qualitative, magical, intensively alive way of working with the starry realms.

In Star Genesis terms, Jupiter is the founding planet of a new eon. It is the spark inscribed in each one's brow, marking out a destiny that awaits the crumbling of all false structures, the end of the mind's duality-negation syndrome. It is the gathering force of future evolutionary seers, who make way for limitless realms by working back into darker times and there seeding sparks of life triumphant. Jupiter thus is the foundation stone for all that is more encompassing and whole to sweep back into more fragmentary times (and the cycles of more obdurate planets) and to be the prevailing current.

In Star Genesis, Pluto embodies a cosmically divergent system, one that has been brought into the Earth since 1925 to get underneath the entire existing system, and to rework all of its premises, undo its falsehoods and distortions, and give it a total self-recycling capacity. This means that the Moon and Saturn are being re-forged from the holders of the lineage, and restored to their original and ultimate purposes. But Pluto does this for any planet with which it comes into contact. It takes that planet, casts off its encrustations, and gives it back to itself, entirely from the inside, as a spark of pure cosmic essence.

When Jupiter and Pluto come together in Scorpio, the sign that Pluto has specialized in absolutely reworking, it is an indication that all momentum is shifting markedly from what had been assumed to be the way it is, into an entirely different inner path. Late in 1994, the crawling forward pace of 1994 will start to accelerate. Jupiter will begin to be truly empowered from within to throw off the doubt-frequencies, and to take us towards the future full-bore. Pluto will have much greater access into consciousness, and will change our mind about where we are and what is now possible.

All of the years when Pluto was in Scorpio, from the mid-1980s to the mid-1990s, have also marked a time when Pluto is within the orbit of Neptune and the closest to Earth that it ever comes. This means that Pluto has been working hard during these years to dismantle the corroded old systems, to create a vacuum or open space around what had been so cluttered and saturated with negativity, and then slowly to bring an entirely different energy into place. This had actually already seriously eroded the grip of the Lord of Death over his domain, so that my act of standing up to him was a final blow that had to come from somewhere. Like him, all the other shady characters are on their way out.

In Star Genesis, Scorpio is the sign of volunteering to go all the way inside the darkest and heaviest collective karmic waste dumps, and then to penetrate through to where something different can come up from underneath. So this sign is the perfect one to take the Pluto challenge in deepest measure. It has been the destiny of thousands of souls in the last nine years to dive into places nobody wants to be, finding out whether they have it in them to stay down long enough to find the lost treasure buried under all the layers of history—the treasure of who we really are, awaiting the intrepid depth-adventurer.

1995 is the year of Pluto moving into Sagittarius, gradually undulating into a new sign, seeking out another area to re-work from the deepest insides. Sagittarius is a good one from which to do this. It is the one sign that has been able to hold out entirely against all efforts to break through its fundamental crack. Only Pluto can reach that crack and fuse it back into a whole sign.

The Sagittarius crack massively impacts the collective undersoul. Sagittarius carries the memories of the downfall of Atlantis. That downfall has leaked into all of the lost connections ever since. Sagittarius is shadow-bound to stick with an underlying subconscious quagmire of complete stoppage, in passive acquiescence to an overwhelming common fate, while laying over that a thick coat of eager, spontaneous wit and drive for all the best things. But this is what will be reworked by Pluto.

I have seen in the future what happens. The key component is turning around an energy awareness stance that says: We are against ourselves at every angle, and we are forced to be, by the undertow of what has been before. Pluto brings in a wipe-out of the basis for such assumptions, at first leaving in its wake a great void. Then new creative forces can begin to weave a different destiny, no longer shadowed by past mistakes. This will be quite a deep reworking, because Sagittarius is so chronic and tough to get at. In fact, 1995 begins the sweeping-away of all the most stuck places in the collective psyche. It is clean-up time in the shared depths.

1996 is the year of Uranus moving into Aquarius, following up on its great overthrow-of-death journey through Capricorn. All the foreshadowings of the Aquarian Age will be with us in the last years of the twentieth century and the first years of the twenty-first century. But what has the Piscean Age really been about, and what will the Aquarian Age truly inaugurate?

Because these are the fixed-star constellations involved in the Ages, and because very few involved with astrology have any cosmic vision of the constellations, we must begin by seeing what the fixed-star constellations are all about.

The source point for all cosmic or star patterns is what used to be called the "mind of God," but what I shall call the inner vision of the creative beings. That inner vision is carried through by God, held in His mind, but it originates in a place beyond our present comprehension, this place I am here calling the inner vision of the creative beings. These beings set all of the cosmos into motion as direct emanation of who they are.

There are three distinct layerings of star patterns—universal, local, and immediate. The universal layer is ultimately timeless and qualitative, but it descends, or externalizes, as far as the fixed-star constellations in the night sky. The universal layer oversees the larger pulse of evolution.

The local layer is the planetary system, and the signs linked with the orbital relations of the planets. This layer links with all aspects of destiny from the ultimate to the most personal.

The immediate layer is the houses formed strictly by a particular time and place. This layer is directly bound up with the body and its karmic structure and dynamics.

When we look into the Ages and the fixed-star constellations, we are not looking into the destiny domain but shifting into the larger pulse of evolution, the vaster design. We have lost our feeling for this level. But we will get it again in the start of the Aquarian Age, less than twenty years from now. So we must future-stretch here. I will help with experiential images.

As I raised my vibrations to this level after death, I saw geometrical shapes forming and reforming into vast and intricate subtle structures, each of which was alive, supple, and sustaining itself by the Breath of the Divine. Because I had never previously realized that geometrics could come to life, I studied these carefully. I found that there were universal archetones that were being struck or moved through in the most evocative fashion. It felt like beings of great majesty could orchestrate a realm of consciousness whose life-pulse would then form our world. And the twelve Zodiac animals were behind these, but in a far more formative design and ever-shifting wonderment than the way we think of them and freeze them in time.

The one of these twelve that has been prevailing for the last 2,000 years or so is the one that the Christ-Being inscribed with His blood. The Cosmic Fishes swim in the limitless waters of vast timelessness, and can take on whatever inscription is needed for a given Age. This one was the aspect of existence that dwells far beyond the Earth, the Father Realm, seeking to manifest all of its power and light through another aspect of existence that could touch down into the Earth—the Son. This Pisces ritual drama was to then allow all of the dwelling beyond realms through one fish, and all of the touching-down into depths of Earth realms through the other fish, to cross-fertilize each other, and eventually to merge at the very end of the Piscean Age.

Previous to the Piscean Age, these polaric realms were always held far apart from each other. The Piscean Age has been strictly incarnational, keyed to the Christ-ray of radical embodiment of spirit. It has hit such vast resistance that only in its final moments does the true Piscean Age come into its own.

Aquarius is a very different cosmic constellation. Its shape and feel on the inner levels is highly abstract and finely evolved, the most intricate and fine-tuned of cosmic designs. The Waterman represents the realms beyond this world, sending forth a seed-stream of those who can renew evolution at its source. It is a massive infusion of a different kind of knowingness and beingness. This is the integral consciousness. All of the polaric tensions that have dominated the Piscean Age give way to the whole of existence being known and sensed and honored, as we expand into a much more developed inner condition.

The raw human is supplanted by the refined inter-dimensional. And that within the human which is true and essential is not only sustained in the new age but brought into its truth entirely.

In 1996, we begin to know the dimensions of all futures, and to enter the futures that are closest to us. It is fortunate that the sign of Aquarius can carry some of the destiny power of the Aquarius Constellation, and invite us into sixteen years of final preparation for Aquarius and culmination of the Pisces merging experience.

The old world ended in 1993. The new world begins to show its colors in 1996. And during 1994 and 1995, we are standing between the old and new worlds, in order to free up the old and make way for the new.

As a cosmic radical, I must add that I am going to skip the preliminaries and move on into the Aquarian Age now. Those who wish to do this can do so as long as they fulfill three stringent criteria:

1. You must, with all of your inner willingness, die to all of the old patterns that have stopped you in the past, and you must do this without delay or excuse—cleansing away the dross is vitally basic.

2. You are called upon to welcome in the new ways with a spirit of gratitude and joy freed up from all the world-weary angles and avoidances—ringing in the new is the core of the matter.

3. You must agree to serve those who have yet to move all the way through, and to give them what is truly called for, free of judgment or sentimentality—giving freely unto all is the path to stay with.

Come join me in jumping off on the first wave, if you dare!

March 4, 1994, 12:30 p.m.

The Creative Spark Casting Off the World Shell

Dear William,

The Earth is now enveloped inside an egg. That egg is protecting the world against any disruption of its rebirth process. But the egg becomes a shell which restricts. This happens when the human intelligence is massively committed to Earthbound thinking. The auric egg then contracts into a solid shell of holding to what has been before. Then there must be a force that can cast off this world-shell and allow for a different perspective, a new way of life, to come roaring through.

That force is the creative spark. This is the power of inner fire to turn Outer Earth into what it is meant to be, by bringing back into play here the cosmic elements that have been kept away. The outer skin must now split open, for that which is burning inside to burst out.

I have a very unusual, in fact unique, perspective on this situation. My body became so shell-like that it developed tumors all over. At the end, the fires inside of me pushed me right out of that decaying shell of a body into the infinite surround. And when I looked back, the body shell was relieved to have me out of it. The body was burned three days after death; it could go free, and I could go free. We were very ready to part.

Because my destiny ties me to the Living Earth in foundational ways, I came back to do something about the collective situation, so that the world-cancer does not need to destroy the Earth-body. I have been scrutinizing the world-shell, finding its cracks and fissures, and uniting myself with the creative spark, seeking the ways that we can cast off what has become our corpse.

I have found a distorting intelligence that forms and maintains and insists upon the thick consistency of the world-shell. This intelligence is an alliance of infernal thinking, intraterrestrial thinking, and the most regressive side of human thinking. Demons and little insectoid creatures and the human shadow-mind all combine to think the world-shell into being, and to hold it there as solid as their shared thought-form can make it. This is a situation that reached critical mass in the 1990s, and the creative spark began to be alerted to its imminent call-up status. But we are so very familiar with the world-shell that we know it in our bones. We are not so familiar with the creative spark. The one thing world-shell consciousness excludes is any reference to the creative spark.

Cosmic forces are intensely involved within the Earth. They are as omnipresent and pivotal an influence as they are considered by shell-mind to be remote and irrelevant. And their most potent expressive vehicle is the creative spark. This is a force that underscores what we call fire, that is cosmic warmth concentrated and distilled. It is the enlivening power that allows something new to come into being. It is working in each moment to activate that which is creative, alive, fresh, and direct from the cosmic source. The creative spark is the free intelligence that will supplant the shell-mind when it is time.

The most intensive manifestation of the creative spark I have ever witnessed happened in me before, during, and after my recent death. I have written elsewhere of the play of the Fire Beings and of the Fire Ladies behind my heart and in my belly, who gave me the immediate fire access. But it is now time to reach into the heart of creation, to courageously tell how the creative spark spoke to me, and redeemed my suffering and my impossible plight.

A future-force began to take hold of me in my final days, and to tap my innermost reserves. I thought, and it seemed medically, that I had used up my reserves. But that was shell-thinking. The future-force burned through me, revealing to me that on the spiritual levels I had not yet touched my inner supply. This was a shock. I had been working as hard as a human being can work for a month of total dying. I was used up, burned out, consumed. The body had become tumors, everywhere. But my spirit had not even started to do what it could do.

That same future-force gave me a very different task to perform. It was no longer possible, in that last week, to try to make the body turn around its self-destructive trend. Nor was it necessary. I had agreed to this death, and it was rightful. However, there was another work to do. I needed to bring as much of my being as possible onto inner levels of awareness, to forge a creative spark between my deep chakras and the deep chakras of the Earth Being.

I had already been kundalini-awakened, and so I had free access to the fire of the deep body. Now I had to pierce to the center of the Earth, pierce to the center of my being, and wield a force that could allow both centers to merge into a oneness that death could not then overturn. This was deep core magic. The future-force guided me to do this seemingly impossible task, and in the process I made several key discoveries.

The first of these was that the creative spark, so long dormant, so utterly ignored, was capable of miracles of the grandest scope. It was a harder job to fuse my being with the being of the planet than to vanquish the cancer tumors. But the creative spark was more than up to the task. It could do it because it was rightful to do. The way the creative spark works is that it can do what is rightful with total will, and nothing else. Rightful or synchronized miracles are its specialty. There is no limit to the forces it can draw upon, as they come from a future-source that can never ever run out.

The second of these was that I-in-me, the true, deep core self, had always awaited this opportunity, was trained towards it, prepared for it, and was herself a creative spark incarnate. This was her first opportunity to tap her own essential way of being. She became so entirely mobilized and enthusiastic that, as we shall see, she could not stop there. The future-forces were drawing me into touch with my own distinctive creative spark, the I-in-me, and as I deepened and strengthened that connection, I came to realize that dying was no problem at all, that I could never be destroyed, my fire could never go out, and that I would burn all the brighter because of what I was then enduring.

The third and most important of these discoveries was that the creative spark that keeps our planet burningly alive in its core manifestation is a spark off the same wheel that each other planet and star is created from. All the interspaces among the planetary bodies, instead of being void or chaos spaces, are actually a turning-inward of this creative spark into a latent or dormant form of itself; each breath, fiber, millimeter of existence is sparked through and through with this incredible, everlasting creative spark. The burning is the same in me, planet, space, you, God.

This is what shell-mind calls a mystical realization, which is supposed to mean that nobody else can understand it, that somehow I happened upon this, and so what? In actuality, my edge-of-death cosmic awareness and awakening was a future event. It opened the door into the common future. This is because the creative spark is intent on becoming known in the human kingdom, and chose me to herald its coming force. I was in on the first wave of the fires that will cast off the world-shell and set us all free.

Ever since that time of fire burning me homewards, I have been burning brighter and brighter, and still brighter. I am just now getting started.

When I emerged into the world beyond the body, I was so fired up inside the creative spark that I could not leave the world behind, or go somewhere special. I could only carry the same force wherever I was assigned or chose to go (which are the same thing). The creative spark, the I-in-me, now held total sway, and I could no longer contain it inside the world-shell at all. In fact, the shell was entirely gone, never to return. My strongest impulse was to bring this limitless fire back with me, exchange it for the highest of Earth fluids, and engage in a free-flowing stream of Earth/cosmos and present/future bridging and cross-fertilizing. That is what I am now doing.

I do it everywhere, in every possible way I can find, but I have been directed to concentrate my strivings, at least at first, primarily upon those I can most fully and drastically impact. So I am working very strongly with the few, somewhat with the many, and ultimately with all-of-existence.

What is this cross-fertilizing exchange really like? How does it work in its fully concentrated form? Do I encounter resistances from within the world-shell as I work in this way?

With my closest friends, I wield a creative spark incarnate, the I-in-me, as a laser instrument of the most advanced kind. My intent is what directs it, and I keep my intent as concentrated as can be upon a very few areas, so as to have optimal effect and lasting results. So far, my primary areas of concentration are those where the world-shell puts up such enormous resistance that you would think I would stay away. But I most certainly do not, and will not.

If there is one thing the shell-mind has convinced itself about most chronically and persistently, it is that sexuality and the life-force are chaotic, dangerous, destructive, and addictive. I am working strongly and closely within the life-force and its sexual expression, in order to prevent it from fulfilling the self-fulfilling prophecy of the shell-mind. Much of this activity is so deep and internal that its impact is hard to depict in mental terms. But there has been such a clamp upon the passionate expression of life-force that it is first a matter of breaking this clamp away.

The clamp has imposed an entropic, regressive fate-loop onto life-force expression. The life-force has been able to come alive expressively for brief, feverish moments, but it has not been able to sustain itself over longer stretches, and thereby to come upon its underlying core truth of being the creative spark in direct activation. Instead, it has remained under wraps as survival instinct, sex drive, and so on.

When the clamp is gone, broken clean away, the soul in the body is for the first time naked, returning forcefully and vibrantly into the garden of paradise. The creative spark starts to radiate far more directly, almost transparently. Instead of two souls held fast in dead bodies, there is the palpable presence of two creative spark bearers, both in similar resonance. And then the final resistance comes into play.

Remember, it is the mind that is the most seriously infected with shell-consciousness. When the mind observes this onrush of utter spirit-breath, without any barrier, it wants to hook back into some form of security, memory, or control. If this is not ready to hand, the mind will contrive to invent it. Shell-mind tries to hastily fabricate a wall around this resurgent creative-spark life-force. At this point in the cycle, I start to bear down with a ferocious zeal. I burn away the shells as fast as they come on. Soon, the regenerative life-force prevails, and the shell-mind is forced to loosen its grip upon the one or two who are being unclasped, liberated, allowed to breathe at last.

Variations on this theme arise often. Each form of laser activation of the creative spark offers the chance for fully conscious emergence from the world-shell. I learn as I go how far to go, how fast, and what will really do it. So far, I am finding that it is the subconscious memory banks that hold the grip of shell-mind most formidably. It is there that the leap beyond tight little worlds must be first made.

What is most encouraging in my creative-spark insurgency is that none of these things have even been tried before, so the shell-mind has no set system to explain it all away or shrug it off. As soon as it gets one, I will shift tactics completely, and move onward. I am infinitely more flexible and fluent than the shell-mind could even conceive, much less allow in itself. So I am free to keep doing the impossible. It does not bother me how much time or effort it requires. I do see quite far ahead. I can tell when something is going to carry through, and if it will, I stay on it.

I can tell you what I have learned in the ultimate sense about the creative spark or, better said, within the creative spark. I now realize that the Spirit that made this world and kept it alive forever has never fully been tapped. The infinite resource has been kept back under. Civilization robs all the secondary sources of energy, and leaves the fire life-force alone. This is because it cannot be misused or abused. It only works within what is rightful.

Not only has it never been fully tapped, it is presently grossly unknown and negated. The shell-mind thinks it has looked everywhere. But it has looked nowhere. The magnificence of what is awaiting exploration is awesome.

I am exploring it now. The creative spark is the seed bearer of future realms unlimited. It is actually sent back to us from a future world in which it is limitlessly abundant. There, in the twenty-second century, it is so abundant that they are exporting it back into these time-frames where everybody is starving for the lack of it.

I come from that twenty-second-century world. I live there, for the most part. And I bring the creative spark directly here from there. We know it as the Light that we meet inside each one—the very thing we always focus on as them. We find it to be the way we truly are inside. It is neither mysterious nor out beyond us. It is who we are, all the way through. Only the shell-mind, in its obstreperous self-clusterings, keeps this from being self-evident.

We meet the shell-mind as an ancient remnant, a final condensation of a state of not-being, an anti-life force that ran the world for far too long. We know all about this. But it does not scare us or impress us. We have seen right through it, we have walked right through it, and we have built our world upon the creative spark, the very thing the shell-mind tried to destroy. But it never really found the creative spark, which knew how to disappear when approached by a secret assassin.

The future realms live in such abundant grace that we must share it with those who still have their shell held tightly around them. We cannot take your "No" and your "Never" for your answer. We see right through the words and the actions of negation. And we come back again, ever and again, to offer you the rare spark that is as common as the world and burns through to you, invitingly and infinitely bright. We welcome you homeward, and we shall not be sent away again.

March 9, 1994, 4:00 p.m.

Fire on the Spot Burning through the Human Blockade

Dear William,

It is so very ecstatic, and the stuff of my expanded journey now, to tap the flames that are in the heights and the flames that are in the depths, and to bring these together entirely within myself. Fire plays with me and I work very hard with fire. This is a labor of love, my fire-dancing, the ways I bring fire into the Earth and among human beings.

The fire of the gods, the heights-fire, has been under blockage for centuries. Very little of it has gotten through. Now I bring with me so much that it can no longer be blocked. We are burning through the human blockage by concentrating our fire into one laser beam, on the spot coming at you.

But nobody knows about the blockade and nobody knows yet about this fire beam. This is new information. So I will slow it down, and bring it to you in doses, phases. Listen carefully and heartfully.

The human blockade against the cosmic fires was begun because we would never be able to develop our own independent inner fires if we were always zapped by the thunderstorms of Zeus. We needed to be stepped down from the bombardment that had always been there. It took us a very long time to succeed in blocking off all the cosmic forces. We started this in the so-called Dark Ages, and we achieved complete humanism only during the nineteenth century. Then we got better and better at it. By the 1920s, we could deny altogether the greater dimensions of our experience, and push everything down under.

The pathological and decadent phase began in the 1940s. Now we were so good at neutralizing all spirit-breath, and especially the full power of the spirit-flames, that the old Atlantean black magicians came back in force and numbers, trying again to follow through on their original ideas and impulses. This time, they got a lot further.

This Earth started to divide off between the human intelligence and all else that goes on here. It was horrible. The story has yet to be told. Here is the brief version.

Hundreds of Atlantean black magicians—the bulk of them— came back as world leaders, as great corporation heads, as the super-rich, and as other power-brokers. They banded together along the telepathic electricities of their shared cause. Merely the outer edge of what they were about would be enough to frighten any spirit-alive being. Those of us who were spirit-alive stuffed it worse than we ever had previously, because we were so frightened by the sinister vibration in charge of world affairs. Probably the heaviest toll came onto the bodies of women.

One of the heavily instituted programs was to turn the human body into a performing machine. There is that within the male body that can almost do this. But it runs hard against the reproductive system and several subtle sides of the feminine physiology. When women attempted to make their bodies perform as well-oiled machines, they began to reap a whirlwind of self-destructive illnesses, injuries, and psychological addictions. This was epidemic in proportion, and almost wiped out the spirit-in-woman.

So many other devious conditionings were allowed to be promiscuously experimented with that the collective undersoul became a waste-dump of failed scientific and technological experiments. No matter what was tried, it never quite worked all the way. When you keep the heavenly fires at bay, and substitute extensive and intensive reliance upon the subterranean fires, you come up against several problems. The primary one is that the gut instinct of every human being is to overthrow limits and distortions.

Black magicians do not believe in such an instinct. They project the thought that all the so-called lower forces in us run toward the destructive and the degenerative. But that gut instinct toward life and love and freedom has always been the salvation of humanity, each and every time we have been invaded, which is so many times that we rarely have been independent of one invasion or another.

Eventually, these latter-day incarnations of black magicians ran out of ideas for how to achieve mastery over the population. This resulted in the 1960s explosion of alternative forces. As soon as they realized they were losing their grip, the Dark Powers grabbed everything back. However, the world-snake was now turning over in new directions of evolution.

Something had shifted, in the seven short years from 1966 to 1973. When everybody became stuffed back into their tight, suppressive shells during the rest of the 1970s, the conforming to plan and experiment continued to seem much more obvious and thin. Human beings were not going to put up with much of this. We contracted for twenty years, one single generation, and then something very drastic began to happen.

During 1993, the human blockade against the fire of the heavens was breaking down, all year long. A primordial force was on the loose. Nobody understood it. Nobody knew what to do with it. But it was here amongst us. And it was burning-hot to the touch.

During 1993, I went through the burning fires of hell myself. My body had taken on the worst of the experiments, and it was burning out fast. I got to participate in that year-of-years from the most intimate possible place. I did get to see what this burning-hot primordial force really was.

We now had alive amongst us the depth fires, which would no longer simmer down. They were coming up in our bodies, in our souls, and all throughout our surrounding environment. These depth fires were restive to reconnect with the height flames they so missed and longed for. Earth had become almost barren. Her fire body was exuding the power that would never again submit to being tamed. The animal Earth was fulfilling the prophecies, and starting to assert her own desire and will.

Because these things are so very far from the ideologically impoverished consciousness of those of us who have endured so much tyranny for so long, nobody knew what this was, or could feel all the way inside of it. But I could—I had to. My only possible rebirth route was to unite so deeply with the fires of the deep that I would be blasted through death into a new life beyond all deaths. So I did it. I worked as hard as anybody could, and I succeeded in making myself one with the depth fires. I'll tell you my one incredible discovery as I did this.

We had always learned in school, and then the media hammered it into us further and further, that human beings are the only ones who fill the foreground around here; that all other beings and forces, no matter who and what they are, are merely background factors. This is the very center of our black-magic conditioning. It makes us tune out everybody and everything that could help us to evolve beyond the slaveries of modern times.

When I met the depth fires of 1993 in a direct reckoning, with no mental bias in the way, I was scorched by the living power of the Earth's fire body. I found that She of Earth bears a dormant fire capacity that is awesome. She will use it to wake us up. She was declaring in 1993, in alignment with the Capricorn planets of mountainous changes, that her inner fires were now ready to arise. And the only way she could agree to temper her charge was if a few among humanity could break through the human blockage and bring down the cosmic fires to meet her and renew her being.

As I died, as I let the body I had worn out become consumed by flames, I was pulled beyond the magnetic suction of the fires of the deep, directly towards the infinite, blessed radiance of the fires of the heights. What a journey! There we were, my I-in-Sara and the remnants of me, traveling together at warp speed into the very fires that the human blockade had so totally made to seem distant, remote, and beside the point of who we are and what we are doing in the Earth. If I thought the Earth's depth fires held a charge far beyond the levels I ever dreamed were there, I was in for a much bigger and far more sudden surprise now.

The cosmic fires are made up of myriad beings, who have been called the gods. Each such being is a warmth vessel, a fire-breather. Instead of having retired to some infinite elsewhere to reminisce, the greater gods were right there, busily cooking up the way for human beings to access them in freedom and independence. That is where I came in.

I was so burning up with the love I had become in Earth that I merged my newly wide-open being with the being of each one I met, wherever I could find those who burned with the fervor of who they are inside. We met in such wondrous and complete ways that they quickly knew that it was time to implement the next stage, and that I could help.

In the midst of a love radiance that was dazzling but inwardly warming and grounding, I was shown how to turn myself into a being of light who could forge a laser-beam of heavenly fire into my heart's expression and then bring it back alive with me. I was equipped with enough fire-power to keep blasting through, and never to say die. However, there was one severe limitation placed upon me.

The true gods do not ever work from a place of power and arbitrary authority. Their entire stream, especially since the time of Christ, is that love is the force that must prevail. So I could never be a "Star Wars" zapper. I had to learn how to wield every ounce of my cosmic fire-power with love, as a current that could draw forth what lives within. And so it is.

I soon came back with my fire heart blazing, and with it all harnessed to the ways of love. As I returned into the human blockade territory of 1994, I was greeted by the very same forces I had left weeks before. But I was so different now, so radically transformed, that my experience of the Earth was entirely fresh and new.

People I approached would either ignore me as best they could, or deify me and keep putting themselves down. But I was prepared for this. It did not deter me for a moment. I began to work in earnest.

I knew as well as anybody ever knows anything that I would gradually be able to impact all of Earth and humanity, but that I would need to start small, and build very well, and let the entire momentum unfold in its own destiny design. So I devoted the bulk of my love-force and fire-radiance to working within and through William, my twin flame, then through a handful of others secondarily, and then through hundreds of those I had touched in my recent lifetime in whatever measure I could. Love is patient and endures faithfully. And so I did.

I am thrilled to be able to report that this method is working miracles. Most of them have yet to surface, but in the depths and in the heights, the fires are burning bright around here. William has taken up the impulse to align with the cosmic fire of the gods and with the depth flames of the Earth, and to bring the two together in very strong measure. Our very closest friends are also realizing this way of life as their own. Let me try to say how the fire-beam itself is activated and doing its work.

The overwhelming pressures against even survival in recent decades have taken a great toll on everybody here. But the worst damage has been done to human sensitivity to subtle forces. It is truly remarkable to witness how thoroughly shut down the deeper and higher human being is right now. Because of this desperate situation, the only forces that can have any enduring impact are those that are highly condensed and concentrated, those that can muster a relentless, tireless ability to wield that concentrated power from every conceivable angle, until it breaks through in so many places so rapidly that it can no longer be blockaded.

We are therefore forging our fire combination in two specific areas. If we try to do everything, we accomplish nothing. If we try to let the regenerative forces come through in just these two areas, we shall have our enduring impact. It has already begun.

Our first area of concentration is on the destruction of all polarization trends and their replacement with the creative spark, each one in their heart moving toward a unity of approach to those polarities most critical in their own development. There are many ways this can manifest, but the two most common areas are:

The gender wars between the sexes—the polarization at its worst—is being broken up by all those who are open in their hearts becoming aware that they must surrender to a love beyond all qualifications, and then bringing that kind of love to their close bonds, in order to free up the stuck energies of centuries of intimate battles involving revenge, murderous suspicion, and the absence of love-getting-through as an aching, common experience.

The past-forces of spirit-attunement and the future-forces of still-greater-spirit-attunement are becoming cross-fertilized and revealed as simultaneously alive, in contrast to the mid-twentieth-century blockade against all inward aliveness. Past and future are forming a serpent circle that spins the human soul into self-remembrance and the incredible ability to start all over again at the very beginning, which turns out to also be the end of an old road—the full-circle dance of time is learned by heart and danced in vibrant joy and self-recognition as surviving even the times when all was done and forsaken—the fire returns at full breath.

Besides this busting-up of all polarizations, we are placing immense emphasis upon one other area. When the human blockade became so hard and tight in the 1940s, immense confusion arose about the above and the below. We were alienated from spirit and lifted away from Earth, and were so far from both that we no longer knew which was which, who was who, or what we were missing where. Very often, when people would claim one of these along a path or journey, they would miss the other one altogether.

We are entirely dedicated to bringing Heaven and Earth together within ourselves. This is a radical path. We seek to bring into immediate, conscious fine- tuning our awakening link with fire above and fire below. And we shall not be content to connect ourselves with either direction and ignore the other one. Instead, we are using all of our laser-beam concentration to pierce the barrier between depths and heights, and thereby arrive here in the surface realm entirely alive to both directions.

This is the shift that William and I are especially keen about. When you have gone through what I have, you have to go this way. First I fused my being with the Deep Earth fires, and discovered just how hot and strong they are coming to be. Then I merged with the Fire Beings of the Heavens, and took all through me their rapture of spirit-presence. I must bring both together, as fire on the spot burning through the human blockade—I'm not going to stop for anything now.

March 11, 1994, 10:30 a.m.

Families, Ancestors, and Holders of the Lineage

Dear William,

In the nineteenth century, families split on themselves. Ever since, those who grow up in families have also split and split on themselves. It is now hard to remember or imagine what a family was like in any whole sense. The late twentieth century mind says: To live in a family is to experience multiple internal and external divisions, all of them compounding each other.

After the nineteenth-century split, the foreground family took on more and more of a nuclear-fission mentality, breaking down radically so that each family member became cut off from the others in all meaningful ways. Eventually each family member became so many different people that they could no longer stay connected with all of their facets. But this foreground family itself became a false front, a shop window that shows the best of what is in the store but grossly misrepresents what you will encounter inside.

The background family became hidden, secretive—seen rationally as not even there, as a superstition or myth. This background family is the ancestors, the family line, the cohesive group of those pulling back on the line to hold everybody in their rightful place. The mother line and the father line both form ancestral clusters that operate behind the scenes. As these were banished from serious consideration and turned into ghosts, the ancestors began to get their revenge for being neglected, denied, and denigrated.

The ancestors stayed in the family home, filling up the attic and the cellar with their presence, influence, and power. The attic held the memories, and kept the lid on all that went on in the house below. The cellar took on the nightmares and the forbidden parts, sucking away vital energy from the ground-floor, foreground family members.

Some of the ancestors stuck around a long time. They could no longer find their way into their own destiny beyond the Earth, as these realms after death were so denied and suppressed. So ancestors stayed with the foreground family and became a major background factor, gripping each family member by the root and by the crown, and pulling back against progressive life-currents that they could not understand or move with.

These splits mask more radical dilemmas. The foreground conflicts in contemporary families are often perpetuated as a relief from undercurrents and overtones of other conflicts and difficulties, deep in the blood and trying to seep through.

Within many modern families, there is one ancestor who is the holder of the lineage, the central figure in the entire family line. When such a person is Earthbound, lost here in the Earth and unable to fulfill their own life-after-death, we are presented with what has become known as the dysfunctional family.

Naturally, the busy mind looks at foreground factors to account for dysfunctional family patterns. But how often is the alcoholic father in a complex interactive field with his own father who died, but who stayed around carrying the family lineage and will not let his son be? And how often is the worried, anxious, and controlling mother embroiled in a subconscious battlefield with her own mother who died, but held the family lineage and wielded it against her daughter, not budging from her contentious position?

We like to kick the dead out, to think they just go away. But this is absurd. If we fail to respect the dead, they will return the favor. When we do not fulfill our part in the universal connecting links, we reap consequences that are extreme, painful, and that could be avoided if we were really paying attention.

Of all the dead people we miss the boat with, it is family members, our ancestors, who are the pivotal ones. They take on shadows and destructive, regressive ways, partially because we walk around in our trance of rationality and dismiss whatever our narrow band of awareness fails to track with.

I have followed out a few of these situations from my perch where I can see into both worlds freely, and I have found that the situation is wasteful, short-sighted, and wildly fear-struck. Families are full of fear they don't even know about. The foreground image of even the well-adjusted family usually masks a lot of family-dweller action, of ancestors pulling strings, of people in the family splitting on themselves in serious ways, and of everybody being ill and miserable.

The only thing that makes this picture a bit less overwhelming is that there is usually one family member, whether mother or first-born child, whether father or later child, who bears the future seeds of family renewal. This single family member acts to change the entire situation, just by being who they are and not entirely succumbing to the subliminal pressures and strains. Their light redeems the situation, lifts the energies and spirits, and prepares for changes ahead.

Let us look further into what happens with the future seed-bearer.

She—let us say she—finds herself surrounded and enveloped by a shared atmosphere of doom, of critical mind prevailing, of everybody being captured by the same negativities and reactivities. But she does not feel the same way as the others. She insists upon her solitude and when she is alone, she clears out the family stuff, perhaps not suspecting that she is clearing it for everybody. It is natural to who she is and to the task she has agreed to perform to act this way, to open the inner spaces so that a breath of fresh air comes through the dank family gloom.

Even if she is in an ultra-casual and fast-paced contemporary family in the suburbs, where little real interaction takes place any longer, and where it looks like nothing heavy is going on at all, her position is very similar. The overt style of family life has little to do with it. The key lies in how the body really feels when sitting in the common family space.

She has in her body the antidote to the family poison. She bears in her soul the counterweight to the escapisms and splittings. She perhaps even knows in her spirit-self, her love-essence, that she can move beyond all these traps and ultimately mediate the others' emerging as well.

It is because of this one family member and her alignment with the future that the situation is open-ended and subject to the grace aspect of family life. Even if a power struggle is unfolding behind the scenes between the holder of the lineage and the future seed-bearer, there is a lot of room for hope. The future seed-bearer somehow knows the way to prevail. She is the one least intimidated by that overbearing pull-back force.

The contemporary family is transparent to ancestors, to invasion by the media, and to myriad other currents. It is blind to these, willfully and obdurately rejecting all evidence that it is an open target. The most ironic part is that the strongest and most powerful enemy of the family's health and well-being is often a group of ancestors who insist upon suppression, who make the world look bleak, who hook family members into safety and security obsessions, and who most of all take revenge for being pushed out by asserting central control in a blind and headstrong fashion. Rare is the family that escapes such a fate. It is fortunate that the future seed-bearer is there as well, to give everybody a chance to journey onwards from these regressive patterns, and to discover how to live, who to be, and what it means to be free.

It is the intimate details that count most in ordinary family life. Among these details are gems that can be mined, clues to the mysteries of what is going on.

Let us say that a family power structure is firmly in place in a given family, and that age and gender determine status, with one family member invisibly placed at the top by these criteria. In a matriarchal family, this would be perhaps the mother's mother. At the bottom perhaps is the youngest boy, the future seed-bearer, who is countering inside himself the family influence of the holder of the lineage, his dead grandmother on his mother's side.

Because of the set roles, and the hierarchy being so rigid and tight, this little boy finds himself viewed as too small, too young, too fragile to do anything other than absorb the power maneuvers of other family members. Behind it all is the mother's mother, pulling strings and instilling fear, doubt, and mutual mistrust.

One day, little Billy, six or seven years old, realizes that he is himself. He is simply walking along the street, and suddenly understands that he exists entirely within himself, and that this compacted family pattern cannot overcome his own nature or destiny. And Billy vows to himself that he will endure through the family trials, get away as soon as he can, and be true to himself no matter what.

When he returns to the family fold, this small factor has changed, with deep and subtle consequences for everybody in the family. It is soon obvious to everybody that Billy can no longer be bullied or persuaded against his will. As all are thus forced to lighten up on Billy, they start to learn each day how to be a little freer and clearer. Billy is their teacher. He has assumed his true role in the family, and that is his focus from that point onwards. He never returns to the dog-house.

What does this show us about the family and the ancestors? That their power is subordinate to the greater destiny of each one, if each one takes that up. If they do not, the consequences are severe.

What would have happened if Billy had failed to listen to his angel, and decided to hide out in the family basement? He would not only stunt his own growth, the family structure would also grow more rigid, the grip on it by his mother's mother would get worse and worse, and eventually the family would be a far more constricting reality for everybody. He had to do it as the future seed-bearer; all depended on him.

We can see that the ancestors are one key factor and the future is the other. These balance on opposite sides of the apparent foreground family drama. If the past predominates, the family energies sink like a stone. If the future wins out, everybody starts to unfold more freely and genuinely.

I was in a family myself, and I was the future seed-bearer. When my cancer tumors were killing me, I had to look hard and long into the structural foundations of my own illness, and to come to terms with the Ancestral Karmas, the deeper substrata of the family con-stellation.

What I discovered was that it was not just a matter of the holder of the lineage, and certainly not merely the psychological factors of early environmental situations. Built into my hereditary genes were certain karmic crystallizations that matched and exacerbated my per-sonal karmic predispositions. I was at the mercy of these patterns in the blood and in the cells, and my own efforts to serve as the family future seed-bearer were only partially successful. I could handle the obvious factors that the contemporary adolescent looks into, but there still remained the Ancestral Karmas.

The further I journeyed inside these crystallizations of genetic structure, the deeper and more elusive their path became. I had to enter the micro-world, the intimate places that few ever go. There I came upon the roots of what I was up against.

Our family was processing the collective karma of the races. My matriarchal roots went back to pure Hawaiian royalty. My patriarchal roots were white Western. And there were many British characters on my mother's father's side. When the races mixed, and especially when the Hawaiian women were taken away from their land to become well-educated and civilized, something horrible happened. The ripping-away of our roots did not result in any forward development in the truest sense.

This feeling of being ripped away from one's roots was so close to my own previous life experiences that when I took all of this on as a child, the future seed I was bearing became pushed much further off into the future, and I became captured under the spell of the existing family pattern. I could not bring the alternative energies in any strong way. I was crushed under the weight of history, until I woke up to what all of this anguish had been about.

As I did come to realize the power of the genetic patterns and Ancestral Karmas to mold me into less-than-myself, I vowed to work to overthrow all false limitations that bind human souls in this way. I did in the end erode these structures in myself, sufficiently that I could not be held back by them at death but could leap at last into that future seed I had always been here to carry. When I did so, the deep healing in the family line began. I have worked on this further since death, and I shall continue to support and encourage the expansive possibilities of each family member who survives me. This is an important part of my path now.

The Ancestral Karmas are not yet acknowledged in our culture. When they are looked into at all, they are always reduced to obvious outer factors. The idea that the ancestors might actually be living after death in Earthbound states is too much for most of us to cope with.

The ancestors dwell in regions of the world-after-death. They are set far apart from most of the rest of what goes on. Those who pass over and are not caught in these frequencies never meet them. But those who have remained under ancestral compulsions during their Earth lives are susceptible to getting lost in the ancestral chambers.

Fortunately, all of these enclaves are now rapidly becoming cleared out. Soon these suppressive activities really will be of the past. But there are many walking the Earth today who must still come to terms with their own Ancestral Karmic self-entrapments.

What about the future seed-bearers? They will leap to the forefront of families as the blood-stigma falls away, and the family angels will begin to do their work with far greater freedom, joy, and responsive participation by family members. The sad history of families is giving way, and those who are born to bring their families forward will have a much better chance than I did to do what they came here to do.

The very best attitude or stance that a contemporary family member can take to other members of their immediate family is that this situation has been chosen, not imposed, and it is the optimal situation to see mirrored all of the places that need to be cleared fast. Therefore, one can be grateful to the others, because all have agreed to enter these fires together. One can even be grateful to those who continue to show the old, stuck places. The reminder they give us is much-needed.

We are still pulling out of the ancestral enchantments. We are still subject to falling back under them. But we are nowhere near as susceptible as we were just a short time ago.

The veils are parting. The structures are crumbling. The worlds are opening up everywhere. The family mansion is being sold, and the ancestors must vacate. They have hung around long enough. They all have their own journeys to take, beyond these mutual down-pullings.

The families have split open. The ancestors are going away. And the communities of the future will know not to trap and bind their members. We will reap the lessons of the old family feuds, and we will move on into the open air.

April 10, 1994, Noon

Pluto's Incision into Core of Earth

Dear William,

Star Genesis is the future star visioning that supplants the astrology of old. In it, the planet Pluto occupies a far more prominent place than in the old astrology.

It is the bias of astrology to be quantitative/mathematical, and so to equate everything with everything else. It is the sure knowledge of Star Genesis that certain things take precedence over certain others. Pluto is the ultimate key to this solar system, and especially to the riddle of Earth's destiny.

When Pluto was confirmed as really there among the planets in 1930, this marked the launching of the very end of all false civilizations which hyped themselves intensely for sixty years and then had nothing left in the 1990s. When Pluto slipped inside the orbit of Neptune in 1979, this allowed the deeper resonance of Pluto to begin to get all the way inside each and every human being walking the Earth inside a physical body. When Pluto entered the sign of Scorpio in 1984, this meant that it was time for the old order to die and for a new internal existence to arise from the lost depths of time. When Pluto came its closest to the Earth in 1989 and 1990, this accelerated tremendously the inner clock of drastic endings and beginnings. Now, in April 1994, as Pluto's orbit converges with Sirius A and Sirius B coming where they come closest together in their cycle, the climactic point of the entire Plutonian incision into the core of Earth evolution is at hand.

Because astrology has put all but the outer mind asleep by its monotonous linear depictions of the way self and world operate, I will avoid its path altogether here and plunge directly into the heart of Star Genesis.

Pluto is the underworld initiation, which takes hold of the deep root in body of human and Earth, and teaches it how to plant itself afresh in the core of experience. The ways this is accomplished are myriad. The most preferred ways are physical and emotional, rooted in undersoul realms, barely accessible to surface consciousness. Rituals, internal journeys, dreams, vision quests, and other metamorphic pathways become the Plutonian ways in and through. But because I have been given so many keys into the deepest mysteries here, I shall show you what I myself am directly accessing through my own journey, starting in 1979.

In 1979 I got desperate, as William began to show me that I was living a lie and that I needed something far more nourishing than others' surface acceptance. By 1984, I was living with William, and my death of personal selfhood was becoming a daily agony and inner necessity. 1989 and 1990 were when cancer tumors began to develop inside my body, lurking under the surface, aiming to get me to relinquish my very ancestrally poisoned and karmically doomed body, and to set out on my greater initiatory journey at the moment of death. I am now reborn on the most radical levels, and I am now starting to orchestrate the universal human metamorphic path for total breakthrough on all levels of existence.

But between 1990 and 1994 lies the tale. How does one take up the inner journey and not stop anywhere? These past years and months have shown me that there is a Light Being who lives in the darkness of the eclipsed and afflicted consciousness of our times, who is ready to arise through the levels and to reassert its place of incarnational presence. This Light Being is entirely free and clear. Its nature is to unfold limitless gifts when accessed. However, most of us are very troubled and anxious about having spent several thousand or so years in a bondage of the personal self lost in the outer world. It takes destiny shocks of Pluto's kind to get us going.

My shock came in April 1991, three years ago, when William, my own close love, was about to be dragged away by another woman into a place where he would lose all his powers, cut our connection with our spirit sources, and lay waste to our union with each other. As I watched him do this, a characteristic Pluto phenomenon occurred. The world we were inhabiting together slowed almost to a halt, perceptions blurred and distorted, past lives were imprinted in very subconscious multiple ways onto the present time scene, my body broke out with breast cancer, and each one of us took on such archetypal images and roles that we virtually lost our own specific identity of any kind at all.

However, because I had been living in the Santa Cruz mountains for seven-and-a-half years already, and because I had endured one-and-a-half years after the great earthquake had generated a permanent Plutonian energy vortex in the area, I had already become accustomed to these particular phenomena as a daily manifestation, and their intensification became for me far more of an internal shake-up than a terminal freeze-over. That is to say, my soul had been learning from the depths of Pluto, in the land and in my body, to take all drastic and extreme sensations and impressions as a sign to pay very close attention, and not as an excuse to go into the deep-freeze of reactivity and abandon myself.

As I gathered my forces to ask myself: What is this that is now turning my world into a whirlpool suction downwards? I was given the Pluto refracting-mirror of everything suddenly getting far worse, so that I was compelled to take my inquiry further. Finally, as I said to myself, "I am going to die here," William went through his own Pluto awakening, as his body absolutely refused to tolerate this woman's savage attack any longer, and his deep body voice surfaced with its get-us-out-of-here instructions, leading right away to release and relief.

My body was still traumatized and headed straight for death, and I had to work very hard to slow down its destruction and turn it into immortality pathways beyond death. But I could fulfill my destiny in the situation, because I kept on responding to crisis and to destruction, at each and every juncture. I was becoming a true Plutonian, a dimensional re-weaver, moving fluently among all worlds, rejecting none of them. The fact that I had to discard one body and take on special tenancy in another was not so very strange in here, although it looked like it from the outside. When you agree to the ways of Pluto, you start to experience a great deal of warp between how it looks outside and how it feels inside. And if you get really honest with yourself, you altogether unhook your sense of well-being from how it seems, and rivet your attention with great fervor into how it really is in here, even though how you turn out is worlds apart from anything you had ever previously imagined.

Pluto has taken me on a journey into death, as all its imagery would suggest, and on a further journey back from death. We are now starting to learn that "nothing is irreversible," the first law of the twenty-first century. I had to think this put me in an unusual position. But now I realize there are no longer any "usual" positions—just those that appear that way. In here, where the feelings and sensations are, the existence of an anonymous world of regular people is long past. Instead, we are all learning how to die, and how to move much further in than we ever could go before we discovered that we are far from alone in here.

The message of Pluto inside the Earth is that the deepest and darkest places contain the most directly relevant and brightest paths to stay with. I signed up to help with this Pluto journey from every side, because I realized that being under and inside the world would get us where we needed to go. Now we are all in here together, so I guess I'd better share with you the lay of the land.

Being all here is the only way we're ever going to get out of here. And when we get out of here, we will be so entirely transformed that we will be on our way into further adventures, revitalized and refreshed for greater journeys beyond this world.

First, we must devote ourselves to being all here. The Pluto signal system suggests that this involves the reversal of racial instinct. The lunar code in the instinctual body antennae, located deep in the pelvic girdle, wards off danger and what is alien, and welcomes in what is safe and friendly. This is firmly settled in our clan nature, in that which ancestral blood supports and sustains. We all know we must follow the lunar code.

The Pluto signal system tells us that what has seemed most safe and friendly is now the block to our emancipation, and that what has felt most dangerous and alien now becomes our closest ally and companion. This is an extreme situation. I resisted it hard and long, but eventually I knew it was true. The safe and friendly pulls away from the deep changes needed, while the dangerous and alien contains the desire and the capacity to travel onwards from here.

As soon as the Moon has lost its tight grip of stay-with-the-familiar, we are compelled to confront Saturn's monumental fixed memory of each and every time we or somebody like us could not carry through when it counted—and a bound-and-gagged determination to avoid falling short like that again. Pluto seeks to sabotage this tight old place inside by drawing in such outrageous situations and dilemmas that even Saturn cannot be sure which ground to retreat to, because there is no ground left anywhere.

But do you realize what we are talking about here? A century ago, rumors were spreading that God is dead. It's now time to spread the rumor that Mom and Dad are dead, and the family homestead is deserted. The location markers, all the fixed points—these are the places where Pluto does its dirty work. We are uprooting the entire lost-self system, so that the Light Being inside can rise and return.

We are driven now to be all here. The full weight of the world of the dead and of the death journey are behind this drive. The dead will not be content to inertly witness their deaths being in vain. They want a world to return into, or a world they can bless, or a world they can interchange with fluently. They cannot be talked out of this. The Lord of Death for so long kept them drugged and "out of it." But we are closing down his operations and setting the dead free, to demand of the living a really strong shot at being all here, so that the whole journey of the soul can be restored.

What is the April 1994 Pluto cycle with Sirius A and B doing in the entire late twentieth-century Pluto blitz? The Sirian system is the instigator of large-scale, long-term collective changes. The Pluto incision is the immediate, short-term, all-at-once catalyst of changes, both individual and collective. When long-term meets short-term, a ninety-thousand-year rarity, we have all of the multiple Pluto changes of the past fifteen years seeding a much broader, deeper, universal change-cycle in the next fifteen years. The year 1994 marks the midpoint of a thirty-year timing in which the biological self must make way for a different kind of self hidden within. The previous fifteen years were primarily an ebbing of the old. The next fifteen years are essentially the rising, waxing, and emergence of the new.

I make this rare excursion into current timings because I have been witnessing an explosion of events among the dead and among the living that needs to be acknowledged. Recently, I have become so excited by these changes that I can hardly work fast enough. I will give you one example of why I feel this way.

William, my twin flame and forever partner, has of late metamorphosed to such an extent that he will soon join me in taking on new names. He simply is no longer the person of this lifetime. He died with me, and gave birth to a self that could contain the whole world inside of it, and is representative of more than his own personal identity.

His changes are immensely Plutonian. His Saturn has been a very William-Lonsdale type of character till now, and was jealously guarding so many ancient treasures that it took up most of his deeper resources. But Pluto conjoining his Saturn has been slowly and painstakingly cutting out a circle around this Saturn, and with my dying the whole Saturn structure collapsed and was replaced by absolutely nothing. Meanwhile, Pluto has gone on to invite in a large circle of future friends, all of whom are collaborating to make the common future much brighter and clearer. And Pluto is doing all this by keeping at bay all self-structures, and allowing the totality of the limitless spirit to prevail in their place.

I witness these deep changes, and I see that we are not going to have any place to hide—only our actual destiny path to follow. The elaborate back-drop can no longer convince us that we are the same beings we were. William exemplifies this situation of worlds ending to let other worlds come into being.

My own changes are comparable. As I continue to pioneer in the two-way interchange between spirit realms and Earth depths, I am called to evolve as rapidly as I can. I have taken on the most demanding of pathways. If you take the usual death route, change is consis-

tently geared to match your internal rhythm, with a fine web of protective assistance. If you track with the Earth as it was till now, you
use the difficulties of life in the body to buffer you against the demand
that you metamorphose daily. But if you live between the worlds,
fully anchored in both of them, you must match the most extreme
pace of change in making them one.

William and those closest to us are being called into this same kind
of crucible of Pluto changes. In a time when everyone is changing
super-fast, we are way ahead of the universal schedule. We have to
be, because we are Future Bearers, flying on ahead to open space and
time for all of the others.

What does it all really mean? That each one's best chance is to recognize those old reference points as bitter and rotten. The new world
is already inside of us, and it will have its way if we can let go into it
freely. In order to do this, we need to blast through fearlessly, and
never look back.

Can you feel the changes in the Earth coming up through your
feet, pulling you onward? Can you sense how everybody is in on
this, whether or not they can see it? Can you get in touch with how
deep and far-reaching these currents really are?

When I link myself with those most responsive to me, I find that
the entire lower body is becoming charged with a substantive consistency that gives it far greater strength and endurance; that the entire
upper body is turning into crystal light and taking off into a free,
spontaneous flow that is mobile and completely alive; and that the
mid-body is opening and opening into both directions and providing a meeting- and crossing-place in between. And I find that the
soul is reborning into its no-longer-needing-to-suffer place. The spirit
is coming in for a landing, in a body that lets it come all the way in,
to be truly all here.

I look around, and I find that so many others are here assisting
the process. What a time! We are swept up in a great wind, and it is
blowing the old house down. But the new house comes up from
beneath, and is one that can let all the worlds converge. I sit inside
the new house, I gaze around, and I know this is only the beginning.

April 26, 1994, 1:00 p.m.

Theanna and Ellias as Future-Bearers

Dear Ellias,

Time traveling is not just a science-fiction plot device. It is common, ordinary, and frequent. But very few of those who engage in it are human, and most have little to do with humanity.

Those few human beings who can time-travel are those who are given a task, from greater galactic origins, that involves becoming human but not losing entirely the faculty for journeying through time. Then such ones can move fluently forwards and backwards in time, and thereby access realms otherwise far from the awareness of 1994 human beings in Outer Earth.

Two of those who are doing this now are Theanna and Ellias. We are especially working to bring into active presence the gifts and treasures of several different future-time frequencies. One of these is near future. One is far future. Another is the twenty-second century. And another is beyond time, but manifesting into time as an indeterminate future frequency.

I am going to describe our activity in relation to all four of these future-time frequencies. This is a basic depiction of what each stream can activate in present time. All I shall do is introduce the particular qualities of each frequency.

The near-future time frequency is working out of an early twenty-first-century time base, and is tunneling back into the present time-world an intensive, full-on, drastically accelerated special tone for those who are the most tuned-up and tuned-in. A vision has formed within this stream that anything is possible in the Earth now, that the patterns the human mind conceives as fixed and determined are not, and that all effort must be made to pull everybody forward into a radically transformed way of life by 2020 A.D. This most radical of future streams is likely to succeed. Theanna and Ellias and close friends are working strongly within this frequency, and it is astoundingly capable and adroit in meeting and addressing the lingering dilemmas of late twentieth-century humanity.

But what would it be like to live in this frequency, to make it one's own rhythmical timing reference point? This one is dedicated to freeing the human life-force in synchronization with a freeing-up of the planetary life-force, so that the violent conflict between the human and the Earth will turn around altogether, and they will move together into an entirely charged lifestream. Each human being, and in fact every sentient being, is here conceived as harnessing a force of life that is naturally and entirely true and pure and whole. Because this is opposite to the current dominant world-view, I must hasten to add that this radical near-future stream has probed into the way people view life right now, and has determined that this view is an alien superimposition from afar, and that human beings have no idea what they would think if they thought for themselves. This alien stream blocks out light and substitutes mental activity of a negative and destructive cast, which cognizes life to be impossible.

Theanna and Ellias and friends have determined that this is correct, and that the near-future stream is the direct antidote to the poison of an attacked and invaded Earth. We are now infusing ourselves and our world with the antidote. It is essentially ordinary. The form that it takes is to harness the human and Earthly life-forces in tandem by surrendering into a love so entirely felt and experienced through every cell that it roots out the mental program of life-negation, and brings in its place a heart force of life-affirmation. But this love is itself a future-time-frequency power.

When love has hatred or mistrust or fear mixed in with it, the love becomes poisoned and does not renew life. But when love is permeated with recognition, with a fiery vision and knowingness of the other-as-self, and of the self-as-other, something incredible is born. Psychology has flattened out this picture to make it look like a purely interpersonal cross-fire. And the poisoned love does fixate upon the overt interpersonal field and its behavioral dynamics.

The love this near-future stream is sparking and igniting is sacred love. The otherness becomes again, as it was in ancient times, a god-power, a feeling for worlds beyond. So other-as-self is no projection but is the Beloved, known inside one's own heart. Self-as-other is the realization of infinite worlds within one's own being. The blending and the fusing is entirely within. Both of the lovers indwell the same sacred space, and they love as one. Then the life-force shoots forth from their circle, and becomes fertilizer for all who thirst in the Earth of today.

The far-future time frequency is Christ-centered, and it is absolutely intent upon following the original design for this Earth and humanity. Working from vast times ahead, this stream is now stripping away all vestiges of the Old Earth and the Old Heavens, and is bringing in their place a void, a vast, empty place, which most of humanity is misapprehending. When there has been an over-full-ness everywhere, then there must come an emptying-out, a laying-waste. But this is only temporary. As soon as the void is universal, it becomes possible to draw through a transitional condition, a Heavenly City or Heavenly Jerusalem-sphere within which the Old Heaven and Earth pass away, and the New Heaven and Earth are seeded. This is now happening.

Humanity dwells upon the threshold of the infinite, and each one's inner life is impressionable to this threshold with all of its intricate streets, events, and heraldings. Most access this realm in their dream life at night, whether recalled or not. In general, the outer or psychological interpretations pass over this new dimension and interpret it away. Many will be trained soon to penetrate deeper into dreams, to reveal the heavenly city inside. The mind tends to remember the overt drama, but to forget the internal revelation it cloaked. Symbolism and myth are not involved. Instead, this is a synchronized-with-soul, unfolding-freshly domain.

Others move into the threshold by near-death experiences, which are vivid imagings of the light and the life of the Heavenly Jerusalem. Most return with the same overlay of externalization that destroys dreams. All such experiences are neither literal nor symbolic. They are inner journeys, which must be lived through again in non-trance inner states of realization in order to be accurately recalled. If they are, such experiences will prove to be doorways for all to walk through, into learning how to be in tune with the lifestream unfolding toward the future.

Still others meet this threshold-realm in actual dying and death. Theanna did this, and what she learned was that worlds are now being set aside for massive retraining of the human soul. Many who die now will not enter the worlds traditionally described, but instead will be held up on the threshold to explore the Heavenly City, and to become the people of the future. This path is arduous, but it is optimal for long-term changes on this planet. The idea is to reinstill the most essential life-giving qualities into the inner soul, and then form a New Earth and a New Heaven within which this soul can live and make its way freely.

Theanna and Ellias and friends work with this far-future, Christ-centered time frequency especially in linking with family, karmic buddies—those who are more towards the mainstream of contemporary life. We build bridges into the broader evolutionary stretchings, and offer a prayerful vigil at the gates of the Heavenly City with all of those who need to find their way into their lost touch with the core of existence.

The twenty-second-century time frequency is anchored into a time encompassing a renaissance of the human spirit. This stream celebrates, enjoys, lives into the resurgence of the human within the vast cosmic design. Ellias has worked within this frequency as his primary focus for more than a century, so I will describe the heart of his experience.

He has given himself over to infiltrating the contemporary culture in as human a fashion as possible, becoming so good at this that he could take on every malady and disturbance that is circulating and spreading in the late nineteenth and twentieth centuries. It was necessary to do this in order to sense in the body and emotions how it feels, what it is really like to be dead to spirit and obsessed within the personal.

Theanna also joined this work at the end of her recent lifetime, and got down to the point where the devoid-of-living-spirit soul condition could eat away at her body and reveal to her its dread mysteries. But why would a stream that celebrates and enjoys the twenty-second-century resurgence of the human/cosmic dance be intent upon research and investigation into the lost regions of the contemporary human being?

This future stream is convinced that humanity could easily fail to grasp its opportunity, and could sink into a stupor of time-lock and never emerge. Nothing is ever certain in the realms of time. So this stream appoints its adherents to journey back in time, to become field-operators extracting the essence of human suffering, illness, and distortion, and then bring these forward in time to be combed through and used as guidelines for working closely with those in present-day humanity who bear powerful future-seeds within them.

The twenty-second-century time-frequency broadcasts open messages to all who thirst for the living future. It gathers them into clusters and groups, encourages and fosters sisterhood and brotherhood and universal synchronization within and amongst them. Its pivotal effort is to seed visions, realizations, and impulses that are realistic about the existing conditions, but also aware of and responsive to an expanding sphere of future possibilities and probabilities.

I have worked only recently within this frequency, but have made it my home base, as it is for Ellias. My striking impressions are that this stream is enthralling, infinitely graced and blessed with regenerative forces of a massive kind. We work and play and live together in an eighth-dimensional world beyond the world, which feeds back so infinitely directly into the very midst of contemporary life that this stream could and did, for example, rescue me from the usual death dramas, and draw me forth into an exquisitely crafted future working that would not have been possible without them. These friends are a circle I value immeasurably. As Ellias would say, the golden promise they emanate is the beacon shining brightest on the human horizon.

The beyond-time, indeterminate future-time frequency is complex and intricate, and very hard to describe in contemporary terms. It is engaged with the vastest cosmic dimensions by far of any of these streams. Its signature is a fire, a great warmth and light, which draws the human spirit into the highest, clearest, and most exalted of time frequencies.

Theanna and Ellias are in the largest picture from this sphere. We journey in time ships through all times and places, and we do what is most needed. We are twin souls within a larger cluster here, and we work as one. I shall attempt to describe the indescribable.

Our beyond-time frequency is most at home within the infinite future. From there, we could say that the early struggles of the many inhabitants of this galaxy have been our primary concern forever, and so we went far back to give aid to those sickened by the galactic virus, or to those seeking to do something about it. We infiltrate in times and places like Earth in 1994, and we offer something a bit different from what the other three future-streams give.

The only thing we bring is a vast and limitless awareness. We simply know who each and all are, as we know who we are. This treasure has a singular impact. It jars loose the inward, suspended ones from the grip of their outward, apparent conditions, and sets them upon their destiny pathway. This is all it does.

We treat cultures and civilizations in the same way that we treat individuals, couples, and small groups. Each has a destiny, an intrinsic pattern or design that needs to be fulfilled. If a virus or scourge, physical or mental or spiritual, is wiping out the destiny potential of a civilization, we bring our vast awareness to bear upon the situation, and we go to whatever lengths are necessary to balance, harmonize, and integrate the situation. Because we are not serving the cause of a specific future, we simply set each and all loose to retrack with their original, intended destiny.

Because the current Outer-Earth situation is too close for comfort, let us take an example from another place and a different time-

sensibility. Say there is a small and infinitely precious planet or civilization dedicated to living true to the Infinite Creator. In this culture, the Creator is known to be directly inside of each moment,
every situation, so the life pulse is vibrant with such all-pervasive love
that it is a hard place for anybody from afar to visit, because they will
not want to leave. But this domain, which does exist, is in the same
galaxy that has become permeated with a virus that saps the vitality,
the life dynamism, of each and all. Because this culture is wise beyond
most others, it simply contracts into a ball, casts over itself a shell,
sends out a few emissaries to find the cure, and waits in a timeless
reverie of bliss. From an ordinary point of view, this might not seem
like a situation that needs help from us. But that is a misleading and
loveless point of view.

We certainly will leave alone its restful, suspended population to
maintain its lifestream in embryonic perfection. But as we follow the
fate of the emissaries, we see this is a hard stream to take along into
other worlds. So we link up in a very powerful fashion with one of
these emissaries, assisting her to find in the Earth the root syndrome
of the virus, where it is being universally studied to get to the bottom of it.

Most of all, we unite with her in her own peoples' fashion, in order
to optimize her own self-renewing love capacity, and to keep her in
tune with her mission. We bring to her only awareness—the vast and
open awareness of destiny that is ours. We can share many things,
work within all of these future frequencies together, but ultimately
and essentially, we simply endow her with the lucid and luminous
awareness to see and feel what the galactic virus is, at its worst, which
is the 1994 Earth version, and to find together with us the total, permanent antidote to the poison, which we can then catalyze into universal availability. She can return to her people and place a drop of
crystal liquid into the center of their embryonic life-wave, and their
enchantment shall then be over, and they can emerge into a further
octave of who they are together.

This example reveals much. Working within the beyond-time
future frequency lets us work within all future-time frequencies,

exploring every viable option for moving forward from the current impasse.

May 1, 1994, 10:30 a.m.

The Dream That Came True

Dear Ellias,

I am Theanna. But when I was Sara, the woman who died all broken up, I was possessed by dreams, gripped by dreams, driven to the point of immensely powerful internal resolution by dreams. So many dreams, and so little life left to live them out! That was how it seemed.

In truth, the dreams were just beginning, and the possibility of living them out was at last real. Dreams were going to be become fulfilled. I knew it. So I could not despair. I did not despair. What was I dreaming? Well, it was about everybody, and it was about me, and it was about what everybody had in common with me. My cancer tumors made tangible what had always been my condition—I was all broken up, absolutely multiple. There were "me"s everywhere, but no "I" in sight. And everybody shared this same condition. I met it everywhere, as broken mirror fragments revealing to me that there was no way out, because all of us were caught in the same jagged shards of glass. We were all lost to ourselves, and we could not get out of here alive.

However, there was a stark contradiction in my plight. I was in love with a man who was not all broken up, and who was so much not all broken up that he pulled me toward wholeness, more strongly than I pulled him toward fragmentation. William, my twin and husband of that time, was this man. He showed me, by tuning-in to Circles of beings on the inner side of life, that there were many whole sources that could reflect my own integrated, unitive self, and say to me: You shall become whole, as we are.

Because William was there anchoring this message by his own closely gathered self, I was forced to admit that I could become whole. So I dreamed and I dreamed of becoming whole, and of sharing this wholeness with all broken people. I saw myself transmitting messages of many kinds—verbal, deeply penetrating, and through touch—to convey in different languages what it is to move from all-broken-up into becoming whole again. I knew this could come true, although my mind was dead-set against it. Its argument was that I could barely express the most ordinary inward experience to anybody else, so how could I ever transmit fluently to all of the world the paths to wholeness? But my mind was barely able to get any audience from me any longer. I was far too engaged in dreaming and dying to worry about arguments and reasons. The dream would have to come true. Everything depended on it.

After I died, I dedicated myself to realizing all of the corners of this dream. But as I moved toward being able to fulfill it, I ran into William's dreams as well. While I had been raptly absorbed in my future dreaming, so was he.

William's dream was of a different order altogether. He had been guided and led by these Circles of beings on the inner side of life to dream with them the great dreams of universal transformation. He was given over to picturing and living into a time and a place and a combination of forces which could allow the innermost destiny of all of us to manifest rightfully. He was as deeply inside this dream as I was in mine.

He had it very detailed and precise. There would come a time when every future-frequency could combine into one encompassing present-time realm. There would come a place where every world, each dimension of existence, could be merged into one world, one life-current. There would come a combination of forces which would passionately fertilize this time and this place with a way of being that celebrated and fused within all that could be. Somehow, when I was dying and all seemed lost, this dream would not go away, but kept growing bigger and more insistent, and it said: You will fulfill me, do not fear.

When I ran into this dream after death, I knew right away that just as we were to merge, our dreams would merge and become more than themselves. My dream of transmitting the path toward wholeness was heating up as I became whole, and William's dream would give me a total context to move into. William's dream, in turn, of a synchronized situation for radical transformation was heating up as he began to conceive my after-death journey and what it was leading towards, and my dream could point him toward a stark, direct, simple place to start. Our dreams were as drawn to merge together as our beings were.

There was still more. As I began to rededicate myself to fulfill our combined dreams, I ran into the dreams of one more being. Let me introduce her properly here.

My final weeks in the Sara body were dominated by physical pressure, discomfort, pain, and surges of rippling sensation in many directions. William could never quite imagine into most of these experiences, because they were all linked with a woman's body. But women friends were there to know my experience and to share it. One of these was Safiya, and she tuned in deepest and furthest. We became incredibly close, sharing many moments of sisterhood which were as alive as any human connection can ever be. Safiya was carrying a buried treasure in her broken heart, one I linked with so entirely that I brought it with me through my death and worked it thoroughly.

In my re-dedication time after dying, this treasure turned into a dream, and I was compelled to heed its call as strongly as I was heeding the combined dream of Sara and of William.

Safiya's dream was in a very different direction than either Sara's or William's. Her broken heart still carried, locked away inside, a vision, a knowingness, that had become a dream because it had slipped away from certainty and fallen into the dream-place where it could live on and hold its power. When I collided with this dream, it absolutely turned me around, several times over.

It was Safiya's dream that people would be able to love in a way entirely divergent from the man/woman knot of this time and place.

Instead of two people owning and narrowing and pulling each other back, it would be all together, worlds and gods and beings, loving through two, loving through three, loving through any number who could become the shared vessels of love. Each one of these would bring into the circle the realm they embodied, and that realm would be given fresh force through the love that was shared. This ecstatic and freeing love-energy would behold and witness the absolute essence of each one as beautiful and great, and would hold nothing back from giving each one's great beauty back to themselves and to their realm, so that worlds and beings could be healed and renewed.

When I searched out the source of this dream and met with the beings who seeded this dream in Safiya, I knew that this one was the key to the fulfillment of the other dreams. This one was being dreamed always and fervently and with all of Safiya's being. It was the truth of who she was. And I knew from my communion with her before and after dying that she stood by this dream and was to fulfill it with William and with me.

All three dreams needed each other. They could cross-pollinate. And all three beings needed each other. We would merge. It was a destiny of stars and gods, of cosmos and Deep Earth. The dreams would lead us to a fulfillment beyond even these dreams themselves. At last, the time of dreams coming true was at hand.

When sacred dreams come true, they turn out differently than could ever have been imagined. We can never imagine the X-factor of how each part impacts each other part, and how each being who is involved will impact the others who are so deeply involved.

Sara's dream became Theanna's dream. I could not stay Sara. She was the broken one. I was now the whole one. When I became Theanna, I reworked Sara's dream. She vastly underestimated herself because she was frightened that she would be back in classical Mayan times, again burning up with grandiose schemes. So she kept her dream bare and stark and minimal. She pictured herself becoming whole, but she did not let herself see that she would be entirely vibrant, a new kind of being altogether, and that she would transmit to everybody a vast spectrum of evolutionary possibilities, not just basic integration. The more her dream fused with William's and Safiya's, the more it turned out to be a dream of new worlds coming into being, the seed of where we all are going together.

As I became Theanna, Safiya began to lose her own coherence, her own woman-of-sorrows mask, and to become the buried treasure, to dig it out, and to heal her broken heart with its balm of remembrance of why she came to Earth, and who she truly is. Then she could not be Safiya any longer. She became Alita, a bright and vast presence. Alita created the path of fruitions for her dream.

However, in the living of it, as it merged with the two other dreams, Alita's dream turned out very differently. She also had been too modest. Not only could the three of us begin to live inside a more-than-traditional, more-than-merely-personal phase of connection and bonding, but we could do this with such natural ease and flow that this way of loving quickly became the springboard for something else altogether. Love proved to be a key in a lock, and when the key was placed in the lock and the lock was opened, all that had been locked away along with love was released as well, and the world began to spin into another octave, a different keynote altogether.

Very soon, William was breaking down his entire self-structure. He could no longer be the solitary individual, the lone force holding out against the lies and distortions of fallen worlds. This position itself became the lie. It was time for William to give way into his total destiny, which would lead him entirely beyond the limitations of William Lonsdale. And so he became Ellias, a master of stars and infinite dimensions.

Ellias stepped forth and created the fruition of his great dreams. These dreams, when merged with the Theanna dreams and the Alita dreams, could not hold their form. Ellias had never counted on the love-force filling Alita, and what it would do inside of him. He had never fully realized what Theanna's expansion into all of herself would instigate and catalyze in both himself and Alita. And he had not reckoned with his own overwhelming imprint within the depths and core of both Alita and Theanna.

The time of all futures converging did take hold. The place of all worlds becoming fully present in this world did indeed manifest. The fertilizing streams of wild blooming into fullness of passionate living were fleshed out and sensuously explored. But there was too much love in it to stop there. And there was too infinite a Theanna in it to be just another dream fulfilled.

Most of those who live in physical bodies in Outer Earth in 1994 have become massively cautious and skeptical in their approach to human relationship. It is commonly and almost universally believed now that other people will always let you down, and you will let the others down, so steer clear of too intense an intimacy and mutual impact. The strategy is to back off and reconcile to what is more realistic and likely, and you will not be hurt so badly.

The pioneers in human evolution are currently feeling charged with a regenerative life-current that reverses this trend. It reveals the occasion for a fresh start in human sharings, with the man/woman bond first on the agenda. It is this radical life-current that runs directly through the middle of the Theanna-Ellias-Alita dream fulfillments. However, we are taking this further than others can. This is because I, as Theanna, am constantly infusing this shared stream with a cosmic force that is fed into me from limitless sources who cannot yet access Earth and humanity directly. Thus, I am a conduit for a greater level of regenerative life-force than even the pioneers are drawing through. I can bring this into the All, but first it must be brought full-on into the three of us who are dreaming the shared dream of something-else-altogether.

It would be prudent to leave it at that. But I am not prudent. I must also now reveal the two other rare ingredients that make our shared dream further out on the edge than would be possible with others as yet.

Alita is starting to pull in a heart-force from her own origins that has been latent and dormant for many thousands of years. The Earth has need of this homeopathic dilution of the finest love-force in the galaxy. As Alita is needed and loved, she in turn calls forth this hidden stream, which ripples through into this all-worlds-in-one-world, all-futures-in-one-time, all-fertility-in-each-gesture shared dream fulfilled. It becomes the matching energy for Theanna to grow stronger and steadier each day. Nobody ever could receive and respond to this limitless and selfless reverie of love before, so Alita's world stayed back as the buried treasure. But now this treasure is finding real currency, and all three of us together are reaping its heritage of wonder, awe, mystery unfathomable, and bright, audacious delight.

Ellias as well is in the early stages of activating the ultimate offerings that are his. His star-mastery involves bearing the synchronized bounty of all future times and vast spaces as a fertility of soul that becomes himself. He *is* the rare ingredient of creative worlds, boundless and eager. As he starts to bring all of this through him into direct impersonal and personal expression, he especially strongly charges the three of us into amazingly potent next stages, over and again, as if there were no limit whatsoever to our shared capacity. Ellias is right. There is now no limit whatsoever to our shared capacity to dream a common dream that comes truer all the time.

What happens when three such beings, who pull in such mighty force of three different and complementary kinds, are catapulted into fully active sharing? Well, we are starting to find out. I can only speak from the initial point of free discovery.

At first, we keep having to grow accustomed to staying with such an accelerated and empowering life-current. As we do so, we find that it in itself is so sweet and flowing, so graciously in tune with every current emerging in this world, that the sustaining force predominates. We feel like grace-vessels, blessings-bearers, whose life-gesture is to give, freely and joyously. Our greatest shared rapture lies in giving everything away, and each time having more to give away. This dream comes true for everybody, and soon it is not our dream at all, but the world-dream coming true.

May 3, 1994, 8:00 a.m.

Midwifing the Future

Dear Ellias,

Women in the Earth are in a sisterhood with women who have died and become tuned-in to what women in the Earth are needing. The rites of passage are one key part in this missing link. When I gave birth to my daughter, I entered into a sphere that nobody around me understood. When I gave death and rebirth to myself, I emerged into an existence beyond the scope of those trying to help me from the Earth side. As significant as the birth-gap was, the death-gap was far greater and more crucial. I wish to correct this for others.

The planetary soul called She of Earth, the awakening Earth Being, is in the process of becoming a death-and-rebirth activator. She will be moving into her own great passage onwards, and she will be triggering many communities, families, and singular beings in their immense transitions from one era and way of life to another. She bears future-seeds for those who are going to participate in an evolution that is dynamic and quite drastic. And she is going to activate every seed soon.

It is these three perspectives that must be combined if we are to midwife the future. The link between women of Outer Earth and women of spirit-central is our foundation. The personal experience of birth, death, and rebirth in its unfolding mysteries is our subject matter. The birth pangs of She of Earth in her edge of great changes is the occasion of our involvement within this realm of discovering how we can participate fully in the need of woman for assistance and mediation as she moves beyond all previous conditions.

I will give a full description of what I went through when I took on both death and that which naturally follows death if the dying is entered into completely. For me, the rebirth following death was there from the beginning. I do not believe in death as such. I see it as a necessary passage, but I do not in any sense accept or embrace the generally assumed conception of death as grimly unavoidable. My interest always lies in new life, in every form. Because my death-journey has been saturated with this allegiance, the stance I take toward dying is intensely committed to not stopping at any point, and going all the way through.

My own dying was far more prolonged than it seemed. I was participating in an experiment that involved how to die into freedom. One of its facets was to train me in the sleep state, and in higher dimensions, to learn thoroughly the death rhythm and the rebirth rhythm, and to practice them in my sleep. I was dying for months ahead of time, and also becoming reborn many times over. This generated an atmosphere of charged immediacy and deep readiness when the body's signs of advanced cancer tumors began to reveal to all parts of me that I was on the way out. It was then that I began to declare to all who would listen that I was going to come back, and that I could not be dislodged from Earth and love and body and the struggle to evolve forwards here. I had already organically integrated the truth that death is one side of a larger rhythm which also includes rebirth, in whichever mode is appropriate and needed.

As I started to apply the lessons in dying and beyond dying that I had been absorbing, I entered the final weeks with their far more overt dramatization in physical form. I developed a rhythm, a characteristic flow of life-force, that was in a different direction than anybody had previously witnessed or participated in. It had a boldness, a sharp discovery curve, a perpetual will to deepen and take up further levels of the process. It was keyed to a letting-go energetics and feeling tone that was the most radical part of all.

Over many years, I had been cultivating the art of letting go of separative ego and personal mind confusion and blockage. Over many months, I had been guided to take this a lot further into great depths of death-forces which, if you could let go into them, were far less pressurized and overwhelming. Now, in the final weeks, I let myself remember from ancient times, and to be coached by my inner-plane midwives in the fine art of releasing myself completely into deep body places, moving into the death contractions and often moving right through them. As the death-vise gripped my body and kept pulling me under, I did not resist, and I did not turn the experience back upon myself as "deserved" suffering. Instead, I bore down and did everything I could to appreciate and acknowledge those guiding beings of death itself, the death angels, as they applied their surgical skill in loosening my body from my inner soul.

I even succeeded in collaborating with them, despite the fact that the collective instinct of pulling away from them desperately wished to assert itself. This instinct was my most tenacious adversary, and I had to get down so low to the ground to counter it that I was in my last days all Earth, way under, almost buried in densities of letting-go, far inside. Eventually, even the collective recoil instinct gave way, and I was home-free, to experience purely the collaborative efforts of all the beings involved. I discovered that the death angels, the midwives of rebirth on the inner side, and the body's ultimate power of letting go were each other's sisters and allies, and that there were no destructive factors left. My death was turning out to be utterly affirmative of life and of the complete cycle of life, death, and rebirth.

How did the rebirth forces play into this rhythm of surrendered dying? The inner midwives were bearing a realization and vision of my rapid and total rebirth after death, and they were transmitting this into my impersonal soul forces, which were bearing this knowledge as their entire focus. Even as my body became very death-capable and fluent way deep, my soul loosened towards its separation from the body. Instead of the parting of the ways being a splitting-apart followed by a recovery and integration cycle, I was engaging in a dance of soul-merging-with-spirit totally at the moment of the body's snapping. Only this could turn the death trauma from the morbid side to its newly awakening rebirth dimension.

One final assisting and mediating force came through at the end, profoundly masculine in its strength and clarity. The Master of Time, a limitless being who had agreed to draw me across the threshold and walk with me from there, began to be involved in the last moments, and to charge the death-field with the flame of rebirth. This came across to me as a lightning bolt so mighty that I at last had to gaze up into his shining countenance. As I did so, the body convulsed into orgasms of sacred dying breaths. The greatest release imaginable, absolutely uninhibited and free, catapulted me into merging with the Master of Time in an ultimate reunion of the human and the divine. My journey from there was sealed; I was liberated from all duality-holding places. I would soar beyond the world, and I would return to be here again within the world. Death had become the passage it was meant to be. I was absolutely home-free.

When I gave birth to my daughter, Amy, I was alone. There were the helpers all around me, but I was alone. I needed to be.

When I gave death and rebirth to myself, I was one with all attending. I had overcome all separativeness. I could be reborn into all-of-us-together-here.

It is the journey from our solitude into our sisterhood that I celebrate and mediate. It is the magnificent opening into our ability to let go into the infinite dance of the whole life-cycle that I wish to assist in every way I can.

My allies in this venture are the women who live beyond death, the great beings who work with this project from spirit realization, and She of Earth in her rebirth pangs at the end of the twentieth and start of the twenty-first centuries. The women who are veterans of death's journey ardently wish that the path beyond dying be traversed far more fluently and universally. The spirit-beings who have prepared this path are certain that this change will key humanity's breakthrough into a new biological condition. She of Earth needs us to do what she is doing, and to assist each other in moving with this, far and fast.

I must now address the gap, the barrier, what it is that stops us from doing this life-and-death dance in its free form. I can best illustrate through my giving-birth experience, back in 1977 when I was captivated by karmic forces of every variety.

It was entirely obvious to me at that time that I could not give birth. I had wandered too far from my innermost path of destiny, and I was in a web of mother, grandmothers, aunts, great-aunts, great grandmothers, and other ancestral feminine beings. All of us together were poised to give birth, but I could not do it in myself. If I depended upon all of them, as I had to do, I had no choice but to withdraw into my own secret recesses, in order to have any place at all to be. So this is what I did. I became overtly synchronized with all the women who had ever given birth within my ancestral feminine bloodline, and inwardly withdrawn into a void space of brooding intensity. However, I was well-trained by this time to give the behavioral cues that were expected, so I expertly and fairly smoothly gave my body over to the birth process.

What was missing? What was wrong? My daughter was a breathtaking creature, the child I craved and was destined to be so intimate with. My husband of the time did bond with our daughter, and become the finest of fathers I could ask for. Friends and family and helpers were all wonderful. What was lacking here?

I myself was gone. I had contracted into a tight little ball inside. It was impossible for who I truly was to give birth in the fashion of the times. This fashion dictated that I do it all from the outside in. Giving birth was an ultimate performance, and everybody knew it.

The birth angels and all of the beings who wish to bless the birth from higher levels are immensely frustrated by such an atmosphere. They still come through, but not at full power. Instead, they hover and offer what can be received. They are treated as distant, remote, and questionable presences. All of the emphasis is upon the apparent foreground action. No being is invited. Even the child's beingness is outraged and deeply impacted by the circus atmosphere we consider to be optimal.

Variations on this theme can be rung around births, deaths, and other rites of passage. Rebirths are not even given their place in this culture. They could not be. What is the very essence of the barrier or gap?

We distance ourselves from the deep body in woman, and from this deep body's natural processes. Whether it is birth or lovemaking, death or rebirth, we feel and sense these depths to be dark, heavy, fallen. We surround these passages with a feeling of shame and exile.

The very worst of this is in the death chamber.

When you lie dying, you are coming toward yourself at last. Your body is fulfilling its final function, disgorging you into a larger state of soul. Your body is needing to be loved into its release. No body is despised and scorned more completely than the dying woman's body. After all, it is in decay and has been used up. It is natural to feel a rejecting energy towards that body. Or is it?

The dying woman's body is actually in its final glory. It is accomplishing the destiny task set for it, and in the right timing. If this body could be loved and acknowledged for what it has done, is doing, and is about to do in its final days and hours, the life-cycle would complete itself far more gracefully and harmoniously. The soul could go free, onto its beyond-death journey, and perhaps even unto rebirth.

Midwifing the future is taking such shifts as this one to heart. It is making sure to give massage and music, tone and touch, to the dying woman, the birthing woman, the rebirthing woman. It is insisting upon restoring the life-instinct beyond the web of those ancestral lines that have become captured by socialized constrictions.

Those who participate in the initial stages of this inward midwifery will start always within themselves. They will need to encounter and free up those places where they hold back from giving birth, giving death, and giving rebirth. They will especially need to face together the devaluing of the deep body, and the estrangement from the life-process at its most primal levels of suppression and negation. But we are not interested in blaming men and systems and all of the convenient alibis. This is a matter of universal evolution and revolution. Everybody is in this together.

Do you see how crucial this is? How can we expect to be any kind of viable species if we forget how to begin, how to finish and complete, and how to start at the next spiral? Who are we to concentrate on the middle and leave the pivotal points in the life-cycle to "experts" and exploiters?

My own experiences in these realms lead me to be the one to call us together now. I shall lead women, and later everybody, in reclaiming the ground of life/death/life. This is a ground I now know very well. I am so thrilled to be able to introduce it afresh to those who have lost this shared way and are hungry to find it again together.

She of Earth will show us all how. But we will need to be responsive to her cues. Her deep body must not be alien or repulsive to us. She is not a wild, hysterical, dangerous force. Neither are we. Her wildness and our wildness are rather in the direction of opening into brightness. We have a lot of life, and a far more vital dying to play through, left in us. The wheel is spinning, and we are that wheel.